KHRUSHCHEV: *A Career*

KHRUSHCHEV

A CAREER

by Edward Crankshaw

New York · The Viking Press

Published in 1966 by The Viking Press, Inc.
625 Madison Avenue, New York, N. Y. 10022

Printed in U.S.A.

Contents

ILLUSTRATIONS

following page 184

Nikita S. Khrushchev (*photo:* © *John Bryson from Rapho Guillumette*).

Khrushchev with Stalin, 1936 (*Sovfoto*); with young miners, 1936 (*Sovfoto*); at the 1937 May Day parade, with Stalin and others (*Sovfoto*).

Khrushchev with Timoshenko, 1938 (*Keystone*); visiting Moscow, 1938 (*Sovfoto*).

Khrushchev with Timoshenko, 1942 (*Sovfoto*); at Stalingrad, 1942 (*Sovfoto*).

Khrushchev at Kiev, 1943 (*Sovfoto*); with Marshal Konev, 1944 (*Sovfoto*).

Khrushchev with Malenkov (*Sovfoto*); with Bulganin (*Keystone*).

Khrushchev in Belgrade with Marshal Tito (*Ralph Crane*—Life magazine, © *Time, Inc.*).

Geneva, 1955: Khrushchev, Zhukov, and Bulganin (*Hank Walker*—Life magazine, © *Time, Inc.*).

May Day Parade, 1957: Zhukov, Khrushchev, Bulganin, Kaganovich, Malenkov, Molotov, Mikoyan (*Sovfoto*); Mao Tse-tung and Khrushchev (*Keystone*).

Khrushchev with Mikhail Sholokov (*Wide World*); with Harold Macmillan (*Keystone*).

United Nations: Khrushchev, Gromyko, Zorin (*Wide World*).

Khrushchev with Charles de Gaulle and with Fidel Castro (*Keystone*).

John F. Kennedy meets Khrushchev in Vienna (*Keystone*).

Madame Nina Khrushchev (*Keystone*); Khrushchev at a collective farm (*Sovfoto*).

Khrushchev in Yugoslavia: at play and with workers (*Keystone*).

Acknowledgements

Books, periodicals, and newspapers referred to in this narrative are acknowledged in the Notes. But I am under an especial debt to Mr. Lazar Pistrak for his book, *The Grand Tactician*. This embodied much pioneering work in tracing the early career of Khrushchev, involving, among other things, a close and comprehensive reading of the Russian and Ukrainian press over many years—a monumental task in itself. I particularly thank Mr. Pistrak and his publishers (Thames & Hudson in London; Frederick A. Praeger in New York) for allowing me to use translations of a number of excerpts from newspapers and periodicals inaccessible to me. I must also thank Harcourt, Brace and World for permission to quote from *Conversations with Stalin* by Milovan Djilas, who, alas, at the time of writing, still sits in one of Marshal Tito's prisons.

Most of the material for my own book was gathered over a long period and in a number of countries—above all, of course, the Soviet Union. I cannot thank by name the many who have helped me, and those who still live in Russia and Eastern Europe would not be pleased if I did so. I am grateful to them all the same. It would be pleasant if, twelve years after Stalin's death, I could acknowledge assistance from "official" Russians; but from these, as always during the past twenty-five years—save for one startling gesture from Khrushchev himself—there has been nothing but obstruction.

—E. C.

KHRUSHCHEV: *A Career*

CHAPTER ONE

From Log Cabin to Red Square

ONE EVENING when Khrushchev was at the summit of his power he was holding forth in one of his more ebullient moods to a group of Western diplomatists at a reception in Moscow. Suddenly, irritated by their professional coolness and evasiveness, he checked himself and exclaimed, "When I find myself talking to you gentlemen, I also find myself wondering. . . . You all went to great schools, to famous universities—to Harvard, to Oxford, to the Sorbonne. I never had any proper schooling. I went about barefoot and in rags. When you were in the nursery I was herding cows for two kopeks. I had no diplomatic training. . . . And yet here we are, and I can make rings round you all. . . . Tell me, gentlemen, why?"

That story is no doubt partly apocryphal, like most good stories. But like most apocryphal stories it strikes at the heart of the matter. Nobody in that little circle cared to hazard an answer to Khrushchev's interesting question. It is worth trying to answer it now.

[2.]

He was born in 1894, the child of peasants who were later driven from the land, the family home, by poverty. The family home belonged to his grandfather: it was a mud hut, or *izba*, with a ragged thatched roof, in Kalinovka, a poor village in the very rich Government of Kursk, where Great Russia borders the

Ukraine. The grandfather had been born a serf, the absolute chattel of his master, who could sell him, or exchange him for a pony or a gun dog, without anybody asking why.* His son, Sergei, was one of those many peasants who were defeated by the consequences of the abolition of serfdom by Alexander II in 1861, soon after the Crimean War. There was not enough land to go round: only the strongest, the cleverest, the most predatory among them could make a decent living from their own land; the rest scraped a subsistence, got hopelessly into debt to the inevitable greedy and acquisitive village kulak, spent their energies toiling for a pittance on the big landowner's fields, or drifted to the towns to better themselves. Sergei Nicaronovich Khrushchev was one of these. Leaving his wife and children behind in his father's *izba,* he went seasonally to work for the winter as a carpenter in the coalfields of the Donets valley, and returned in the spring to work on the land. His great ambition, Khrushchev was much later to say, was to buy himself a horse, but he never saved enough for this, and in the end the whole family moved for good.

Thus the infant Khrushchev was one of a vast family of nearly 100 million peasants, mainly illiterate, lately liberated from serfdom, who then formed four-fifths of the population of Imperial Russia. Nobody knows where the name Khrushchev came from. But there was a wealthy landowning family of Khrushchevs in the eastern Ukraine, and it is likely that Nikita's own forebears lived as serfs on the Khrushchev estate, taking their name from the master, as was common in those days. Nikita himself was christened Nikita Sergeievich, Nikita son of Sergei, after his father. He was a child without a history, and as an infant he was lucky to survive. There was nothing in his background to distinguish him from 100 million other peasants, so primitive and backward in their attitudes and standards that

---

* It is impossible to be certain of anything about the origins of Bolsheviks who joined the Party after 1917, so important was it for them to be able to claim a working-class or peasant background (as, increasingly, it is for English politicians today). But it is highly improbable that Khrushchev's grandfather was a landowner fallen upon hard times, as has sometimes been stated. It takes more than two generations to achieve the quintessential peasant as exhibited in N. S. Khrushchev.

they belonged to a different world from ours. Sixty years later, nevertheless, he was to become the autocrat of the Soviet empire, now the home of 220 million souls, disposing of a massive and complex economy and a vast and modern Army, Navy, and Air Force, and presiding over the launching of the first man into space.

His opportunity was the Revolution of 1917, which shattered the framework of Russian society and threw the field open to all the talents, heavily favouring the workers in the towns. But there were still more than 100 million peasants and workers for Khrushchev to compete with. He was twenty-three at the time of the revolution, and his education had been limited to two or three years in the village school. He did not join the Bolsheviks until 1918, when he was twenty-four. It would be evident from this brief record alone that Khrushchev was a man of extraordinary gifts and also of obvious limitations. Yet when he began to emerge as the supreme leader of the Soviet Union in 1954 there were many who could not bring themselves to believe that he was a man with the secret of leadership and power. He was contrasted unfavourably with his predecessor, Stalin: a pygmy, it was said, had succeeded a giant.

[3.]

To understand how this mistake could be made, and to appreciate the character of Khrushchev, it is necessary to range far and wide over the landscape of Russian society, moving away from the record of the man's immediate activities, and back again: he was formed by the Russia which he himself sought to mould. And because in a book of this limited size it is out of the question to bring the whole country, for so long terribly convulsed, alive, we must from time to time select certain keys to the general situation.

For example, it is useful to bear in mind that Nikita Sergeievich Khrushchev was born at almost precisely the same moment in time as the fictional hero of Pasternak's great novel *Dr. Zhivago;* the Russia into which he was born and the times through which he lived were thus the Russia and the times of Yuri Zhivago. But Zhivago was a bourgeois and Khrushchev was a peasant. When Yuri Zhivago was riding about the Russian countryside in an open carriage with his uncle, visiting wealthy and cultivated rural notabilities, the young Khrushchev, nine years old, had already left school and was herding the village cows.

Uncle Kolya was interested in the land problem, and on one of his excursions, with Yuri Zhivago at his side, he reflected aloud to the driver on the dangerous mood of the peasants.

"People are getting pretty rough here" [he said]. "A merchant has had his throat slit and the stud-farm of the *Zemsky* has been burned down. What do you think of it all? What are they saying in your village?" . . .

"What do you expect them to say? The peasants have got out of hand. They've been treated too well. That's no good for the likes of us. Give the peasants rope and God knows we'll all be at each other's throats." [1]

Uncle Kolya's driver was a jumped-up hanger-on of the Russian intelligentsia, himself precariously separated from the immemorial masses by a veneer of education. Nikita Khrushchev was a child of those peasants. The year was 1903.

Again, in the civil war after the Revolution, that fearful, confused, anarchic, treacherous struggle in which Zhivago found himself unable to aim his rifle to fire at a fellow countryman, even when under fire himself, Nikita Khrushchev, now twenty-five, a new Bolshevik, was a Red Army man, ready to fight ruthlessly and violently and urging ruthlessness and violence on his softer comrades.

Much later, when Lara, Pasternak's beloved heroine, was taken away by the political police to perish miserably, Nikita Khrushchev stood at the right hand of the man who caused her to be sent away.

One day Lara went out and did not come back. She must have been arrested in the street, as so often happened in those days, and she died or vanished somewhere, forgotten, a nameless number on a list which was later mislaid, in one of the innumerable . . . concentration camps in the north.

Those are the closing words of *Dr. Zhivago,* except for the Epilogue. Khrushchev was later to do away with many of those concentration camps, but when he attained supreme power he retained a number of them. And it was he who allowed Pasternak, the creator of Yuri Zhivago and Lara, to be persecuted to death; and when Pasternak was dead he allowed the real Lara, one of the models for Pasternak's heroine, who had in fact survived the labour camps, to be picked up and arrested on a trumped-up charge and sent away again, this time with her young daughter.[2]

He also brought Russia into the twentieth century, though even now, over large areas of the country, peasant life is as wretched as it was when he himself was a child.

CHAPTER TWO

The Child, Then the Man

AT THE TURN of the century, when Khrushchev was six years old, the revolutionary ferment among the students, among the intelligentsia, and in innumerable families of the nobility was building up a dangerous head of force. There were two main revolutionary parties: by far the largest were the Social Revolutionaries, who believed in violence and individual acts of terror, and who found their main strength in the provinces and the countryside; smaller, but more coherent and cohesive, were the Social Democrats, who took their inspiration from Karl Marx and, eschewing violence and assassination, looked for support among the urban proletariat. These had no faith in the ability of the peasants, overwhelming in numbers as they were, to effect by violence any useful change: revolution must come, but it could come only when the town workers, the urban proletariat, had grown numerous, strong, and desperate enough to turn against their masters and seize for themselves the means of industrial production. It was this party which, in 1903, was split by Lenin into two wings: his own, the Bolsheviks, on one hand; on the other, the Mensheviks. The Bolsheviks, like Lenin himself, were opportunists; the Mensheviks, more theoretical, were better Marxists.

The lives of the villagers deep in the interior, often hundreds of miles from any railway, connected with the outer world only by rivers, frozen in winter, and by dirt tracks, monstrously rutted in the heat of summer, impassable because of mud for long periods during the spring thaws and the autumn rains, were hardly affected by this ferment. They had their waves of violence and then subsided into brooding. When Khrushchev's father was a young man there was a great movement among the students and the intelligentsia of Russia to go to the peasants, to educate them by precept and example, to prepare them for the day when they could rise up in an organized manner and demand for themselves a decent life. But these missionary efforts were not well received.

It was not for nothing that the peasants were called the Dark People: cunning, sly, inured to a centuries-old burden of suffering, primitive in their cultivations, they had a profound instinct for ultimate self-preservation and they regarded with hostility, suspicion, and contempt the efforts of the starry-eyed idealists to help them to better ways. In famine years they were stricken, and this was the will of God: what could man do about it when week in, week out, the sun blazed down from a brassy sky and withered, then scorched and burnt to nothing the crops that were to sustain them for another year? In years when there was no famine they were so accustomed to hunger as a routine affliction before the new crops could be gathered in that they accepted this as part of the rhythm of life. Ridden by priests but not helped by them, superstitious in their religion to the point of idolatry, living to themselves in tight family networks, often drunk on cheap vodka, treating their wives like cattle but submitting to the absolute rule of the grandmother, the *babushka*, they resisted all interference from outside. Their revolutionary feelings, which sometimes fitted in with the programme of the social revolutionaries, were limited in expression to sudden uncoordinated outbursts of terrifying violence, in which, usually drunk, they would "slit the throat of a merchant," or burn down the landlord's house. Many an ardent political and educational missionary from the towns was also set on in this way.

For the rest, they lived in their *izbas* with mud or wooden walls, their animals under the same roof, spending interminable hours and days and weeks of the long dark winters on the wooden benches which were the only furniture, with the grandparents and the children stretched out on the stifling heat of the big flat clay or brick surface of the cooking stove.

It was not all misery. Long spells of idleness would alternate with bursts of pent-up energy as they set about cultivations and harvesting, trying to cram a year's work into the all too short season during which the land could be worked. They used wooden ploughs and mowed and harvested with primitive scythes and sickles and threshed with flails. In the forested areas they were clever with the adze and the axe, which were also deadly weapons. Their feast days were frequent and long-drawn-out and full of song and drunken horseplay. Every funeral was the occasion for a village wake.

Yet Khrushchev, like many more besides, became a revolutionary and in due course found himself first working with and for the intelligentsia whom he as a peasant despised, then turning on them and helping to kill them off, then triumphantly ruling over their successors, whom he needed for his rockets and sputniks and other ornaments of high civilization.

[2.]

The bridge between Khrushchev and the active revolutionaries was the industrial town. Russia under Alexander III and Nicholas II was beginning to industrialize itself, largely with the aid of foreign capital and under the direction of foreign entrepreneurs; but other than in certain quite exceptional centres, above all St. Petersburg, there was nothing yet in the way of a settled artisan class: most of the factories and the mines in the new centres were worked by peasants, like Khrushchev's father, whose hearts were still with the land, who kept their places in the village communes warm, and who drifted purposefully to and fro, on foot, by sledge, by unsprung peasant cart, over quite surprisingly long distances between their remote villages and the new industrial centres. The feeling of attachment to the land was so deep and compelling that it was a common thing for men who had risen high in the government service and were permanently resident in St. Petersburg, Moscow, or Odessa, whose children were born in city apartments, to pay their dues to the *mir* of their native village and thus keep open for themselves their claim on their tiny shares of the land—which one day, in a country run by arbitrary force, might suddenly come to be their only means of support. This ambivalence, this absence of a hard line between countryside and town, persists even to this day, after the transformation of the country by the Five Year Plans into a largely industrial society: officials in dark suits, with briefcases, who spend their days in city offices, still keep their precious ties with the collectives, the *kolkhozy*, which work the land where they, or their fathers, were born.

Khrushchev's father, as we have seen, made his way regularly each autumn to the coal mines in the valley of the Donets, the Donbas, where he lived hard, with thousands of others like him, separated from his family and sleeping in corners or in the crowded dormitories of bleak and ugly workers' barracks. This seasonal segregation of the sexes was one of the peculiar features of the Russian industrial revolution, and it had a good deal to do with the slow growth of industrial towns. There were fewer than 30 towns with a population of 100,000. Except in St. Petersburg, Moscow, and a few other places, where industry was tacked on to an existing city, there was an air of the provisional about all Russian industrial centres, an air, indeed, of the camp, with a marked absence of all those amenities—churches, chapels, public houses, meeting halls, music halls—which are the expression, however seedy and inadequate, of a settled communal life. And, indeed, this tradition persisted in postrevolutionary Russia: the workers' barracks were very much a feature of the new industrial centres of the Five Year Plan period; during the great reconstruction after the Second World War segregation was so marked that for a period of years the fields were worked almost exclusively by women, boys, and very old men; millions of the able-bodied men were dead, millions more were hard at work rebuilding industry.

In the early days of this process the young Khrushchev (he was fifteen at the time) was transplanted from the countryside to become a settled urban worker. His boyhood had been rough, but poverty and hunger and long hours in the fields were mitigated by the deep satisfactions of country life. The boy had no boots, but at least he could feel the hot sand of the dirt roads and the spongy grass of the pastures between his toes. He could fish, even if it meant poaching and being caught and beaten by keepers; he could drink in the sounds and smells of the broad, ever fluid Russian plain. Kalinovka was not far from the Turgenev country; it, too, had its nightingales, its long summer twilights and early dawns. At fifteen he left all this finally behind him, and for the rest of his life he was to be a dweller in towns. But he never escaped from the countryside, and his peasant background was to move right into the foreground of all his activity when, as a world statesman, he showed himself happiest talking to farmers, peppering his speeches with peasant wit, and, out of his own deep understanding of peasant backwardness and stubbornness, conservatism above all, knocking peasants' heads together and telling them what to do to make a better living for themselves.

His childhood days had been rough, but they had the glow of life. His adolescence was rough with no redeeming feature. It was lived out in a squalid mining town, or encampment, called Yuzovka in the Donbas.

Yuzovka was later to become Stalino, the very heart and capital of the Donbas industrial complex: the German occupation of it in 1941 marked the destruction of the whole vast industrial area of the Ukraine, upon which, until that date, the economy of the Soviet Union had very much depended. After the war it was rebuilt as an urgent priority, in spite of the great transfer of industry to the Urals and beyond, and it is now a great city of massive buildings and a strong, if rough, communal life—renamed, since Stalin's posthumous destruction, Donetsk.

Yuzovka was named after a Welshman called Hughes, who built the iron works there in 1869. By the time of the Khrushchev migration the town and the whole region round it were effectively in the hands of foreign concessionaires.

I worked [Khrushchev himself was later to say] at a factory owned by Germans, at coal pits owned by Frenchmen, and at a chemical plant owned by Belgians. There I discovered something about capitalists. They are all alike, whatever their nationality. All they wanted from me was the most work for the least money that kept me alive. So I became a Communist, and all my conscious life I have worked

with my whole heart and all my energy for my party. I was not born
a Communist any more than you [he was speaking to visitors from
abroad] are born members of your own parties. But life is a great
school. It thrashes you and bangs you about and teaches you.[1]

This is an oversimplification. It was 1909 when Khrushchev
settled with his parents in Yuzovka, six years after Lenin had
quarrelled with his fellow Social Democrats and founded the
Bolshevik Party. Khrushchev did not join the Bolsheviks until
1918, when he was twenty-four and when Lenin was already in
power. Soviet sources, and Khrushchev himself, prefer to blur
this point, and we have not been told why Khrushchev took so
long to make up his mind to follow Lenin. But there was nothing disgraceful about this hesitation. Khrushchev was a rebel
long before he became a Communist, and he was in good company. The great majority of the most ardent rebels in those days
were anything but Bolsheviks, including most of the dedicated
humanitarian idealists and many of the fiercest destructive spirits
—among them Leon Trotsky.

[3.]

If we do not know why Khrushchev did not join the Bolsheviks,
or any other revolutionary party, sooner, we can at least guess,
putting together what we know of those sullen, restless times
and what we now know of the character of Khrushchev himself.
All through his public life, familiar from 1953 onwards, quite
well documented in outline, as we shall see, but unfamiliar to all
but specialists for twenty-five years before that date, he was to
show a remarkable sense of timing: it was not an unerring sense
(he made his mistakes), but it was keen to a degree. During that
epoch of his career, the last twelve years, which was lived out
under the eyes of all the world, this gift, this sense of timing, was
often obscured by the continuous noisy running commentary, a
kind of glorified conjuror's patter, which accompanied and
partly covered all his actions. But it was very much in evidence
underneath the blarney and the ballyhoo. And it was a gift
which went hand in hand with a very cool and cautious and far-
sighted mind. Time and time again, first as a provincial boss

with great powers, then as a metropolitan figure, then as a national chieftain, finally as an international statesman, he showed that he could withdraw from the scrimmage, quietly watching the state of play with almost perfect detachment, and then move in to strike at the critical moment. Often and often his most compelling exhibitions of apparent indiscretion were no more than cover, a sort of smokescreen, for these spells of intent and purposeful watchfulness. At the same time he was always a great learner. He was constantly talking about learning from life and he was, indeed, one of life's most eager and rewarding pupils. He even had the gift, so rare among politicians, of learning from his own mistakes.

He must have always been like this: the youth of eighteen held the pattern of the autocrat of sixty. Rough, impulsive, coarse in his language, inclined to bully he must have been then, but also watchful and cautious—and learning. He had a great deal to learn.

[4.]

In biographies of Western statesmen, whose lives from childhood onwards may be reconstructed and documented in some detail, the usual method of procedure is for the biographer to start at the beginning and go on to the end, building up the character of his hero as he proceeds. But the early lives of Soviet politicians are not documented at all, and we are told next to nothing about them. Khrushchev used to talk about his own life, or parts of it, more freely than any other postrevolutionary Russian politician, but he did not tell us much, and it is not until he began making important public speeches in his middle thirties that we can begin to trace the development of his career and his way of thinking with certainty. Thus, in order to understand the sort of person Khrushchev was when in 1918, at twenty-four, he became a Bolshevik, we need the clearest possible picture of the mature public figure. Only then can the scanty information about his early days, and the few extremely revealing photographs of the young Communist boss, begin to make sense.

All the world has seen Khrushchev on television and knows what he looked like at the height of his power and how he spoke. But television performances conceal as much as they reveal. We can do a little better than that: we can catch Nikita Khrushchev as he appeared before he achieved confidence as a world states-man; we can catch him, also, speaking not to a mass audience or even in carefully calculated indiscretions to foreign diploma-tists, but to a small group of people whose brains he was trying to pick—as far as he knew, unobserved by any outsider.

The occasion was Khrushchev's first visit to the world outside his own closed society, that celebrated pilgrimage to Yugoslavia in 1955, about which we shall have more to say later. With Mar-shal Bulganin, titular Prime Minister, cheerful and blowzy and very much in holiday mood, and Anastas Mikoyan, grimly sar-donic and fathomlessly bored, he had gone to Belgrade to make up the quarrel with Marshal Tito, whom Stalin had so viciously and vainly sought to destroy, using every method short of mili-tary bombardment or invasion. He found himself with a harder task on his hands than he had expected. It was clear from the moment he stepped from the plane, a squat little figure with flapping trousers, that he was taking it quite for granted that Tito would be flattered and overjoyed by this grand gesture of reconciliation—the leaders of mighty Russia abasing themselves before the master of a poor, weak country. Tito must certainly have felt triumphant, but he showed no joy, and he made it clear at once that he was standing no nonsense of any kind at all. The first nonsense was when Khrushchev in his speech at the airport said he had come to bury the hatchet, that the Soviet Union had behaved badly towards Yugoslavia, but it had all been the fault of Beria. Tito knew it was the fault of Stalin, who had not then been pulled from his pedestal, and he knew that Khrushchev, Bulganin, and Mikoyan had been among Stalin's chief aides. He was not going to have the whole affair, which had been a matter of life and death for Yugoslavia—nearly death—smoothly blamed on the chief policeman of the Soviet Union, who had been executed by his colleagues less than two years ear-lier. He showed his displeasure: he interrupted the interpreter who had started putting Khrushchev's speech into Serbo-Croat, and stalked off, waving his Russian visitors on, to the waiting car.

This was Khrushchev's first mistake. He swallowed its consequences and never made that mistake again. During the next few days he was to make so many mistakes that the onlookers, the diplomatists and the journalists, began to write him off as a clumsy nonentity who could not possibly last long. What they appeared not to see was that Khrushchev registered his mistakes as he made them, digested them, and never made the same mistake twice. What most of them never had a chance to see was Khrushchev at his ease, concentrating on a job in hand which he really understood.

Tito made things as difficult and awkward as he could. This man, who himself went about in fear of assassination, decided to show off by conducting his visitors through crowded streets in an open car. Khrushchev was used to bulletproof cars with shaded windows, tearing in convoy through the cleared streets in Moscow. But he blinked only once before stepping into this death-trap of a vehicle, and then settled down, waving to unresponsive crowds, as to the manner born. In private meetings Tito declared himself ready to resume cordial state relations with the Soviet Union, but he would have nothing to do with the Soviet Communist Party as such: Khrushchev was there not as prime minister (that was Bulganin) but solely as First Secretary of the Soviet Communist Party. At a grandiose reception in the White Palace, Tito put all his senior officials into dinner jackets and their wives into full evening dress. The Russians had no dinner jackets and arrived, to be kept standing in the glare of Klieg lights, still dressed in their clumsy Russian summer suitings: Bulganin looked foolish; Mikoyan looked daggers; Khrushchev simply blinked a little and stood, quite passively and patiently, his hands clasped loosely in front of him. Tito insisted on racing Khrushchev about the Adriatic in a high-powered motorboat. Khrushchev was not sick. He must have had a most humiliating time, but he came through it, and he became, at the end, enough himself to get noisily drunk at the Soviet Embassy reception: it was the last time he was ever to get seriously drunk in public.

And in the middle of it all, in spite of many harassments, in spite of innumerable snubs by his host, he was able, when necessary, to concentrate on the job in hand.

One day, after being rushed all over the Yugoslav countryside, he had to visit a factory at Ljubljana in Slovenia. The factory made turbines; it was new and up-to-date, and the construction of prestressed concrete with a finely arching cantilever roof was beautiful and impressive.

There was a large assortment of Western journalists waiting for the arrival of the Russians; only two were to receive permission to join the party on its tour of the factory, and in the end the correspondent of *The Times* of London was chosen, a young woman of a startling elegance and beauty not readily associated with Printing House Square, as was the present writer, the correspondent of *The Observer*. We were chosen because *The Times* spoke Serbo-Croat and could understand the interpretations, while *The Observer* spoke a little Russian and could, it was hoped, listen in on Khrushchev and his colleagues.

There was the usual immense procession of officials, engineers, hangers-on, East European journalists, and the rest. Khrushchev and Bulganin leading, the procession made its way at a brisk pace through the vast central aisle of the swept and garnished building, with great chunks of recondite machinery in various stages of completion and assembly dotted about the floor in a surrealist manner, or suspended from overhead rails.

Khrushchev was not interested in the machinery: he had that at home. What he was interested in was the building itself, which was a model of functional design and light as air. For some months past, in Russia, he had been touring the country on one of his crusades, this time a crusade for the use of concrete, especially prefabricated concrete units, for industrial and institutional building; the Soviet press had been full of nothing else for weeks, as, earlier, it had been full of nothing but talk of corn as the universal panacea. Khrushchev, to hear him, might have invented concrete. Well, here concrete was, in a perfect object lesson in what it might do. In the middle of that vast hall Khrushchev stopped and proceeded to deliver a lecture to Bulganin, Mikoyan, Shepilov, and anybody else who cared to listen. They had heard it all before, and they looked as though they had heard it all before. But this did not deter the master: he had talked to them about concrete, now he was showing them concrete. Would they kindly pay attention to what he said, make a note of what they saw, and get on with the manufacture of concrete and the construction of concrete buildings when they got home?

Bulganin emerged from his perpetual purring dream for long enough to look intelligent and reply that indeed he would see to it. Mikoyan said nothing. The Yugoslav conducting officials (Tito had demonstratively stayed behind in Belgrade) were a little taken aback. They had wanted to show off their turbines, of which they were very proud; they wanted to talk about their Workers' Councils, in which Khrushchev was not interested: they were presenting a splendid picture, and here was Khrushchev insisting on praising the frame. They had also expected Khrushchev to have something to say to the workers grouped round their machines. But this working-class master of the original workers' paradise seemed unaware of the existence of the workers: like a caricature of a capitalist tycoon, he poked around and prodded, never addressing a question to the men on the job, behaving as though they were not there. This was a shock. It was also another mistake. By the time that tour was over Khrushchev had registered this mistake: the Yugoslavs took the line that the workers mattered; very well. Next day, at a factory in Zagreb, he remembered the workers and talked to them a great deal.

At the end of this little tour the Yugoslav hosts had arranged for the Russians and a handful of Yugoslavs to move into the factory director's room for drinks and conversation. When the time came for this, the correspondents for *The Times* and *The Observer* were both just behind Khrushchev and just in front of Mikoyan; it was the easiest thing to infiltrate with them before the barrier was closed. The chief Soviet and the chief Yugoslav security men looked a little surprised, but the Russians must have thought the newspaper people were accredited Yugoslavs, and the Yugoslavs must have thought they were accredited Russians. There were only a dozen or so people in that room, but both correspondents were offered drinks with the rest. Bulganin from now on could not take his eyes off *The Times*. While Khrushchev talked technicalities, his eyes strayed constantly. In the end he could resist no longer. He leant across to where *The Times* was standing, patted her gently, raised his glass, beamed moonily, and murmured: *"À vous, madame!"*—words he had clearly been rehearsing for some minutes past. He went on beaming. Khrushchev's eyes, a little startled, flickered across; but he had seen beautiful young women before. Mikoyan looked disgusted. The meeting proceeded.

The real interest was Khrushchev himself. He sat down in an armchair in front of a round table spread with blueprints. He drank freely and absently, but he was a man transformed, no longer the public clown, no longer the bullying demagogue, no longer the man showing off about concrete; his whole immense vitality was concentrated on the job in hand. The job in hand was twofold: first, to understand the details of the concrete construction and to make sure that these details were conveyed to him in Moscow in such a form that they could be readily and completely understood by Soviet engineers; second, to tell the Yugoslavs that all their ideas about a workers' democracy, about workers' participation in factory management (the famous Workers' Councils) were so much nonsense, and why: workers had to be told what to do and made to do it, and that was that; any government, any managerial staff, which shirked this responsibility in the name of democracy was heading straight for trouble.

All this was done very quietly but with an authority which was absolute. This little man, no longer a comic figure with badly fitting clothes, had become, without emphasis, without raising his voice, the born and unquestioned master. There are some great men who, in a group, achieve their ascendancy by, as it were, radiating vitality, by giving out. Khrushchev gave out nothing. He was learning, and at the same time commanding. He became at once the still centre of that small and powerful gathering and instead of giving he took. It was as though all the energies, all the vitality, of everybody in that room were being drained from each individual and absorbed into this small figure who knew just what he wanted and was going to get it with perfect economy of effort—and knew just what he did not want: it took only a barely perceptible wave of the hand to divert an eager torrent of explanation, which he did not want; it took a single word to turn the conversation in the direction he required. Another man who had this quality, this capacity to subdue, to draw out, to pull the essence of other people's specialized experience almost physically into his own mind, without lifting a finger to dominate, was the late Ernest Bevin—who could also be garrulous and bullying and histrionic on occasion. It was impossible to watch this performance without being convinced that behind Khrushchev the showman and the extrovert there was a man born to supreme authority. It explained a great many things.

[5.]

It explained, when one came to think of it, his early career. We have to reconcile two images: on one hand, the rough, loquacious, joking, bullying extrovert, impetuous to the point of recklessness; on the other, the calculator, withdrawn into himself, watching, learning, waiting. The supreme authority which he was to show in that Ljubljana factory by the carriage of his head, the exactness and economy of a gesture, was a quality which obviously developed in later life. But those other qualities must have been present in quite early days. The side he then put forward was the rough side, and even when he was forty years old and making a distinguished career in Moscow he consistently presented himself as a rough diamond, hectoring and familiar in his public speeches, more of a coal miner's son than he had ever been in real life. At a time when his senior colleagues were beginning to spruce themselves up, Khrushchev went about in a cloth cap spectacularly hideous even by Soviet standards, as though to emphasize his proletarian origins. Indeed, these were of the greatest value to him. The higher reaches of the Bolshevik Party were not rich in proletarians. Stalin himself was a cobbler's son; but he was a Georgian, a member of an elite tribe, and he had been educated for the Church. Molotov,

Malenkov, Zhdanov, Beria, Bulganin, were all born into bourgeois families, high or low. The most distinguished of the old Bolsheviks whom Stalin killed off belonged to the intelligentsia. Khrushchev, with one or two others, was able to exploit his contempt for the bourgeoisie and the intelligentsia, and he did so.

When, at fifteen, he went to work in Yuzovka, he was gifted enough to keep out of the pits and to turn himself quite soon into a skilled worker of sorts. He moved from factory to factory. He got himself trained as a fitter, and on the eve of the 1914 war he was in charge of the maintenance of a pit-head installation, the elevator in which the miners went up and down.

Various attempts, frequently contradictory, have been made to present the young Khrushchev as an active revolutionary worker in those early days: these include remarks made by Khrushchev himself from time to time and, more particularly, romanticized accounts of his youth put out for foreign consumption on the various occasions of his foreign tours. But there is not a word in the dry official biographies to substantiate the claims that he was engaged in large-scale strike activity, or that he undertook negotiations with the management on behalf of his work-mates. Indeed, Khrushchev himself once said that he had never played any part in the trade-union movement.[2]

That he was in a rebellious frame of mind goes without saying. Yuzovka had a great tradition of belligerent labour going back to the 1880s. But after the 1905 revolt, with the shooting down of the loyal and silent demonstrators in front of the empty Winter Palace and the severe repression which followed, the labour movement in the Donbas, as elsewhere, fell into a decline. When the fifteen-year-old Khrushchev started work there in 1909 things were very quiet indeed. There were strikes in 1912 and 1913. But in 1914 over a third of the miners were conscripted into the Army, and it was not until 1916 that industrial action began to get out of hand in protest against the sharp deterioration of living and working conditions produced by the war.

During all this period, until 1916, the Bolshevik Party, numerically small, played an unimportant part. The main fomentors of revolt in Yuzovka were the Mensheviks and the Social

Revolutionaries, and it was the slow recovery of these parties from the post-1905 repression which brought about the strike movement in 1912. In that year, too, *Pravda* had begun to appear openly, and there were groups all over the Ukraine, in Yuzovka too, engaged in trying to whip up subscriptions to the Bolshevik paper. But the Mensheviks and Social Revolutionaries were far stronger, so strong, indeed, that in the Ukraine they completely dominated the workers' councils after the March Revolution in 1917 and continued in a majority even after the Bolshevik seizure of power in October. It was not until six months after that that Khrushchev joined the Bolsheviks.

There is one particular reason for being certain that Khrushchev had no connection with the Bolsheviks at all until, seeing which way things were going, he joined them. In 1916, when Khrushchev was twenty-two and doing well, Lazar Kaganovich came to Yuzovka to run the Bolshevik group there. Kaganovich, a Jew from the Kiev region, was only a year older than Khrushchev (and fourteen years younger than Stalin); but he had been an active Bolshevik since 1911, when he was eighteen, in and out of prison for fomenting strikes, and generally a fighter who had gained such ascendancy over his fellow workers that when he was sacked from a shoe factory at Dnepropetrovsk they had carried out a successful six-week strike to secure his reinstatement. In Yuzovka this brilliant and powerfully built young Jew must have been an outstanding and romantic figure. His job, in which he failed, was to turn the workers away from the Mensheviks and Social Revolutionaries and capture them for the party of Lenin. Any worker remotely sympathetic towards Bolshevism must have come in contact with him, and, once one was in contact with him, his persuasive ways, backed by an extremely strong personality, must have been hard to resist. Years later, in his steady upward climb, Khrushchev was to be very much a Kaganovich man: first his protégé; then, in one job after another, his assistant and successor; finally, in 1957, his destroyer. Any association between Khrushchev and Kaganovich, however tenuous, in those Yuzovka days, would, until 1957, have been underlined in red in the official biographies. No such association is mentioned. And all this can only mean that, if Khrushchev played any part at all in the prerevolutionary workers' movement, he must have been on the side of the Mensheviks or the Social Revolutionaries; this is a thing that would not, could not, be mentioned after 1917. It is a big "if," however. The signs are that the young Khrushchev was too busy bettering himself to risk his future in organized revolutionary struggle.

He was doing well by his employers. Although young and able-bodied, he was not called up in 1914, clearly because he qualified for exemption as an indispensable worker. He married in 1915 and had two children by his first wife, who, according to his second wife, Nina Petrovna, whom he married in 1924, died in the great famine of 1921–1922. At a time when the young revolutionaries were fanatically active educating themselves in political theory, in history, in everything, the young Khrushchev seems to have been quite happy without book learning. And when the Revolution finally came, in 1917, his first recorded action "in the name of the Revolution" took place not in Yuzovka at all, but back in his own village of Kalinovka. Suddenly he appeared there as chairman of the peasants' committee engaged in parcelling out among the peasants the land seized from the landowners.[3] The picture we receive is of a tough, watchful, calculating mechanic observing the impact of the Revolution and, leaving his bench, hurrying straight back to his native village to make sure that when the land was divided there would be some for his family.

It was not until 1918 that the victory of the Bolsheviks in the Donbas over the rival revolutionary parties was clear for all to see. What Khrushchev did, in effect, was to apply for membership in the ruling party.

Not all the workers at that time hurried to join the Bolsheviks. On the contrary. But those who did were on the side of whatever authority there was. In January 1918 Lenin had dissolved the Constituent Assembly. It had sat from 4 p.m. on January 18 until 4:40 a.m. on January 19. It was the cherished symbol of all revolutionary aspiration, the first truly democratic parliament Russia had ever known.* But it included only 175 Bolsheviks among its 700-odd elected deputies. This would not do for Lenin. For a brief moment he had control of the only coherent force in Petrograd, the mutinous soldiers and sailors who, on the Bolsheviks' behalf, had raided the Winter Palace and swept away the unfortunate Kerensky's Provisional Government. He now reposed himself on that force. "All Power to the Soviets!" (the soldiers' and sailors' councils) was still the slogan. If only he could disperse the parliamentary opposition and thereby shatter the cohesion, such as it was, of the Mensheviks and Social Revolutionaries, he, Lenin, could master the Soviets and transfer their power to himself. This is what he did. The new Russian democracy functioned for exactly twelve hours and forty minutes. Then the dictatorship of the proletariat took over. The two revolutions, the popular rising of March 1917, which had swept away the tsarist autocracy, and the Bolshevik *Putsch* of October 1917, which exploited the chaos and the discontent induced by Kerensky's determination to keep Russia in the war, had been carried through with very little bloodshed. The blood was to start flowing once Lenin, as Chairman of the Council of People's Commissars, started to consolidate his own dictatorship. It was at this point that Nikita Khrushchev became a Bolshevik.

---

* The Provisional Government which was installed after the March Revolution and the abdication of Nicholas II was, of course, infinitely more democratic than anything hitherto dreamed of in Russia; hence its vulnerability to the undemocratic Bolsheviks. But it was not a government elected by the people. Lenin saw to it that it did not have time to sort itself out and appeal to the country.

CHAPTER THREE

Revolution, Chaos, Civil War

THE NEW young Comrade Khrushchev had nothing at all
to do with the feverish manœuvring in Petrograd whereby
Lenin and his trusted (also some not so trusted) colleagues organized some sort of government and set about the seemingly
hopeless task of subduing a vast country to their will, while at
the same time holding the foreigner at arm's length—sometimes
a very short arm's length. Outside Petrograd, Moscow, and one
or two other centres, there was chaos. Yuzovka was part of that
chaos.

Khrushchev was not there. We do not know where he was—
perhaps for a time at Kalinovka. Yuzovka was deep in the
Ukraine, and in 1917 the Ukraine, together with the Cossack
lands along the Don and the Volga and on the coasts of the Black
Sea and the Caspian, rejected Bolshevism. The newly formed
Red Army had only just completed the military subjugation of
the Ukraine at the end of January 1918 when Trotsky, on behalf
of Lenin, signed away the whole of it to Germany under the
Treaty of Brest-Litovsk. Then, until the Allied victory, it was
governed by a German puppet, the Hetman Skoropadski. There
was no room in the Donbas for a man who felt himself neither a
Ukrainian nationalist nor a pro-German. Khrushchev's first appearance as a Bolshevik was as a Red Army man in the civil
war.

What he was doing is not clear. Once again the propagandists
sought, years later, to magnify his position. He served, they said,

as a *politrabotnik* with the Red Army.[1] It is hard to be convinced of this. A *politrabotnik,* or political worker, was even in
those days an active Bolshevik whom the Party could trust: his
job was to keep the Red Army volunteers and conscripts up to
the mark and instruct them in the inner meaning of Bolshevism.
It was a necessary job. Trotsky's Red Army was a very mixed lot.
It included not only a mass of workers and peasants who joined
it voluntarily, either out of conviction or because they saw in
the Bolsheviks their only hope of stopping the landlords from
coming back to claim their lands, but also, in hundreds of thousands, conscripts rounded up as the Red Army established itself
in new territory, or men from the armies of the Whites captured
by the Red Army and given their freedom to fight for it against
the Whites. Untold thousands who hardly knew White from
Red changed sides in this way, often many times.

It was an appalling struggle, conducted in a mood of desperate savagery on both sides. Atrocity, designed as Terror, was the
order of the day: massacres of sleeping villages, public hangings,
summary executions, murder and rape and looting, systematic
arson and destruction, complex and vicious treacheries. There
were formal cavalry actions, sweeping and terrifying incursions
by armoured trains, artillery bombardments, hand-to-hand
fighting in the style of trench warfare. And behind the set pieces
there went on all the time incessant guerrilla warfare, sniping,
ambushing, torturing, and throat-cutting, in the forests and in
the towns. The Red Army had to face three separate major
threats: Generals Denikin and Wrangel from the South, Admiral Kolchak from Siberia, General Miller from the North. The
White armies were supported by the Western Allies, who started
their intervention with a landing at Murmansk in June.

The Entente powers had welcomed the March revolution and
the fall of the tsarist autocracy: Russia, the great dumb ally,
would be purged, freed of the bonds of tyranny, would fight all
the harder for finding her soul. The United States Secretary of
State, Mr. Robert Lansing, went so far as to declare to the Cabinet in Washington that the Russian Revolution "had removed
the one objection to affirming that the European war was a war
between Democracy and Absolutism." But when, just seven

months later, democracy went under to Lenin and his Bolsheviks, who had already indicated that their first task was to take Russia out of the war, benign approval of Russian progressiveness was succeeded by embittered consternation. Nobody quite knew who the Bolsheviks were. Lenin, they did know, was an extreme revolutionary who had been brought back to Russia in the famous sealed train by the Germans—was thus, inevitably and reasonably, highly suspect. He was surrounded by a number of very conspiratorial-looking figures, often bearded in an outlandish manner, often Jews, born equivocators who were also rabble-rousers. It was natural to assume that an extreme left-wing party in a land given to revolutionary terror and assassination should be more addicted to violence than all other parties; and, indeed, Trotsky, Zinoviev, and certain others looked just the sort of men to carry bombs in their pockets. In fact the Bolsheviks in opposition eschewed political assassination, not for moral reasons but for reasons of expediency; the Social Revolutionaries were the terrorists. To this image were added Lenin's actions: his denunciation of all established governments and his appeal to all the workers of the world to unite and overthrow their masters; his denunciation of all existing treaties; his immediate trampling down of the first tender shoots of Russian democracy and his imposition of what amounted to a military dictatorship; his disgraceful separate peace with Germany.

The Allied response was emotional rather than reasoned. Troops were sent to bolster up any Russian government which would fight the Germans, but soon they were helping the White generals to overthrow the Bolsheviks in favour of a government pledged to continue the war, and thus keep the German armies from moving across to the Western front, then desperately hard-pressed; they were also required to prevent the vast dumps of war material supplied by the Entente and piled up at Russian ports from falling into German hands. The Allied intervention was never in the least intended to restore either the monarchy or the landlords.

In this context it should be remembered that the Whites were not the only ones opposed to the Bolsheviks and to the separate peace. The Social Revolutionaries, who had filled 370 seats in the short-lived Constituent Assembly, to the Bolsheviks' 175, were also fighting hard. They were still in being as a party and at the Fifth All Union Congress of Soviets, which met in July 1918, four months after the peace of Brest-Litovsk, they sponsored a motion declaring renewed war on Germany. This motion was defeated, and the Social Revolutionary leaders were immediately arrested. But the party was far from dead. On July 6 it organized the assassination of the first German Ambassador to the Soviet Union, Count Mirbach, in order to provoke the Germans to military action against the Bolshevik government. At the same time it launched its own military action against the Moscow government, which failed. The troops who went over to the Social Revolutionaries and joined in this ill-fated march on Moscow were indistinguishable from the troops who fought against them in the Bolshevik cause.

Somewhere in this phantasmagoric mix-up was Comrade N. S. Khrushchev, allegedly a trusted political worker from the beginning, in fact a raw recruit to the Red Army. The Red Army was indeed short of political watchdogs and instructors, but Trotsky, its organizer and commander-in-chief, had high standards. A rough mechanic of twenty-three pitchforked into the Red Army, then fighting for its life, would have to prove himself under the eyes of existing political officers who had joined the Party before its seizure of power: only then would he be trusted. Comrade Khrushchev, strong, rough, energetic, and at the same time calculating, as he then must have been, no doubt set himself to do precisely this. It is certain that by the time the civil war was over in 1920 he had in fact started to emerge as a useful and loyal figure, but still not a politician. And there is nothing at all in his official civil-war record to compare, for example, with Malenkov's performance. Malenkov was eight years younger than Khrushchev, but he joined the Red Army in 1919, when he was only seventeen, and was almost at once (he was an educated bourgeois, not a mechanic) put to political work, even before he formally joined the party—as the *politrabotnik* first of a squadron, then of a brigade, then at HQ Eastern and Turkestan Front. These are the kind of details which are included, when they exist, in all official political biographies of Soviet leaders.

But it was not until Khrushchev had achieved supreme power, and not until he had destroyed Malenkov himself, and also Kaganovich (who knew everything about him), that the propagandists got to work to rewrite this bit of history and build up for him a civil-war legend.

When the civil war was over, Khrushchev went back to Yuzovka to help get coal production going. Malenkov, in contrast, at nineteen was called straight to Moscow to be trained at the Higher Technical School. Kaganovich, the young Ukrainian revolutionary, was already working hand in glove with Stalin and was sent off to Turkestan to put down the separatist movement before, in 1922, being called back to Moscow as head of the Personnel Department of the Party Central Committee.

[2.]

Khrushchev had last seen Yuzovka as a mechanic in the employ of a foreign capitalist. He returned to it as a member of the ruling party and as assistant manager of one of the expropriated mines. The Bolsheviks were in control of the country, but now they were ruling by terror. Terror, which Lenin had found inexpedient when the Bolsheviks were in opposition, became immediately expedient when they were masters of the prisons and the machine guns. The Cheka (the Extraordinary Commission to Fight Counterrevolution and Sabotage) had been set up by Lenin in December 1917. The Red Terror was formally inaugurated in December 1918. The Cheka soon found plenty to do, and within a matter of months had become a virtually autonomous force. Its autonomy was formally recognized in September 1918. "The All-Russia Cheka is absolutely independent in its activity and is invested with the power to carry out searches, arrests, and executions." [2] But if the Cheka itself was autonomous, so, in effect, were local Chekist organizations: these were commanded as often as not by thugs and sadists, and the rank and file were illiterate peasant youths whose natural callousness and indifference to suffering were magnified by the unspeakable cruelties of the civil war.

Any aspiring Communist activist was utterly dependent on

the local Cheka for his necessary backing of force—and was himself under constant surveillance from that same Cheka: a false move, an injudicious word, the slightest hint of weakness, of failure of "Bolshevik resolution" in carrying out the harshest tasks, and he himself would be denounced and arrested as an enemy of the people. The twenty-seven-year-old Khrushchev, assistant manager of a mine and now secretary of the Party cell of that mine, was learning in the Cheka school.

We have one glimpse of Khrushchev in his first days as a minor Party activist. It is the picture of the burly assistant manager in his cloth cap haranguing the miners who were demanding their back pay. "Everything depends on coal. How can the factories produce boots and shirts if they do not have coal? All you demand you must get with your own hands. No manna from the sky is going to come down to you. So beat with your picks with all your might." [3]

That story was told to the American journalist Harold Martin, who went first to Kalinovka, then to Donetsk (late Stalino, late Yuzovka), to see what light he could find on Khrushchev's origins. Not all the stories told Mr. Martin by men and women who said they had known the young Khrushchev were true; some were demonstrably untrue. But this story has the authentic ring. It is the Khrushchev we know. And, indeed, this is the sort of work Khrushchev must have been doing. There were a million unemployed. The countryside was ravaged by armed bands. All over the country workers were striking and demonstrating sometimes rising up in violent rebellion, because they were not being paid—more often than not for three or four months on end—and because what money they had would buy nothing. And it was the job of the local Party men, backed by the Cheka, to cajole them, to trick them, to bully them, into going on working. There was nothing else to be done unless Lenin chose to abdicate. This he could not do, even had he wished to. He had brought the country through the civil war, largely represented as a quasi-patriotic war against capitalist invaders. In the course of this struggle he had built up an army and a police force upon which his power reposed. He had driven out the Western Allies and the Whites. He had conducted a war against the Poles, which had taken the Red Army to the gate of Warsaw. He had subdued strong separatist movements in the Ukraine, in the Caucasus, in Turkestan. For an internationalist who did not believe in colonialism he had done fairly well: when it was all over he ruled over the whole of the empire conquered by the tsars, less only Poland, Finland, and Bessarabia. But that empire was a ruin. It was on men like Comrade Khrushchev, scattered thinly over the whole vast ravaged landscape of the Soviet Union, that he depended to get the economy going again. This had to be done against the background of the worst famine since 1890. There was no light, no heat, no food. The peasants were reduced to eating grass and bark and chewing leather. In extreme cases— but by no means uncommon ones—they ate the corpses of their neighbours.

To force famished and exhausted men to work in these conditions, first to restore what factories there were, to open flooded mines, then to start producing coal, called for a very high degree of toughness and some courage. Comrade Khrushchev filled the bill. His first known contribution to the Communist cause was to help get the mines of Yuzovka back into production. Either while he was still doing this, or immediately afterwards, he started going to school. The date is not certain, but the school, the Donets Mining Technical School, was not founded until May 1921. It was almost certainly soon after that. Khrushchev had seen his wife, still in her twenties, die of hunger and exhaustion. He had two young children to care for. He had found his talent for organizing people and ordering them about. But he was still hardly more than literate. Disregarding the discrepancies between the various official reports, some of which say he worked and educated himself simultaneously, some of which say that late in 1922 he became a full-time student, it seems likely that the death of his wife had a bearing on the matter.[4]

Be that as it may. By 1923 Khrushchev was beginning to emerge as a politician among students. And after that he was never to work with his hands again. In 1923 he became a *politrook,* or political guide, at the technical school. The students lived roughly, in a derelict, half-shattered barracks. It has been suggested that Khrushchev had better quarters because of his

political work, but there is no reason to suppose this: a *politrook*
was the lowest kind of political animal. I was personally acquainted with two or three of them serving in infantry regi-
ments during World War II. Although they were spared certain
fatigues, they belonged to the rank and file, lived in billets or
dugouts with the rank and file, enjoyed no special privileges,
and worked desperately hard: their job, under the battalion
commissar, was to establish a moral ascendancy over the men of
their company, to interpret the news for them, to lecture endlessly: they functioned as a cross between a company education
officer and a police informer.

The young Khrushchev would have done all this besides slog-
ging away at his own studies, sleeping on bedboards with his
fellow-students: until his second marriage he would have had to
farm his children out—whether back in Kalinovka with relations, or with acquaintances in Yuzovka, we do not know.[5] And
it would have been now that he discovered not only a talent for
organization and man-management, to use a horrible phrase,
but also for quick book learning. By 1925, when he completed
his course, he was wholly literate, sufficiently indoctrinated with
Leninist thinking, and expert in the differences between Social
Revolutionaries, Mensheviks, Anarchists, and all other enemies
of the people. For these were the days when GPU interrogators
(the Cheka had been reorganized into the GPU in December
1921) justified their existence by smelling out counterrevolu-
tionaries and often argued like theologians in their attempts to
establish vaguely suspect individuals as Social Revolutionary or
Menshevik conspirators. Later the emphasis was to be on wrecking and sabotage; later still, in the great purges of the thirties
and thereafter, on espionage and conspiring with foreign
powers.

CHAPTER FOUR

First Steps of a Very Long Climb

BY THIS TIME, also, Lenin was dead. He had died on January 24, 1924. For nearly a year he had lain paralysed and inert after the third of a series of strokes, almost certainly the result of the grave wounds inflicted in August 1918 by the bullets fired by Dora Kaplan-Roid, a Social Revolutionary. He was only fifty-four when he died and, after bringing the Soviet Union through the civil war, he had had to retreat from the frenzied campaign to achieve socialism in one sweep, falling back in 1921 on his famous New Economic Policy, which sought to harness the peasants and the remaining businessmen and traders of all kinds to the salvation of the economy by allowing them to work for personal gain. But he was firmly set on the path which Stalin was later to follow. It was Lenin the internationalist who sought to impose Bolshevism by force on all the component parts of the tsarist empire—and who largely succeeded. It was Lenin the philosopher who inaugurated the Cheka and the Red Terror as a calculated act of policy. It was Lenin the champion of the working class who put down in blood and violence popular rising after popular rising and finally broke the hearts of many of his most staunch and idealistic supporters by smashing, at Kronstadt on the Baltic, the very soldiers and sailors who had carried him to victory in October 1917, now turned against him for perverting the ideals for which they had fought. It was Lenin the humanitarian who imposed police rule on that vast and desolated land. His right hand in all this was Trotsky, who was later to spend years of exile bitterly denouncing for his tyrannic acts the man who had had the impertinence to steal the power from him when Lenin died: Joseph Stalin.

Khrushchev never met Lenin. But in his days as a *politrook* at the technical school in Yuzovka he heard a great deal about Trotsky and, increasingly, about Stalin. The battle between these two, one the flamboyant national figure who had created the Red Army, the other colourless and unobtrusive, wonderfully calculating, was already joined—though Trotsky, with all his brilliance and his catastrophic intellectual arrogance, hopelessly underestimated the danger of Stalin's challenge.

To Trotsky Stalin was a Georgian bandit disguised as a revolutionary. He was the man with the "sickly smile . . . the yellow eyes . . . and the hangdog look" who clung to Lenin's coattails and was useful as a bureaucratic organizer. He detested Stalin if only because at Tsaritsyn, later Stalingrad, he had changed his, Trotsky's, plan of campaign at a critical moment in the civil war—and won a decisive battle in consequence; it never seems to have occurred to Trotsky that a junior Bolshevik who dared challenge in this way the creator of the Red Army and Lenin's right hand must possess certain qualities that were worth serious consideration.

We do not know what Stalin thought about Trotsky, who was his exact contemporary but far senior to him in Lenin's eyes. We only know what he said about Trotsky, which is neither here nor there. The probability is that this brooding and vindictive *condottiere*, who was also a most accomplished administrator, regarded with total contempt and extreme jealousy not only Trotsky but also all those émigré revolutionaries who had flocked back to Russia in 1917—above all the intellectualizing Jews, Zinoviev and others as well as Trotsky, who were full of sound and fury but had long been cut off from the Russian land, while he, Stalin, had been fighting and conspiring at home and serving his term in Siberia. At any rate, this is how he behaved.

Lenin used him to sort out the problem of the minority nationalities and then as the first secretary of the Bolshevik Party, to carry out the sort of administrative duties the importance of which Lenin, who had once said that ministers were unnecessary (any butcher, baker, or candlestick-maker could run a Department of State), had always failed to comprehend. And as General Secretary of the Party Stalin saw his opportunity. While Lenin's companions struck the attitudes, roused the rabble, and tried to cope, not very effectively, with problems of state government, Stalin applied himself to building up a bureaucratic machine which under his direction would one day be ready to take the government over. Thus he appointed to his secretariat a number of men, all young, who felt as he did and whose faces Lenin hardly knew. Stalin was thirty-eight, and so was Trotsky. Apart from Lenin, all the great public figures of the Bolshevik Party were in their middle and late thirties. Stalin, for his secretariat, picked the young Molotov, twenty-seven at the time of the Revolution and contemptuously described by Lenin as "the best filing clerk in Moscow"; the young Lazar Kaganovich, twenty-four; the young Andreyev, twenty-nine. He was not content with packing the Party secretariat; he picked other young men to occupy key positions in the provinces—for example, the young Zhdanov, twenty-one. These men and others were all prepared to back Stalin through thick and thin against an older generation when the time came for the showdown.

Khrushchev in these formative years was still at school and coming up to thirty years old. Until Lenin died in 1924 he must have been perfectly unaware of the great struggle brewing behind the scenes in Moscow. But before he graduated and went out into the field, in 1925, the fight was already coming out into the open. It was essentially a power struggle, but it was presented as a conflict of ideological principles, very much as forty years later the great battle between Khrushchev's Russia and Mao's China was to be presented as a conflict of ideological principles. It was also increasingly a struggle between those who, with Trotsky, believed in "perpetual revolution" and saw the new Soviet Union's only hope, backward and ravaged as she was and desperately in need of material assistance from abroad, as the active instigation of revolution in more advanced lands, and those who saw that Lenin's hopes of a general European revolution were illusory; these saw that Russia was going to be encircled by hostile powers for many years, and that if the Soviet Union was ever to mean anything at all and be made viable it would have to concentrate on setting its own house in order first, leaving the foreigners to take care of themselves. This general idea came later to be known as "Socialism in One Country"; a more accurate slogan would have been "Russia First," and Russia First was to be realized by a devious young Georgian from the hills called Stalin, a man with a strong streak of violent irresponsibility, a man whose knowledge of Marxism was confined to what Lenin had told him, a member of a proud and cruel race who dested and despised the Russians as colonial oppressors. It was an improbable situation.

In 1925, when the public fight was in full swing, Khrushchev, thirty-one, was given his first appointment as a full-time professional Party functionary, an *apparatchik,* or member of the apparatus. It was an apparatus of whose existence Lenin had been scarcely aware, and it was controlled by Stalin. Khrushchev had never been nearer to Moscow than Kalinovka—unless one of the retreats in the civil war had swept him back with it for a time. Khrushchev was not appointed by Stalin, but he was given his job by one of Stalin's lesser men, Comrade Moyseenko, Party Secretary of the Yuzovka Region, or *oblast.* He was appointed to be Party Secretary of the Petrovsko-Mariinski District, or *raion,* of the Yuzovka Region, and this was an important job. He had a parish of some 400 square miles, nearly half the size of Warwickshire or Rhode Island, in a predominantly industrial area which, however, contained large stretches of open farmland between the factory towns. Here he was the supreme boss, subject only to Moyseenko in Yuzovka and to the surveillance of the GPU.

It must have been a fairly hopeful job. The period from 1925 to 1927 was a sort of golden age of the Revolution. The peasants were at work, "enriching" themselves; the mines and factories were functioning; unemployment had dropped; the predatory bands of mutinous peasants, soldiers, workers, Ukrainian nationalists, who for years had terrorized the countryside, had been wiped out; all that remained were the wild children, the *besprisorni,* orphaned by the civil war and the famine, who still would not settle down. Some were rounded up and put to work on irrigation schemes, railways, canals (Khrushchev himself is supposed to have started a hostel to reclaim some of these wretched, ragged bands). More were shot. But the country was in working trim, and Nikita Khrushchev was responsible for 400 square miles of it—out of a total of nearly 2 million square miles. His new wife, Nina Petrovna, a schoolteacher, was to bear him two more children and develop into the comfortable, sensible, and dignified figure who years later was to make such a favourable impact on the West. He was quite a personage, and he went to work with a will.

In one of his few references to his early days, Khrushchev told an audience at Kiev: "When I was working as Secretary of a District Party Committee in the Donbas, I used to pay calls on the villages, and I would get into a sledge—at that time we had sledges instead of motor-cars—and wrap myself up in a sheepskin coat, and the frost would not bite me." He was some way out in the country, due south of Yuzovka, and nearly ten miles from the nearest railway station. All his travelling in and out of Marinka, the capital of his little satrapy, had to be done by sledge in winter, by gig or pony-trap in summer. But the interesting thing about that little reminiscence is that even in those early days he got out and about—which is what we would expect from the man who, when all the Soviet Union was his territory, would travel about and get out among the people as no Soviet leader has done before or since.

Russian officials, Russian factory managers, building constructors, farm overseers, or whatever, are notorious for their extreme reluctance to get mud on their boots. For the traditional Russian official or manager, a large part of the advantage of being an official or a manager was that he need never again go out into the mud or the snow or the slush or the summer dust: he had qualified himself to sit indoors in winter, generating a classic fug, or in the shade on the veranda in summer, "managing" or snoozing or drinking away the tedious hours.

The revolution hardly changed this at all. The old Tsarist officials, men with a certain education and a certain social background, were superseded by new men who were only too pleased to adopt the old official ways. They soon had a new bureaucracy in full working order, composed almost exclusively of men who were to make their entire careers as Party functionaries, or *apparatchiki*. Since our hero was to be one of these, in the end supreme among them, and since he moved up through the apparatus—Stalin's apparatus—step by step, it is desirable to have a picture of that apparatus.

[2.]

At the time of Lenin's death, that is, at the time when Khrushchev took up his first appointment in the field, the Party consisted of about 1 million members out of a population of 140 million. These were the elite of the new society. Some two-thirds of them were spare-time Party workers, forming Party cells in factories and institutions of all kinds, as well as on the land. Their task was to set an example to all those with whom they came in contact in their work and their recreation. In 1925 the great majority of these were dedicated men and women, passionately certain that they were building a heaven on earth, ready to sacrifice themselves—and everybody else—to the demands and interests of the Party, to endure unpopularity, to be sent to outlandish regions. They lived for the cause. They were worker priests in a secular religion. It was only later that membership of the Communist Party became a *sine qua non* for all careerists and climbers, for all who wanted to get on.

Controlling this lay army were the professional Communists, the organizers and the actual dictators. In theory they derived their powers from the rank and file. The periodic Party Congresses, the All Union Congress and the separate Republican Congresses, consisted of elected delegates from all parts of the Union and all parts of the individual Republics. At each All Union Congress one of the main tasks was to elect a new Central Committee, to which all power was delegated until the next Congress. The Central Committee, meeting comparatively frequently, elected its permanent officers and standing committees. Supreme among these was the Political Bureau (Politburo), which was the standing policy-making body of the Central Committee—that is, of the Party, that is, of the Soviet Union. There was also a Secretariat, headed by the Secretary General, which was responsible for the execution of Politburo decisions and for overseeing the Party organization. The actual business of organization and disciplining was carried out by other standing committees, the Organization Bureau (Orgburo) and the Party Control Commission. Already, when Khrushchev became an *apparatchik* in 1925, Stalin, as Secretary General, was in virtual control of these bodies; the men who were elected to them by the Central Committee were in fact his nominees. The Secretariat, the Orgburo, and the Control Commission between them were directly responsible for all major appointments in the All-Union Party and, indirectly, for appointments in the separate Republics.

There was then no separate Party organization for the largest of all the Republics, the Russian Soviet Socialist Republic, or RFSSR. Thus the Secretary General in Moscow could himself make appointments over a vast area from Leningrad to Astrakhan, from Novgorod to Vladivostok. He also appointed the key men in the Republics' Party offices—for example, in the Ukraine.

The chain of command worked down through republic to region (*oblast*) to district (*raion*). Thus, in the Ukraine, the Ukrainian Party had its headquarters in Kharkov, then the capital. Under Kharkov there were a number of regional, city, and district committees. But Moscow could, and on occasion did, by-pass the republican committee and put pressure immediately on the regional committees. These had the most critical role of all. They were responsible to the Kremlin for everything that went on in their regions, from industrial and agricultural production to political education, discipline, and morale. They were caught between the rigid and quite ruthless demands of the centre and the hostility and inertia of the masses. They had to rely absolutely on their district secretaries both to squeeze the masses (aided by the GPU) and to persuade them and exhort them, to translate remote paper decisions into practical politics—to keep the wheels turning, in a word. The only active help the district secretaries could rely on came from the dedicated part-time workers referred to above. What the masses had to produce was coal and steel and building materials—above all, food.

It was in this job that Khrushchev soon began to shine. As we have seen, unlike most district secretaries, he enjoyed getting about among the people; he was not afraid of them; he could talk to them and cajole them and bully them; in the last resort he could call on the GPU. He depended for lay help, as it were, on the dedicated Party workers, who in the Ukraine were more thinly scattered than in most areas of the Union, and on the village, town, and city soviets, or councils—seen not as independent democratic bodies but as instruments of Party power. The chief value of these soviets, a value which diminished progressively up the ladder (a village soviet was a genuine parish meeting at which grievances and constructive ideas of all kinds could be expressed, whereas the Supreme Soviet, meeting infrequently in Moscow, was simply a rubber stamp for decisions taken by the Politburo), was as a safety valve, as a means of giving ordinary people a sense of participation, and as a litmus paper. Through the village and town soviets a district Party secretary could easily discover just what the people could bear and what they could not bear. The other great channel of information upwards came from the police, whose reports were remarkably accurate and objective.*

We have no records of the workings of the Party and the police in the Stalino Region at this or at any other time. But we do have remarkably complete—and unique—records of what was going on in the Smolensk *oblast,* in Byelorussia, some hun-

---

* It is commonly believed that police reports to the centre conceal the nature and volume of discontent. The assumption is that it is in the interests of the provincial police to persuade the higher authorities that all is for the best in the best possible of worlds in their own areas. The contrary is true. It is in the interest of the police to convince the government of the continued necessity for their existence. In fact discontent has been so sharp and widespread that it is quite enough for them—or has been quite enough until very recently—to report the actual state of affairs. The Smolensk Archive (see below) bears this out to perfection. The people who were, and are, anxious to prove to the government and Party headquarters that all is well are, above all, the local Party secretaries, the planners and the economic ministries—as Khrushchev in later life was so often and so bitterly to complain.

dreds of miles to the north. And these enable us to get a fairly clear idea of the conditions obtaining at the time when Khrushchev was beginning to make his name as a promising *apparatchik*. For some reason the Party and police archives of the Smolensk Region were neither destroyed nor removed to safety when the Germans approached in 1941. The Germans seized a mountain of paper and sent it back to Berlin, where it stayed, unsorted, until the Americans got hold of it and shipped it to Washington.[1]

Even in the Smolensk Region there was still a great deal of noisy opposition to Bolshevik rule—strikes, demonstrations, the shouting out and writing upon walls of anti-Leninist slogans. And this was an area where the Bolsheviks had long been stronger than in the Ukraine. As the New Economic Policy progressed and the roaming bandit gangs were suppressed and the peasants found that it was worth while to till their fields, things became much quieter. But in the industrial areas conditions were such that the factory workers, far from benefiting from the Revolution, their own revolution, starved of food and consumer goods, were in a perpetual ferment. The Social Revolutionaries, outlawed as a party, were still active. The little band of Bolshevik *apparatchiki* lived islanded in a sullen and hostile land, like representatives of an occupying power. Urged on by the Regional Committee, which had at all costs to satisfy Kharkov and Moscow, detested as the representatives of a remote and dictatorial government by the workers among whom they had to move, the district officials were driven to band themselves into a sort of compact family, buttressing themselves with their friends and living a life increasingly cut off from the countryside as a whole. Since the regional officials depended on them utterly for their own jobs, the whole apparatus became a family establishment. Everybody in it depended on everybody else, and, as in all such closed societies, the moral tone soon began to deteriorate heavily. Everybody covered up for everybody else. The Russians have always been drinkers, and the provincial party bosses had easy access to drink. Drink, indeed, was the only amenity available. They were drunk half the time. After starting off by turning a blind eye to the excesses of their coarser companions, they soon descended to their level. While in Moscow the great "ideological" battle raged between Stalin and his challengers, in the provinces nobody paid much attention to all this, seeing in it nothing more than a quarrel for power among the top bosses, trying to decide with a cool eye where their bread and drink were coming from. Thus, in Smolensk, the Regional First Secretary, Comrade Beika, was said to have a wife in every town under his jurisdiction, and when he was called to higher duties in Moscow in 1926 he was succeeded by an honest worker called Pavlychenko, who continued and developed Beika's practices. "Everyone in the Party organization drinks—from the top to the bottom there's drinking. District Party Conferences were just one big drinking party," said one of the witnesses at the inquiry which followed.[2]

The Smolensk inquiry took place in the spring of 1928. It was conducted by two investigators from the Central Control Commission in Moscow, and the result was that Pavlychenko and his senior colleagues were hauled up to Moscow and demoted. There followed a purge, carried out by a member of the Presidium of the Central Control Commission, who, at a two-day meeting, made a revealing report.

The Katushka factory, which was one of the proletarian strongholds of the province and enlisted 50 per cent of its workers in either the Party or the Young Communist League (Komsomol), was revealed as a nest of bribery and promiscuity. "Female workers were habitually taken advantage of by the foremen. In the Yartsevo factory there had been seven suicides of workers, because of the indifference of the Party leadership to their grievances. Old revolutionaries had turned into drunkards and indulged in sexual licence. One local secretary had had five wives in the course of one year." [3]

Smolensk was no doubt a particularly bad case, but it was not uncharacteristic. In 1930 Malenkov, then making his way upward in the back rooms of the Moscow Central Committee, contributed to the periodical *Party Construction* an article devoted to the shortcomings of the Ukrainian Party. This article contained a particular reference to Khrushchev's own organization as it was at the end of 1927 and early in 1928—i.e., at the time of the Smolensk scandal:

> About two years ago the organization of the Stalino Region went through a deep and difficult crisis in its Party leadership. At the end of 1927 and the beginning of 1928, the Central Committee and the Central Control Commission of the Ukrainian Communist Party (Bolshevik) brought to light the rottenness of the leadership of the Region and part of its cadres. In its resolution of March 1928, the Central Control Commission of the Ukrainian Communist Party (Bolshevik) took note of the systematic drinking bouts among the upper strata of the Regional Party organization, of "self-provisioning," of the ineffective struggle of the Bureau of the Regional Committee against waste, bad management, and the whitewashing of individual responsible workers, of the use of means of oppression by the Bureau of the Regional Committee against comrades who protested against shameful conduct, and other unwholesome occurrences.[4]

Malenkov then dwelt on the purge of the Stalino leadership, which (writing in 1930) he said was still incomplete. It was taking so long because corruption, et cetera, had bitten deep down into the lower echelons of the organization.

Khrushchev himself, in the years leading up to 1927, was emerging as a member of the "higher strata" of the regional organization, which was still run by Moyseenko, who had appointed him to Mariinka. And this was the atmosphere in which he lived and worked. In the purge which followed he was moved to an unspecified appointment in Kiev. He was moved by the supreme boss of the Ukraine, the man responsible for carrying out the Stalino purge, Lazar Kaganovich, since 1925 First Secretary of the Ukrainian Party and, as such, viceroy over 40 million souls.

This move was a promotion rather than a check. It seems unlikely, in view of his later habits, that the young Khrushchev stood out against drinking. There is nothing to suggest that he was "oppressed" by his corrupt bosses. He was very much one of them. But he was also showing himself outstandingly able and outstandingly willing in the cause of Stalin. From 1926 onwards he was already a marked man, and he was already, far more than the great majority of his ranking colleagues elsewhere, deeply involved in Stalin's personal drive for power. His career from 1925 to the end of 1927, when he was transferred to Kiev, was quite remarkable for a raw district secretary.

In the normal course of events he had attended late in 1925 the Ninth All Ukrainian Party Congress, with Kaganovich in the chair. The fact that he was there as the delegate from the Petrovsko-Mariinski District was enough to indicate that he was the true master of that district. He did not speak at any of the formal sessions, as far as the record shows. But his master, Moyseenko, spoke long and loud, viciously denouncing all those, including some of the most distinguished Bolsheviks, who refused to endorse wholeheartedly the Stalin line in the struggle with Trotsky and others.[5] But Khrushchev clearly made an impression offstage, because almost at once he was nominated as one of the delegates to the far more important All Union Party Congress, which was held in Moscow in December 1925. This was the Fourteenth Congress, in which Stalin defeated Kamenev and Zinoviev, his associates in the *troika,* or triumvirate, which had run the Party since Lenin's death. They had been very necessary to Stalin in his initial humiliation of Trotsky at the Thirteenth Congress in May 1924. Now, with Trotsky on the sidelines, they attacked Stalin on the issue of "Socialism in One Country" and on the matter of more liberal agricultural policies. Stalin, for the purposes of this argument, joined forces with Bukharin (who really believed in a liberal agricultural policy), but only for the time being. The really distinguishing aspect of the Fourteenth Party Congress, which was a climateric in the history of the Soviet Union, was the suppression of free debate within the Party itself. Lenin had suppressed free debate within the country by his dissolution of the Constituent Assembly and his creation of the Cheka. Stalin took matters a stage further and suppressed free debate within the Party itself. In December 1925 this was done by rowdyism: the Congress was packed with his supporters, who simply shouted down all opposition, and Comrade Moyseenko is on record as being one of the rowdiest. Khrushchev did not speak, but no doubt he shouted with the rest—and went back to Stalino with Moyseenko, well pleased with Stalin's over-whelming victory: 599 votes to 65. There were 666 voting delegates and 641 non-voting delegates, of whom Khrushchev was one: just over 1300 all told, representing just over 1 million Party members. Khrushchev, only seven years a Bolshevik, was now in the first 1300. In the following year, in October 1926, he made his first formal public speech, at a Ukrainian Party Conference in Kharkov. Under the eyes of Kaganovich, shortly to be called to Moscow as one of Stalin's principal aides, he made a speech which put him a move ahead of Stalin.

CHAPTER FIVE

More Stalinist than Stalin

YEARS LATER, soon after Stalin's death and when our hero was moving to the top, I asked a Russian friend how this man with his incessant flow of talk, public and semi-public, his torrent of indiscretions, had possibly managed to keep quiet and behave discreetly during all his years of more or less anonymous service under Stalin, when nobody at all was allowed to talk out of turn: the strain of silence must have been unendurable. My Russian laughed. "He talked all the time! He has talked without stopping ever since anyone knew him. Sometimes he talked out of turn and was slapped down. Often he jumped the gun. But Stalin let him talk and found him useful. The only thing was that in those days he wasn't much reported."

Going back over the records, such as they are, one can see the truth of this. Certainly Khrushchev talked his way up, at Yuzovka, then at Mariinka and Stalino—much the same bullying, coaxing, no-nonsense talk that he later produced on the national, then the international stage. Then, in 1926, he started talking for the record, at Party conferences (lower down the scale than congresses) and meetings of all kinds. But, as far as the outside world was concerned, his speeches did not exist—though some of them are recorded in the minutes of those conferences.

This first recorded speech, at Kharkov, was a very interesting performance. Khrushchev was thirty-two. He had made up his mind where he was going and what was necessary for the coun-

try and for him. He had moved among the people of his district
in a way uncharacteristic of the junior *apparatchik* of those days.
He had seen some sort of order being produced out of chaos, and
had himself helped to produce it. He had been convinced of the
need for a strong hand—and, by nature, he himself had a strong
hand. Only a few miles outside his district, at the famous Shakhty
mine, demonstrating strikers had been shot down by the armed
police. The strikers were the sort of men that Khrushchev was,
with Khrushchev's background; but Khrushchev was now on
the side of order. He had his own potential strikers to cope
with. Order meant discipline, above all labour discipline, without which nothing could be built. I have no doubt at all that
when, thirty years later, Khrushchev told the Yugoslavs that
their Workers' Councils were no substitute for discipline and
authority he was thinking back to the brutal and chaotic days
when he had helped to break the resistance of his comrades, the
workers of the Stalino Region, if necessary by force—and, of
course, for their own, for the country's, good.

He had been to Moscow and seen Stalin in action, smashing
with his claque and his strong-arm squads at the Fourteenth
Party Congress the theorizing windbags—as Zinoviev and
Kamenev would have appeared to him. He had read *Pravda* as it
dug the grave not of Soviet democracy (Lenin had done that in
person) but of democracy within the Party, under the slogan,
"Against discussion!" forbidding in a five-point programme the
very idea of open discussion within the Party, "because it shakes
the very foundations of the dictatorship of the proletariat, the
unity of the Party, and its dominant position in the country;
because it serves the cause of petty groups which hanker for
political democracy." [1] And this would have made sense to a
man conscious of great practical gifts and with a naturally authoritarian temperament, impatient of subtleties of all kinds.
He had read, in October of that year, the "declaration of submission" to the Party (i.e., to Stalin) signed by the defeated opposition leaders, Trotsky, Kamenev, Zinoviev, Piatakov, Sokolnikov (all of them later to be killed by Stalin), which showed
who the master was. And at the opening of the Kharkov conference, the very next day, he heard Kaganovich pouring scorn

on all those who said that democracy within the Party had
been destroyed. Intra-Party democracy, Kaganovich said with
remarkable semantic agility, did not mean that everyone had
the right to question the decisions of the majority; it simply
meant drawing the masses into political activity under the
Party's wing.[2] And when Kaganovich was sharply challenged
by a comrade from Odessa (the Kharkov conference was by
no means steamrollered by the Stalinists) Khrushchev got up
to speak. While the Central Committee in Moscow, dominated
by Stalin, was going out of its way to conciliate the opposition,
having won its victory, Khrushchev in Kharkov was setting the
tone for the next stage, moving ahead of Stalin: he proved
himself at the same time a polished master of what later came to
be known as Stalinist invective and the Stalinist manner of flat-
tening opponents by imputing bad faith and by brute, unsupported assertions:

It is wholly clear to me that Comrade Golubenko [the man from
Odessa] has intentionally slandered the Party and that he is lying
about the situation in our Party organization. If Comrade Golubenko
says that the changes in our Party organs were achieved only by packing the ranks, then this is barefaced calumny. . . . In my opinion
today's speech of the opportunist Golubenko wholly confirms the
unscrupulous and superficial nature of the declaration of our opposition. Our Party organizations require from the opposition that they
totally submit to the decisions of the Fourteenth Congress and the
Central Committee of the All-Union Communist Party. I believe
that the declaration written by the opposition is not a sincere declaration. Unless the opposition entirely recognizes the decisions of the
Fourteenth Party Congress, there can be no question of collaborating
with them. Should this not be the case, then we ought to demand
from the highest Party organs that they apply repressive measures
against the incorrigible members of the opposition, regardless of
their former merits and positions.[3]

Stalin, it should be noted, had accepted the sincerity of the
declaration of submission—at least for the record and for the
time being. Khrushchev, in questioning it, threw the whole
matter wide open.

What lay behind this performance? Was the tough young

comrade from Stalino, with his bullet head, shaved close, his vehement, bullying style, speaking for himself? Had he calculated correctly what Stalin's next move would be, and was he determined to be first in the field and in at the kill? Was he, in a word, playing a hunch and taking a gamble on impressing Kaganovich? Was his outburst the simple uncalculated outcome of irrepressible moral indignation?

Certainly not the last. Khrushchev knew, because he had heard her at the Fourteenth Congress in Moscow, that Lenin's widow, Krupskaya, a venerated figure, had protested against Stalin's treatment of the minority. She had been silenced and her protests rejected for reasons of expediency, and everybody knew it. Further, it seems unlikely, to say the least, that a young man on the threshold of his career would have taken the risk of speaking out of turn at that most critical moment. It seems far more likely that he was being used. There was no need for him to impress Kaganovich. That must have been done already, otherwise Khrushchev would never have been sent from the Ukraine to Moscow for the Fourteenth Congress. The all but certain answer is that Stalin, while appearing to accept the submission of the opposition in order to present himself in a conciliatory light, was already planning his next move, and that he had seen to it that certain of the more zealous comrades in the provinces would start raising a demand for that next move, to prepare the ground in advance. Kaganovich, already very close to Stalin, would make his dispositions accordingly, and the truculent young peasant from Kalinovka, who had shown that he knew how to combine active fieldwork with a sharp interest in higher strategy, would be given his instructions: he was to say what he no doubt believed, that the Party was being too soft in its treatment of the opposition. It had better look out. In that case the only risk the young Khrushchev took was that Stalin would later change his mind, come to terms with the opposition, and throw to the wolves all those, young Khrushchev among them, who had pressed too hard. Even if this was a large risk (and it was not), it was a calculated risk, very different from the reckless risk involved in playing a hunch, in leaping seriously ahead of Stalin; and Khrushchev was to show in his later life that he was deeply addicted to the calculated risk—which was not really a risk at all: as, for example, when he threatened Britain and France with long-range missiles at the time of Suez, but when he was certain that the crisis was effectively over; as, for example, in his great speech against Stalin at the Twentieth Party Congress in 1956.

He also had the tremendous and uncovenanted advantage of speaking the truth when he accused Trotsky, Zinoviev, and the rest of "insincerity" in their act of submission: it was Stalin in his pretended belief in their good faith who was acting the hypocrite. Of course they were insincere, as all confessions or recantations or submissions obtained by *force majeure* are insincere. Through all the decades of Stalin's rule this charge of insincerity, correct but perfectly irrelevant, was to be the burden of a thousand thousand accusations. Vishinsky screamed it unceasingly during the great purge trials of the middle thirties. It was to outlive Stalin. After the smashing of Molotov, Malenkov, Kaganovich, and all the so-called "anti-Party group" which marked Khrushchev's accession to something like supreme power, his own supporters at meeting after meeting were to accuse Bulganin, Pervukhin, Saburov, and others of insincerity in their "self-criticisms," on the face of things accepted as genuine by Khrushchev himself, and to demand more drastic punishment—clearly indicating that Khrushchev himself at that time was playing with the idea of further action against his own defeated opposition.

It was thus at the Kharkov Party Conference in 1927 that one of the main infinitely recurrent elements of the Stalinist pattern of oppression was established, and it was established by Khrushchev, in league with Kaganovich, Stalin's right hand in the Ukraine, when, on the face of it, he was still no more than a very junior Party officer from Mariinka.

He was on the way up. At some time in the following year he was moved from Mariinka to Stalino itself. And in November 1927 he made another speech, this time at the Tenth Ukrainian Party Congress in Kiev, this time, by all the signs, the outcome of his own thinking. It was a contribution on questions of Party organization, and the main sense of it was an argument for increased centralization of Party control in the provinces; for the independence of the district Party committees to be reduced (Khrushchev had just been promoted to a higher level than the district) and for the curtailment of elections to Party cells and of district Party conferences—all with a very clear eye to the reduction of the number of occasions on which Party members could engage in critical discussion and to the facilitation of authoritarian control from the centre.* The proposals were presented in a fairly innocuous way. They were not discussed at the time, but they were to form part of the pattern of the future.

These two speeches, unimportant in the context of Stalin's own grand design, were of extreme importance in the development of Khrushchev. They show that his character was formed, that he was a convinced believer in authoritarianism, and that his ambition had taken control: he had become a pacemaker for Kaganovich, and therefore for Stalin, and he was already committed by conviction to the development of authoritarian rule which was to be the distinguishing feature of Stalin's career. As a newly fledged regional Party official with a particular interest in Party organization, he had deliberately cut himself off from his less thrusting comrades with their doubts, their uncertainties, their human inertia, and identified himself with the great machine then rapidly taking shape, of which he was still only a very minor part. At thirty-three, in Stalino, he had decided where he was going. He was going where the power lay, and he was shaking himself free from the loyalties of his early manhood. It was at this moment that the great purge of Stalino took place, but Khrushchev was not punished. He was sent to Kiev.

This great and beautiful city, a city of trees and gardens and broad avenues built on a great hill high above the Dnieper, looking out over that historic waterway to Moscow and the East, to where sky and land blend in an invisible horizon, was the birthplace of Christian Russia. It was down that great river that

* This may be seen as the first beginnings of a process which reached its logical conclusion after 1939, when Stalin ceased even to pretend to pay attention to the Central Committee itself and ruled through his Politburo and Secretariat in defiance of the Party statutes. There was not even an All Union Party Congress between the Eighteenth in 1939 (when Khrushchev became a full member of the Politburo) and the Nineteenth in 1952, a few months before Stalin's death.

the Vikings came from the North on their way to Constantinople, and from Constantinople they brought back Christianity to Kiev and founded a dynasty to rule over the Russian settlements clustered on its banks. Kiev was a holy place, more of the West than of the East. Later, under the Tartar occupation, it lost its supremacy to Moscow, the Muscovite princes proving themselves more amenable to the Tartar overlordship and zealous in collecting tribute for the Golden Horde in exchange for privilege. As time went on, the Kiev Russians and the Muscovite Russians, the Little Russians and the Great Russians, developed distinguishing characteristics. Under the absolutism of the Great Russian rulers, their blood mixed heavily with Finnish and Tartar contributions, the Great Russians became the servile instruments of an imperial and military house; the Little Russians on their rich, black soil, laced with their Cossack enclaves, were, by contrast, stubborn, hard-working and proud. Their history grew apart from the history of Muscovy. After the withdrawal of the Tartars they fell under Lithuanian, then Polish rule. Muscovy did not take over until the seventeenth century. But to this day many Ukrainians dream of their own sovereign state and despise the Great Russians as idle and reckless and submissive. Khrushchev, in spite of all beliefs to the contrary, was not a Ukrainian by birth, but it is beyond all doubt that his lifelong association with the Ukraine has had a deep effect on him. Many years later he was to surround himself in Moscow with a solid bloc of Ukrainians of the toughest kind—a sort of counter-colonization.

In 1927, when he went to Kiev as a functionary of the Ukrainian Central Committee, he was moving decisively towards one of the three great centres of Soviet power. These were Moscow, Leningrad, and Kharkov (only later did Kiev become once again the capital of the Ukraine). Leningrad (St. Petersburg, Petrograd) had been Zinoviev's city, and under Zinoviev it started its career as a challenger to Moscow. Lenin had moved the government from there to Moscow to emphasize the Russianness of Soviet power; St. Petersburg had always been the window on the West, as it is today. Zinoviev had been broken at the Fourteenth Party Congress and the city won for Stalin, who put there as his viceroy Sergei Kirov, one of his toughest and ablest supporters, whose assassination, perhaps on Stalin's instigation, was to unloose the great purges of the thirties. The Ukraine had already been won for Stalin by Kaganovich. And it was Kaganovich, as First Secretary of the Ukrainian Communist Party, who drew Khrushchev more completely into his extremely powerful apparatus. The object of this transfer was to give this powerful, impetuous, yet level-headed young tough from Stalino a spell in one of the important centres of the new Party bureaucracy and to see how he shaped as an administrator. Within a year Kaganovich was called to Moscow to be a Secretary of the Central Committee of the All-Union Party, and almost at once Khrushchev followed him. After that, until Khrushchev turned on his old master and destroyed him in 1957, he was never far from Kaganovich's side.

CHAPTER SIX

To Moscow! Perseverance and Intrigue

KHRUSHCHEV was now fast approaching the first great crisis of his life, in which everything he had so carefully built up might have been lost forever. But his personal crisis was so intimately bound up with the greatest crisis of Stalin's own career, which was also a climacteric in the history of the Soviet Union, that it is necessary to stand away from Khrushchev for a moment and look at what was happening to Stalin—and to Russia.

In 1926, as we have seen, Stalin had received the submission of the Zinoviev opposition; but, as Khrushchev himself had said at Kharkov, it had been an insincere submission. And the opposition continued to underestimate Stalin. On the anniversary celebrations of the Revolution in November 1927, Trotsky and Zinoviev still dared to organize public demonstrations and lead independent "opposition" processions through the streets of Moscow and Leningrad. For this act of defiance both men were at once formally expelled from the Party, and at the Fifteenth Party Congress in the following month seventy-five of their sympathizers followed them into excommunication. Stalin had been glad to use Kamenev in his initial fight with Trotsky, but at the Fifteenth Party Congress, in December 1927, he said of his old comrade's speech that it was "the most lying, pharasaical, scoundrelly and rascally of all the opposition speeches that have been made from this platform." [1] At the congress what was later to be known as the "left opposition" was shattered forever; but already a new opposition was forming, headed by some of the men who had most decisively helped Stalin in his previous victories: Rykov, who had succeeded Lenin as Chairman of the Council of People's Commissars, or Prime Minister; and Bukharin, the brilliant but unreliable intellectual of the Party. These were the leaders of the new "Right Opposition"—the opposition of the Bukharinites, so called to distinguish it from the "Left Opposition" of Trotsky, and, later, Zinoviev, et cetera.

The crisis in Stalin's career was not produced by his struggle with the "right opposition." This disintegrated in terror with scarcely a fight. The crisis arose as a result of his struggle with the peasants, who were much tougher than their self-appointed champions among the Bolshevik intellectuals.

Until 1927 Stalin had been devoting by far the greater part of his very considerable energies to manœuvring against his opponents and consolidating his grip on his new Party machine. He had contributed no ideas of his own to the conduct of either domestic or foreign affairs, apparently content to see the country make its slow recovery from the ravages of war, revolution, civil war, and famine under the general direction of Lenin's NEP. During these years he appeared as a moderate in all matters of high policy, contemptuous of extremism either on the right or on the left, and this appearance in all probability coincided with his own convictions. The vast chaotic land, its governing class destroyed, had to be pulled together, and the only way to pull it together was to encourage all classes to work together in their own interests. Intellectual theorists of all kinds he held in deep contempt, though he did not mind picking their brains; fanatical ideologists were beneath his contempt. He had entertained strong reservations about certain of Lenin's teachings, but he would take things from Lenin which he would take from nobody else. In practice, like any ambitious politician, he trimmed. He was against antagonizing the peasants by pushing collectivization too hard; he poured scorn on the idea of expropriating the kulaks; schemes for rapid super-industrialization he rejected as absurd and impracticable; he was in favour of slow, steady, and organic progress towards material prosperity and the development of socialism. The men closest to him were Molotov, young and still obscure, who acted not only as his Bolshevik conscience (it had been Molotov who, at twenty-seven, had striven in the background to keep the Party on the right lines before Lenin's return from exile in April 1917) but also as his chief of staff; Voroshilov, the one-time sergeant-major and hard-drinking hero of the civil war; Kirov, a ruthless young man of immense dynamism, great practical sense, and a certain far-ranging imagination; Kaganovich, the strongest, the most ruthless and most able organizer and manager in the country. With these, and a few others, he took counsel. Behind them, not consulted but eager to serve, were the brightest newcomers, including Malenkov and Zhdanov, already at home at the very heart of the Party machine. Behind these were the tough and violent young commissars—as the professional party workers, the *apparatchiki,* were universally known.

"Everywhere there were new elections," wrote Pasternak in *Dr. Zhivago* of the first winter of the Revolution, "for the running of housing, trade, industry and municipal services. Commissars were being appointed to each, men in black leather jerkins, with unlimited powers and an iron will, armed with means of intimidation and revolvers, who shaved little and slept less." [2] Now, ten years later, the men in black leather jerkins had stolen the country from the revolutionary dreamers. They had the power and they were determined to keep it. They were impatient and intolerant and they were determined to make things work; everything, everybody that stood in their way they would sweep aside with merciless single-mindedness. They dramatized their ruthlessness and, glorying in it, made themselves far worse than most of them really were. They despised the old order with a total and uncomprehending blankness; but fellow revolutionaries who still dreamed dreams, who showed themselves humane, or who argued and discussed and theorized in the traditional Russian manner, they hated and feared. Many of them hated Jews. Stalin, the born organizer, the man with an iron will, the anti-dreamer, was their hope.

And Stalin was going to need them. He had been fairly easygoing: get things properly organized, clear the rhetoric out of the way, and the country would soon begin to sort itself out. But suddenly, in the moment of his personal triumph, he found he had been wrong. The shouting over the Fifteenth Party Congress had scarcely died down when Russia was found to be on the edge of another famine. Unless the towns and cities were to starve, unless industry was to founder, the government had to extract immediately another 2 million tons of grain from the peasants. By the early summer the collectivization was in full swing: Stalin, reacting to a dire emergency with convulsive, almost paranoiac violence, had embarked on a course which he had never planned—which, indeed, he had actively opposed—which was to destroy the lives of millions, which was to bring the country to the very edge of ruin, and which was to shatter the agricultural economy and alienate the peasantry for decades to come.

The story of the collectivization and of the first Five Year Plan is so familiar that it need not be retold. As Stalin himself confessed to Winston Churchill, this terrible action was more critical for the Soviet Union than any of the crises of the Second World War.[3] That is saying a good deal. After what amounted to a civil war against the peasants, with whole villages being driven into the collectives at gunpoint, with the physical liquidation, by firing squad, deportation, or starvation, of all the most able and enterprising villagers, Soviet agriculture lay in ruins. In their bitter and passionate resistance to being forced off their own land, the peasants slaughtered their livestock, destroyed their implements, burned their crops rather than let the state lay hands on them. In the end the state triumphed. But the field of victory was desolation. In 1929 there had been 34 million horses, 70 million cattle, 130 million sheep and goats. In 1933 there was famine of the bitterest kind. Immense areas of land were untilled and unsown (the peasants ate what seed there was). There were less then 17 million horses, 30 million cattle, 40 million sheep and goats.[4] Even when the fields were finally worked again, agriculture was a shadow of itself. Only the poorest, the feeblest of the peasants remained to work the new collectives, and these were sullen, dazed, and shocked. By the eve of the German invasion in 1941 Soviet agriculture had still not been restored to the 1929 level of productivity.

This terrible interlude is of importance to us for three reasons. First, for the light it throws on the character of Stalin, the man whom Khrushchev chose to support, body and soul; second, because of its effect on the development of the Soviet Union, which persists until this day, and on the minds of the men responsible for that development; third, because it was to be Khrushchev himself, over twenty years later, who was to make the first serious attempt to redeem Soviet agriculture, and, later still, to make the first honest admission of its backwardness—though even then without stating the basic cause of this backwardness. For good measure, it was Khrushchev's failure to achieve his agricultural aims which helped to bring about his ultimate downfall in 1964.

It was in 1929 that Stalin first revealed himself as a hysteric. Until then, apart from the reckless episode of the Tiflis bank raid in his youth, he had impressed himself on all his colleagues as sober, calculating, and neutral in tone, if with a marked streak of malice. The manœuvres whereby he had concentrated so much power in his own hands had, to all appearances, been the manœuvres of an organization man with a natural bent for intrigue. The actual policies over which he had presided had been cautious and middle-of-the-road. Now, under the impact of the discovery that the system was not working, that the gradual industrialization of the Soviet Union was on the way to failure because of hunger in the towns, that the poor peasants working their own land were producing only enough to feed themselves, and that the more prosperous and enterprising peasants, the kulaks, were holding the towns up to ransom, all caution was thrown to the winds. It was as though the man who by sheer willpower and ruthlessness had smashed the pretensions of his most able colleagues had suddenly decided that with a further exercise of willpower and ruthlessness he could smash the opposition of millions of unorganized peasants who were standing between him and the fulfilment of his very modest plans for the development of socialism in one country. And the way he set about things showed those who could use their eyes a glimpse of the sort of man he was. Those who were attaching themselves or had attached themselves to him knew by 1931 at the latest that he was a man without principle, scruple, or pity, emotional to the point of hysteria, convulsively domineering, jealous and vengeful, malicious if not malevolent, a manic-depressive in whom fits of gleefully savage recklessness alternated with periods of pessimistic gloom, in whom the gambler in the grand manner alternated with the coldly prudent schemer.

The first really credible picture of Stalin in his maturity was given us by the Yugoslav rebel Milovan Djilas, and the main characteristic which emerges from that picture is irresponsibility. Apart from his natural gifts and drive, Stalin had settled allegiance to no one but himself, and to no idea but the idea of power; "settled" is the operative word. And he was wholly contemptuous of all other individuals except for one or two who were also bold, successful, and strong for power: for example, Hitler and Winston Churchill.

An ungainly dwarf of a man passed through gilded and marbled imperial halls, and a path opened before him; radiant, admiring glances followed him, while the ears of courtiers strained to catch his every word. And he, sure of himself and his works, obviously paid no attention to all this. His country was in ruins, hungry, exhausted. But his armies and his marshals, heavy with fat and medals and drunk with vodka and victory, had already trampled half Europe underfoot, and he was convinced that they would trample over the other half in the next round. He knew that he was one of the most cruel and despotic figures in history. But this did not worry him a bit, for he was convinced that he was carrying out the will of history.[5]

That was Stalin, as seen by Djilas, after the defeat of Germany. He had moved a long way from the lean and hungry revolutionary. This was the man who commanded Khrushchev, his viceroy in the Ukraine (according to Khrushchev himself), to dance the *gopak* at a drunken party;[6] the Stalin who, again according to Khrushchev, might at any moment, at any time, in a moment of anger or irritation or sheer boredom, give the order to his bodyguard to seize any of his closest colleagues and lead them off to prison.[7] This man did not exist in 1927, or even in 1931; but by 1931 the makings of this man were evident. They became clear in the civil war on the peasants, still two-thirds of the population of the Soviet Union, the collectivization. The switch from the moderate, industriously intriguing Secretary General to the arbitrary dictator was very sudden indeed. But there was plenty of time for his loyal colleagues and their protégés (for instance, Kaganovich as one, Khrushchev as the other) to entertain second thoughts about their new leader who suddenly, overnight as it were, abandoned moderation and issued instructions to the Party and police to declare war on the kulaks and then to transform the face of rural Russia by pushing through a gigantic industrial programme in record time. They had no such second thoughts. Molotov stood at Stalin's side, actively encouraging his most excessive actions; Kaganovich lent his strong right arm. Khrushchev was Kaganovich's man.[8]

At this period, when the Soviet Union, slowly but surely pulling itself up by its own bootstrap, was transformed into a madhouse running blood, Khrushchev was in no way a policy-maker, but he exploited in his own interests the terrible mood of the times. His theatre of action was, to begin with, the Moscow Industrial Academy, and it was from this unlikely launching-pad that he took off for higher things. He arrived at the academy, fresh from a minor position in the provinces, in September 1929. By 1934 he was supreme Party boss of Moscow. By 1939 he was a full member of the Politburo of the Central Committee, the supreme policy-making body. The period of his rise, swift, uninterrupted, from a provincial agitator to one of Stalin's closest colleagues, coincided precisely with the ten years of Stalinism at its worst. This man, who was later to become one of the world's senior and in some ways most far-seeing and beneficent statesmen, achieved his eminence at a time when success could be obtained only by atrocious methods and over the dead or broken bodies of innumerable comrades. The Khrushchev story from 1929 to 1939 has been known in detail outside Russia only to those especially interested in what are called the minutiae of Soviet affairs. In other countries minutiae of this kind are commonly known as high politics and fill the newspaper headlines week in, week out, year in, year out. How did Lloyd George overthrow Asquith? How did Baldwin become Prime Minister? How did Kennedy beat Nixon? By what remarkable manœuvres did de Gaulle make himself effective dictator of France? In England and America we discuss these things, however imperfectly. In the Soviet Union equivalent developments may not be publicly mentioned. Events which, occurring in a Western country, would be hotly debated in public for weeks at a time, filling the front pages of the newspapers, are not so much as mentioned in the Soviet Union, and when Western journalists try to point to them and explain them, they are not thanked. The rise of Bonar Law, the rise of Harold Wilson, the earlier career of President Johnson, may not be very important in the eyes of God, but they matter to us. The rise of Khrushchev, and its nature, also mattered.

It started when, instead of applying himself to industrial education, he became active in the academy's Party cell. It was a very interesting Party cell, and what went on in it was an exact pattern on a small (but rather exalted) scale of what was going on in larger Party organizations all over the country: the good were being broken by the bad. Those who were not inherently bad but who, for whatever reason, attached themselves to the winning side were themselves soon forced to behave badly. Arbitrary government operating by force, by terror, must destroy the best, the boldest dissenters in sheer self-defence; soon it finds itself destroying all who, on one hand, do not actively assist it or, on the other, do not passively submit. This process we all know about. But it has another quality which is less generally understood: it turns men who are not born wicked into thugs. It corrupts, usually irredeemably, all those who, for what seem to them quite good reasons, lend themselves to its activities. Khrushchev voluntarily enrolled himself under the banner of a man who was a natural terrorist and murderer. He did this at a time when Stalin's true nature was not apparent, partly from personal ambition, partly because he had a naturally authoritarian nature and was impatient with the vacillations of so many of the old Bolsheviks. When, in 1929, Stalin was beginning to reveal himself for what he was, Khrushchev could have drawn back. He did not, for reasons which are obvious. Soon he was so deeply committed that there was no escape and he himself became an active instrument of terror. He was corrupted, one would have said, irredeemably. We shall soon have to consider some of the things that Khrushchev said and did at the height of the great purges, when he was manœuvring his way to the topmost echelon of the Soviet leadership; we shall find ourselves wondering how any man could conduct himself in this way who was not an un- mitigated villain. That he was not this, we know. Years later, when he had the stage to himself, it emerged that he had— though corrupted in many ways—retained a large measure of his natural humanity. How this could be is the great question mark which hangs over his story. The conflict between his natural hu- manity and the corruption which bit deeply into him during the years of his rise to the top was to be the great drama of the last ten years of his career.

Moscow in 1929 was a strange town. Nothing had been done to it since 1914. It was still a vast city with, apart from certain great churches and the Kremlin itself, the appearance of an overgrown provincial town—but a provincial town now in de- cay. Stucco peeled from innumerable buildings; old palaces and mansions, gutted, taken over by technical institutes or turned into apartments which were really dormitories, presented blank, uncurtained windows to the outside world. In the Red Presnaya district, which Khrushchev was soon to command, buildings burnt out during the 1905 Revolution still stood roofless, gap- ing and deserted. There was no new building. Roofs leaked. Every festering basement and cellar teemed with ragged human- ity. The overcrowding was such that it was the commonest thing to find two or three families to a room. There was little food; heat and light were hopelessly inadequate; infinite hours were spent by hundreds of thousands glumly queuing for the neces- sities of life. There was no soap. And yet the city had vitality. In countless thousands of odd corners sad relics of the old regime, the "former people," kept starvation at bay (not always) by sell- ing in the commission shops, piece by pathetic piece, their last precious possessions. But the workers in the factories, who had recently inherited the earth, were seized in some measure, par- ticularly the young and naïve, with the intoxication of the dawn- ing age of the machine. The revolutionary intelligentsia and the artists, already marked down by Stalin for suppression as dangerous elements, hardly knew yet what was hitting them. Alexander Blok had died, disillusioned, years earlier. Sergei Yessenin had committed suicide in 1925. The Russian Association of Proletarian Writers (RAPP) had established control over all the field in a highly dictatorial manner, the first decisive step on the stony road much later to be known as Zhdanovism. But Pasternak was still writing, and the theatre, especially the theatre of Meyerhold, had not yet been killed. Thousands of artists of all kinds were fighting back, not yet understanding that their cause was lost in advance.

Similarly, although Stalin had crushed the high political opposition, at lower levels, and particularly among students of all kinds (this included students in their thirties, being trained to fill the great gap left by the extinction of the ruling and managerial classes), the fight went on. Those not close to the seat of power had not yet understood the full implications of Stalin's victory, first over Trotsky, then over Zinoviev and Kamenev, then over Bukharin: they did not realize that the battle was lost. They were, moreover, behind the times, still geared to Stalin's own preaching of moderation. When they saw what was happening in the countryside, when they saw that Stalin was launching into a frenzied programme of super-industrialization, regardless of the cost in present suffering, they were outraged and said so.

It was into this milieu that Khrushchev, now thirty-five, was precipitated in September 1929. The Stalin Industrial Academy, an elite collection of the most promising young men and women in the Soviet Union, gathered together into what was intended to be a forcing house, under Stalin's own protection, to produce new leaders in industry and administration in record time, was in full revolt against Stalin. The situation was complicated beyond all measure by the fact that one of the most gifted students, beautiful too, the thirty-two-year-old Nadezhda Allilulyeva, was Stalin's own wife. And Nadezhda Allilulyeva, who went home to sleep in the Kremlin every night, while the Khrushchevs and many more besides packed themselves into their bleak and shabby quarters, was herself in revolt against her husband's policies. She was a member of the academy's Party cell, which was purged again and again for right-wing deviationism, for Bukharinism. Less than three years later, at the height of the great famine produced by her husband's policies, she solved her problem by committing suicide. This was after an evening of bitter recrimination at the home of Voroshilov. The rumour went round that Stalin had strangled his wife with his own hands in an access of rage; many Russians still believe this, but there is not a shred of evidence—unless evidence of character, unless evidence of Russian Tsarist tradition. But the problem for Khrushchev, up from the Ukraine, owing his call to Moscow to Kaganovich, Stalin's right-hand man, and deeply committed to support of Stalin, must have been difficult indeed. We do not know just how he solved it, but there are pointers, and he succeeded brilliantly. By 1932, when Nadezhda Allilulyeva killed herself in despair (she was the gentle and idealistic daughter of an old revolutionary who had given shelter to Stalin in the days of his Siberian exile), Khrushchev had risen to the point where he was second in command of the Party organization for the whole city of Moscow.

When he arrived in the great city to start the dreary hunt for quarters for his wife, his two children by his first wife, and another on the way, he cannot have been oppressed by the physical decay and the dreariness of life in Moscow: it was a great deal better, though more crowded, than life in Stalino or Kiev. He must have been wholly oblivious of the steamrollering of intellectual life: he was himself impatient of intellectuals. The great political battle was over, and he was comfortably on the right side. He cannot have been upset by the rapidly increasing regimentation of life and the command to tighten belts: he was an authoritarian by nature, and he had risen as far as he had by his talent for bullying and cajoling people into tightening their belts. In the light of later events there is no reason to doubt that he was a man possessed by a vision: Russia, the sprawling, the feckless, the anarchic, the inchoate, was to be dragged into the industrial age and transformed utterly. The wretched peasants from whom he had sprung were themselves going to achieve this transformation, the best of them transplanted into factories and fed by their less intelligent and enterprising cousins. They were going to succeed where all the panoply of an antique ruling class had failed. Their children were going to inherit the earth, cost what it might in suffering meanwhile; and he, Nikita Khrushchev, toiling on the side of Marx, Lenin, and history, was one of the chosen few who were going to drag them by their shirttails, kicking and groaning, into the twentieth century—as Peter the Great before him had dragged their ancestors into Europe. He did not know what Europe was. He did not know what the twentieth century was: to him it was machines and monuments to the glory of industry. Industry was the peasantry of Chekhov let loose in a machine shop and producing, God knew how, the machines to make machines to make machines which would one day bring plenty and prosperity to poor old Mother Russia. He did not know what prosperity and plenty were; he had never seen them. But he knew what desperate poverty was; he had never seen anything else. And if it was rough on the peasants to drive them into collectives, and rough on their cousins in the factories to punish them violently for sabotage when they broke machines, admittedly most often through clumsiness but sometimes through malice and bloody-mindedness—well, they had to be taught. And life in Russia was rough and always had been. He did not know what gentleness was, but he knew what roughness was. For centuries the peasants had been bullied and knouted to keep them down; they were still being bullied and knouted—but this time to force them to work for themselves and their children, for the revolution embodied in 180 million idle, garrulous, moody Russians, for the glory of the new workers' state. There was a difference.

In a word, having arrived in Moscow at the age of thirty-five, Khrushchev was shocked by nothing he saw—he was excited and stimulated, rather—until his induction into the Party cell at the Industrial Academy. Here there were others like him, workers and peasants who had shown outstanding talent for leadership and had been hand-picked for training as a new ruling elite, subservient, of course, to the Secretary General and his caucus. These were not ordinary students; most of them had already learned much in the hard school of postrevolutionary Russia and were ten years older than the ordinary run of students, already experienced in responsibility. Besides the workers were sons and daughters of the intelligentsia who had thrown in their lot with the new regime, and men and women who had thought a great deal, far more than Khrushchev and those like him, about the theory of the Revolution and also about ways and means, other than brute force, of building up a socialist paradise and swinging the masses behind the Bolshevik leadership. They talked, discussed, criticized authority, exchanged horror stories, and debated hotly among themselves.

Khrushchev had always been a doer rather than a debater, and though he was a great talker he favoured the monologue, the harangue. For a long time now he had been shouting down all critics, in the interests of getting things done. The open discussions in the Party cell at the Industrial Academy must have seemed to him frivolous and adolescent at best, but dangerous too: the mood was running fiercely against Stalin and his ruthless drive, towards Bukharin. This was dangerous. It would have to be changed, and it would be his job to help change it. And yet, there at the very heart of the unrest, stood the sad, tense, splendid beauty who was the wife of the leader himself. What was to be done? How did one do one's duty by Stalin and the new Soviet state, fighting subversion all along the line, reporting heresy to the proper authorities, without getting into trouble for slandering Nadezhda Allilulyeva, the sort of woman Khrushchev had never met—she might have been a Turgenev heroine.

Khrushchev may have been warned. Kaganovich himself may have warned him (later Kaganovich was to stand by and let Stalin ruin his own brother, apparently without a murmur) that all was not well with the Technical Academy and that Nadezhda Allilulyeva had been countenancing criticism of her husband. It is probable, indeed, that Khrushchev was chosen as the sort of man who could be relied upon to help put an end to the nonsense. The whole interlude of his spell at the academy is mysterious. He entered it, apparently, in the ordinary way. In a short time he had come to dominate it. He can have done little training after his first six months; then it was all politics and agita-

tion. And long before he was due to finish his course he was off
and away and up.

There had been trouble before he arrived, and it continued.
Here are the facts we know.

The academy was one of the key Moscow institutions, falling
under the jurisdiction of the city's first Party secretary. In October 1928 the Moscow Party secretariat was heavily purged. But
the Party cell of the Industrial Academy continued to harbour
Bukharinite ideas, and the cell itself was purged in the late autumn of 1929. Within six months there was further trouble.
In May 1930 *Pravda* went into the attack on the academy, accusing the new Party bureau of right deviationism, of a total
failure to preach to cell members (including Khrushchev) the
urgent necessity for stepping up the struggle against the "rightists" and "conciliators" (i.e., the Bukharinites), and even, in
the case of some unspecified individuals, of spreading "slander-
ous anti-Party rumours concerning the leadership of the Party." [9]
This attack was launched with cries of horror and outrage, as
though it concerned a new discovery. The accusations may have
been a new discovery for the editor-in-chief of *Pravda,* but what
followed indicated clearly enough that someone in authority
(Kaganovich? Stalin himself through Kaganovich?) must have
known what was going on. Whoever it was knew, indeed, from
Nadezhda Allilulyeva of opposition in principle; he must have
known from someone else what was happening in detail, because what followed had all the hallmarks of the sort of manœuvre already perfected by Stalin, later to be developed by
him in the grand manner; later still, when Stalin was dead, to
be employed by Khrushchev in his fight with Molotov on one
hand and Malenkov on the other.

In spite of *Pravda*'s strictures, the Bukharinites in the academy cell fought on. They had the boldness to elect, among
others, eight of their number to represent the academy at the
Moscow Party conference, then in preparation. Their talk was
wild, but to the point. Stalin was attacked, the collectivization
was attacked, one speaker declared that the only solution was to
develop a species of "organized capitalism" [10]—he did not mean

state capitalism, which was precisely what Stalin was in the process of organizing. "It is all the fault of the Central Committee," said one. "The Central Committee does not lead; it lags behind." Another spoke openly of the "bankruptcy of the Central Committee line." When the storm broke, it centred on the head of an unfortunate comrade, A. P. Shirin, secretary of the Bauman District Committee (the academy was situated in the Bauman District of Moscow), who was directly responsible for the Party manners of the Academy. The heretics were put down. More, the cell recanted its errors. The cell bureau was dissolved for the second time in six months. A new one was "elected," its secretary Nikita Sergeievich Khrushchev. His first act was to conduct a new and more drastic purge. Some of the members of this elite body of potential managers were to be expelled from the Party, others were to be expelled from the academy itself. More interesting, progress was to be reported directly to the Central Committee of the Bolshevik Party of the Soviet Union, of which Stalin was Secretary General. Khrushchev, at thirty-five, was now officially reporting to the highest Party organ, and one of the people on whom he had to report was Stalin's wife.[11]

It was not quite the end of Shirin. He had another six months to go as Party boss of the Bauman District: he had not, after all, agitated against Stalin; he had merely turned a blind eye on some of those who had, including Nadezhda Allilulyeva. Within six months Khrushchev had done what he had to do in the Industrial Academy and was ready to move to higher things. Shirin was sacked, and Khrushchev, his course uncompleted, took his place. None of these things could have happened had Khrushchev, in the guise of a student, not in fact been working in the closest liaison with high authority. It was the Kharkov speech, in which Khrushchev went one step farther than Stalin, over again. The dates speak sufficiently clearly. Khrushchev was called to Moscow very soon after Kaganovich had finally established himself there, having left the Ukraine to become a secretary of the Central Committee. In 1930 he became First Secretary of the Moscow City and Regional Party organizations. Poor Shirin was one of his underlings. Kaganovich, of course, was responsible ultimately for the health of the Party in the industrial academy, as throughout Moscow. If one of his underlings failed there was nothing to stop him from quietly shifting him to another sphere or reducing him to the ranks. But the hierarchy never worked like this in Stalin's Russia, and for two reasons: the higher leadership was above criticism, except by Stalin himself, which meant that for every failure there had to be a scapegoat; further, the sins of omission or commission were habitually dramatized, the rank and file, as well as all officials except the very senior, were to be kept on the stretch without intermission as part of a system of subdued terror. There were two theories at work here, and they contradicted each other: one was that the best way to keep officials up to the mark was to let it be understood that at any time a lapse on their part might be visited with exemplary severity; the other was that total obedience from all officials could be ensured only if they knew that the least deviation from the prescribed line would mean their ruin. There was something to be said for the first as a harsh and savage expedient; but the second, as time went on, led to the extinction of initiative and to sycophancy on a monstrous scale, breeding inefficiency and corruption. Later, as we know, Stalin applied this system to his own immediate colleagues, none of whom knew from one day to the next whether they were safe. But in the early days of Stalin's ascendancy, at the beginning of the thirties, he still desperately needed the Molotovs, the Kaganoviches, the Kirovs, and the rest. These were safe. But they, in their turn, depended absolutely on loyal supporters who understood the game and could combine cunning, brutality, organizing ability, and boundless energy. They also needed courage, for they could be thrown to the wolves at a moment's notice if things went wrong, or if the Party line, Stalin's line, suddenly changed. There were plenty who could combine brutality with cunning, many had organizing ability, some had boundless energy, but few could also bring courage. Khrushchev was one of these few. It is perfectly clear that he was the junior partner in an arrangement, a *kombinatzia,* organized by Kaganovich. But there was plenty of room for things to go wrong. If they had gone wrong, he would have been repudiated, disgraced, never heard of again.

But they did not go wrong. It was Khrushchev's courage, or calculated recklessness, which most distinguished him from many of his contemporaries—that even more than the very remarkable combination of a capacity for intrigue (Malenkov had that), skill in organization (Bulganin had that), and a passion for hard practical work in the field (few had that). It was not an accident that he rose so fast: he had, in the context of the collectivization, in which he had very little part,* and the first Five Year Plan, in which he played an important role, and the final consolidation of Stalin's supremacy, to which he was indispensable, well earned his preferment.

His relationship with Kaganovich was a fascinating one. Kaganovich was a working man too, about the same age; but as a revolutionary he was far senior, and he had an attacking, not a calculating temperament. He was also a Jew. Khrushchev in later years showed himself an anti-Semite.[12] He was a tough and unimpeachable Russian *mouzhik*. As Stalin consolidated his position the Jewish revolutionaries, to whom Lenin owed so much, were being beaten down. Kaganovich, the Jew, who was also an anti-Semite, may have found it useful to show as his most useful protégé the very type of the anti-Jewish, anti-intellectual peasant. He must have been aware, too, that Khrushchev, for all his brash and noisy, overbearing ways, had reserves of subtlety and cunning which he lacked, Kaganovich's revolutionary cunning was adequate for his purposes, but it never aspired much beyond the Leninist double-cross. Khrushchev's mind, behind those small screwed-up eyes, was more devious; his nature, behind the bluster, far more patient. He was a long-term schemer, which Kaganovich never was. There is a photograph of Khrushchev taken, judging by the look of it, about this time. He is back in the Ukraine, visiting the scenes of his childhood. It is a group picture, and the little man, his head shaved and his ears sticking out, sits passively among an eager group of local Party workers. He might be sitting on a cloud,

---

* But he knew just what was going on, and not simply from hearsay. Indeed he was actively responsible under Kaganovich for the final collectivization of Moscow Region in 1932. Early in 1933 he was sent out with Bulganin and Malenkov to finish off the good work.

detached, those eyes fixed on a private vision—a vision of power? A vision of achievement? There was even then the air of perfectly relaxed authority which, decades later, I was to feel so strongly at close quarters in that Yogoslav factory. Kaganovich was never relaxed; he never dreamed.

CHAPTER SEVEN

City Politics, Moscow Style

IT WAS JANUARY 1931 when Khrushchev, after only fifteen months, said farewell to the Industrial Academy and launched himself into Moscow city politics. Within weeks of taking over from the unfortunate Shirin the secretaryship of the Bauman District Party Committee he was elected to the City Party Committee itself, a committee of fifteen, dominated by Kaganovich as First Secretary. Kaganovich was already a member of Stalin's Politburo as well as a secretary of the Central Committee, which meant that Khrushchev, at thirty-six, was in direct contact with the supreme direction of the Soviet Union. He was also favoured by it. In July 1931 he took another step upwards, being appointed secretary of the most important of all the Moscow districts, Red Presnaya, while contriving to keep the Bauman District in his hands. In January 1932, exactly a year after his Moscow city debut, he was made Second Secretary of the Moscow City Committee, immediately responsible to Kaganovich.

The *kombinatzia* was showing its teeth. More important, the Stalinist pattern of government was quickly taking shape, and the men now being moved into high positions were those who, with one or two exceptions, were to dominate the Soviet Union for more than two decades to come. The final pattern did not take shape until after the Seventeenth Party Congress, "the Congress of the Victors," in 1934, but already in 1931 the Stalin team occupied strategic positions. Stalin's only contemporary,

Voroshilov, in charge of the Red Army, Molotov, and Kaganovich were already members of the Politburo. Andreyev joined it in the course of 1931. Kuibyshev was soon to die a natural death. Ordzhonikidze and Kirov, two of Stalin's closest supporters, were later to be killed, almost certainly by order of Stalin. Mikoyan was in charge of foreign trade and a candidate member of the Politburo; Beria, after a spell in the Cheka, was Stalin's deputy in the Caucasus. Kaganovich, of course, ran Moscow; Kirov, Leningrad; Kossior, the Ukraine; Zhdanov was master of Nizhni Novgorod (later Gorki), which then occupied the key industrial position later to be taken over by Stalingrad; Shvernik was a secretary of the Central Committee and head of the trade unions. The two chief policemen of terrible fame, Yagoda and Yezhov, were rising stars: Yagoda ran GULAG, the central administration in charge of labour camps, soon to become notorious; Yezhov, by all reasonable standards a criminal lunatic, was to move up to his fearful eminence via the Central Control Commission (the disciplinary arm) of the Party itself.

Others were also on the move, among them Bulganin, a year younger than Khrushchev, whose career was to march very closely with Khrushchev's until, as Prime Minister, he was finally broken by his old comrade in 1958. Bulganin was to form the third member of the triumvirate which completely dominated Moscow. His first appearance as a Bolshevik was in 1918, when he joined the newly formed Cheka. After four years as a political policeman, he was discovered to have a talent for organization and a head for figures. In 1922, while Khrushchev was still in Stalino, he moved to the Supreme Council of National Economy, the forerunner of the State Planning Commission. In 1927 he was put in charge of the Moscow Electric Plant, a huge and favoured concern, which he turned into an example for all Soviet industry. In 1931 he was appointed Chairman of the Moscow City Soviet, or, as he was sometimes called, Mayor of Moscow. He maintained this position during the whole of Khrushchev's Moscow period, and the two worked hand-in-glove together. The Party organization, headed first by Kaganovich, then, in 1935, by Khrushchev himself, provided the drive, the direction, the guidance, the discipline. It was the task of the City

Soviet in its attractive old building on the Tverskaya Boulevard (now Gorki Street)* to work out ways and means of carrying out the Party's directives, or to reconcile them with reality. But there was no clear-cut division between the two organizations. The First Secretary of the Moscow Party organization was the unquestioned boss, responsible only to Stalin; but Bulganin, as Chairman of the City Soviet, was also a member of the Moscow City Committee, thus helping to arrive at decisions which it would then be his duty to implement. These three—Stalin, Bulganin, Kaganovich—made a strong team.

To these were added two others. For five years the young Georgy Malenkov had been working behind the scenes in Stalin's private secretariat. In 1930 he too emerged into the open, backed by an invaluable knowledge of Stalin's *modus operandi* and of the strengths and weaknesses of his most exalted colleagues. He was given a department inside the Central Committee of the All Union Party and at the same time he was put in charge of the Organization Bureau of the Moscow Party Committee, responsible to Kaganovich and a close colleague of Khrushchev and Bulganin. Also on the city committee was Yezhov, later to commit the worst excesses of the great purge; later still to be denounced as a criminal by Khrushchev, his one-time colleague. The team was a constellation. Four of the potentially most powerful men in the Soviet Union were gathered together in one committee under the leadership of Kaganovich, who was already among the first four or five under Stalin. Kaganovitch, thirty-seven; Khrushchev, thirty-six; Bulganin, thirty-five; Malenkov, twenty-eight; and Yezhov . . . The great city was effectively in the hands of these five immensely tough young men, cloth-capped, booted, shirts buttoned up to the neck. It was this team, less Yezhov, executed long before, plus Molotov, then Stalin's right-hand man, which twenty-three years later was to take over the country from Stalin—with the help of the newcomer Beria, whom they were soon to kill. Now they ran Moscow.

---

* Tourists who may not find this building attractive are advised that its modest and perfect proportions were spoiled by the addition of extra stories at a later date.

A strong team was needed. Between 1930 and 1932 the mood of the Soviet Union underwent a change. With the first Five Year Plan under way and the collectivization completed, there were to be no more arguments about ways and means. The course was set, and it had nothing whatever to do with socialism or communism as understood either by Lenin or by Marxists outside the Soviet Union. The dictatorship of the proletariat, which for some time had been transformed into the dictatorship of the Central Committee of the Communist Party, operating through its organs, the Politburo, the Secretariat, the Orgburo, and the Central Control Commission, was now the dictatorship of Stalin, operating first through the Politburo and the Secretariat, later through the GPU. And although this dictatorship was for a time not absolute, it was Stalin and Stalin alone who, in his speeches, could break new ground and set the tone.

In this year Molotov was made Chairman of the Council of People's Commissars or Prime Minister, in succession to Rykov, who had taken over from Lenin and was later to be executed by Stalin. Molotov's first act was to declare his subservience to the Party—i.e., to Stalin. Once upon a time the Council of People's Commissars (after 1946 the Council of People's Ministers), with Lenin as Chairman, had been a force in the land. Now it became merely the executive arm of the Party, and its most important members, from Molotov down, were themselves high Party functionaries. Every activity in the land—heavy industry, light industry, trade, agriculture, transport, communications, et cetera—was the responsibility of the relevant commissariat, and Molotov, at forty, thus acted as Stalin's overseer for the administration and production of the whole of the USSR.

What Stalin in fact was doing was imposing upon the country a system of state capitalism, and for a time his one and only interest was to make this system work. It took him a long way from socialism. It forced him to develop a completely regimented state engaged in carrying out an industrial revolution through dictates from above. The excesses of the English industrial revolution—the forcing of country-dwellers into horrible new towns, child labour, grinding poverty, the stunting of bodies and souls —had been perpetrated by individuals in search of profit and allowed by the government to operate in its crudest form the law of supply and demand because it was considered immoral to interfere with the "natural laws" of economics. The excesses of the Soviet industrial revolution, which led to similar situations, but on a vast and Russian scale, were perpetrated by Stalin's decree: instead of being forced into the towns by the enclosures, instead of being forced into the mines and mills—men, women, and children—by the threat of starvation, Russian peasants were moved about by decree and, when this failed, by the GPU, which under Yagoda constructed vast labour camps filled by arbitrary arrests, on construction sites, in forests, in mineral-bearing areas. Hundreds of thousands would be picked up to labour, and often to die, as slaves on the Baltic-White Sea canal, in the Lena goldfields, in the killing climate of the Magadan region, in the coal mines of Norilsk.

And to what end? It was in 1931 that Stalin abruptly put an end to the last dreams of the revolutionary idealists by insisting on the necessity for steep differences of reward to act as incentives, initiating a policy which was formalized three years later when at the Seventeenth Party Congress he declared that egalitarianism had nothing to do with Marxism, but was a "reactionary, petty-bourgeois absurdity worthy of a primitive sect of ascetics but not of a Socialist society organized on Marxist lines." [1] In 1931, too, for the first time he sounded the nationalist, chauvinist note which ever after was to obsess him: it was back to the tsars with a vengeance:

No, comrades . . . the pace must not be slackened! On the contrary. . . .

To slacken the pace would mean to lag behind; and those who lag behind are beaten. We do not want to be beaten. No, we do not! Russia . . . was ceaselessly beaten for her backwardness. She was beaten by the Mongol Khans, she was beaten by the Turkish Beys, she was beaten by the Swedish feudal lords, she was beaten by the Anglo-French capitalists, she was beaten by the Japanese barons, she was beaten by all—for her backwardness. For military backwardness, for cultural backwardness, for agricultural backwardness. She was beaten because to beat her was profitable and went unpunished. You remember the words of the prerevolutionary Russian poet: "Thou art poor and thou art abundant, thou art mighty and thou art helpless, Mother Russia!"

We are fifty or a hundred years behind the advanced countries. We must make good this lag in ten years. Either we do it or they crush us.[2]

The spirit of internationalism, of world revolution, had departed. From now on all who worked with Stalin were to work for one thing only: the greater glory of the Soviet Union. All ideologies were perverted to this end; all methods, however brutal, however misguided, were directed to this end.

Khrushchev took Stalin as he found him. He knew, all those who had attended the Fourteenth Party Congress knew at first hand, and many more besides from hearsay, that Lenin in his last years had distrusted Stalin and wanted to see him put down. Many years later, in 1956, in the course of his historic attack on Stalin, Khrushchev was to quote from Lenin's famous testament (a document known in the West for decades), in which he had warned the comrades against giving Stalin too much power because of his rough and overbearing ways. In 1956, filled with righteous indignation, Khrushchev spoke as though this testament had just come to light after having been suppressed for more than three decades. It had been suppressed not only by Stalin, but by all Stalin's comrades-in-arms, including Khrushchev, who had heard it read out in Congress and had voted to remove it from the record.[3]

Khrushchev knew who Stalin was and what he was driving at: greatness for the Soviet Union. And this suited him very well. It is improbable that he had ever given the least thought to world revolution. From the very beginning of his career as a Bolshevik he had been, as we have seen, interested in only three things: getting things going and making his part of the economy work, smashing down opposition of all kinds, and forwarding his own career by intrigue and by showing himself more Stalinist than Stalin. He thought in terms of the here and the now and the concrete; his vision of the future was concrete too, limited to the dream of material abundance and prosperity for his own people. There is nothing to suggest that he had thought of the outside world at all, unless as the supplier of prerevolutionary capital for the exploitation of Russian mineral wealth. Stalin's new and uninhibited emphasis on a strong and powerful Russia for the Russians must have appeared to him entirely right and proper, and so must the abandonment of egalitarian dreams: "To each according to his work," the slogan which was to prepare the way for spectacular differentials, so that a Red Army lieutenant would soon be earning a hundred times more than a Red Army private, so that a new privileged class of Communist officials, engineers, industrialists, writers, scientists, and ballet dancers would soon be emerging, would have struck him as self-evident. As for the crash programme of industrialization, cost what it might in suffering, Khrushchev himself was one of nature's shock brigadiers. And, unlike most of his colleagues, he was prepared to roll his sleeves up and muddy his boots, to get down among the workers and show them by precept, exhortation, and example.

This was the period when all over the vast land, above all in the Urals, huge new towns and enterprises were being raised out of the mud for the production of steel. The symbol of the day was the great new steel town, Magnitogorsk. And of Magnitogorsk Mr. John Scott, an American who worked there, wrote:

In Magnitogorsk I was precipitated into a battle. I was deployed on the iron and steel front. Tens of thousands of people were enduring the most intense hardships in order to build blast furnaces, and many of them did it willingly, with boundless enthusiasm, which infected me from the day of my arrival. . . . I would wager that Russia's battle of ferrous metallurgy alone involved more casualties than the battle of the Marne.[4]

This was the mood not only in the great new steel towns but all over Russia where construction work was going on. The young and idealistic, who knew nothing about their rulers, threw themselves into the most heartbreaking toil, suffering atrocious conditions for the sake of a dream: Russia had been stagnant; now, as the smoke and the dust cleared away after the cataclysmic earthquake, they were building. There was purpose behind everything they did, and everything they did was worth personal sacrifice, because what they were building with their own sweat and blood was the celestial city on earth, and in their lifetime this paradise would be completed. Those who were not young and idealistic, those who cared for nothing but their own survival, and those who had once cared deeply and were now disillusioned, were carried along on this almost palpable wave of enthusiasm, were shamed into working hard too, were goaded and bullied by the Party comrades, in the last resort were picked up by the GPU and carried off to work for starvation rations in concentration camps.

This was the mood. It might have been made for our hero; it was the sort of manic mood he liked. He knew how to exploit enthusiasm (he was enthusiastic himself), and he knew how to bully those who lagged. He knew, to the last inch, just how far he could drive these peasants turned construction workers and machinists. He was in his element. Not in Magnitogorsk, but in Moscow, which Stalin was preparing to pull down and rebuild as the most splendid capital city in the world.

[2.]

Khrushchev still had some way to go before he could fulfil himself as the great leader and commander on the construction front. It was not until January 1932 that he abandoned his Red Presnaya District to a smaller man and moved up formally to be Kaganovich's second in command. He had achieved the Red Presnaya District six months earlier, as he had achieved the Bauman District earlier still, by clambering over the ruins of his predecessor, Comrade Kozlov, who had been made an official scapegoat for food shortages caused directly by government policies. Kozlov's dismissal was preceded by the usual *Pravda* broadside.[5] But instead of kowtowing and confessing his sins, he was foolhardy enough to fight back. He went. Khrushchev moved up in his place.

He did not improve the food situation, which was causing extreme discontent and some rioting, but he did begin at once to show himself a master of the "new style"—the Stalinist way of work. The Stalinist way was the shock way, which later led to Stakhanovism. We have heard a great deal about the special and spectacular *ad hoc* mobilizations of whole districts, whole towns, whole age groups, to achieve a particular task in a set time; these formed familiar features of the landscape of those days. The idea was first put into practice in the Red Presnaya District of Moscow in 1931, and it was Khrushchev's own idea. He applied it not only to construction work but to everything he touched. He introduced special days for this and that, and special ten-day periods of supreme endeavour—it might be for digging a new drain, or for improving the training of candidates for the Communist Party. He also invented the device known as the Stalin *Estafette,* which was to breed many horrors. This unlikely term was used to stand for a shock programme designed to enforce and to dramatize the "Stalinist style." Under cover of a variety of euphemisms the new methods meant, among other things, conscription of labour; deprivation of the worker's right to choose or change his place of work; saddling the worker personally with responsibility for the condition of the machines and tools he used. Within this oppressive framework all sorts of devices were introduced for the more thorough exploitation of labour: so-called "counter-plans" to exceed the demands of the official plan; forced state loans, called "the mobilization of monetary resources"; the creation of the notorious shock brigades working on a system of premium and progressive piecework. The Stalinist *Estafette* caught on and quickly spread to the whole of Moscow and elsewhere. It set the pattern which was to be formalized in the draconian labour laws of 1933, which were not to be repealed until after Stalin's death. The standard-bearer of conscript labour was Nikita Khrushchev.[6]

We are still in 1932. It was a terrible year for the people, and it was a terrible year for Stalin. The first Five Year Plan, with its impossible targets, had failed; but an immense amount had been done. A miracle had taken place—except that this "miracle" was paid for by the physical and mental suffering of untold millions and by the sacrifice of individual lives on a gigantic scale. The base had been laid, and the more sensible, second Five Year Plan was to see the raising of the edifice. In 1932 Stalin seems for a moment to have lost his nerve. Worship of Stalin was not yet the required thing; he asked only to be feared. But he was detested too. Some, even, of the men round him were beginning to express anxieties and doubts long nurtured but concealed. There was no conspiracy, but senior members of the government who had actively helped Stalin defeat first the Trotskyists, then the Bukharinites were exchanging memoranda urging that the Central Committee should have the courage to vote Stalin out of office by constitutional means. These included the chief of propaganda, Riutin, and the Premier of the Russian Republic, Syrtsov; with others, they were charged with conspiracy and sent to prison. Stalin had not then begun killing his own colleagues. The Ukraine, Khrushchev's old stamping ground, made safe (forever, it seemed) for Stalin by Kaganovich, was in full revolt. Stalin sent one of his closest friends, Postychev (later to be killed by his friend and master), to conduct a ferocious purge. One of the most distinguished old Bolsheviks, Skrypnik, killed himself as a consequence of that purge.*

It was in November of that year that Stalin's wife, Nadezhda Allilulyevna, killed herself. In the words of the French author Victor Serge:

> There was the man of steel, as he had called himself, . . . face to face with that corpse. It was at about this time that he stood up one day at a meeting of the Politburo and offered to resign. "Perhaps it is indeed true that I have become an obstacle in the unity of the Party. I am ready to go." The members of the Politburo —that body had already been purged of its right wing—glanced at one another in embarrassment. Who among them would take it upon himself to reply: "Yes, my friend—just that. You had better go. It is the best thing you can do." Who indeed? The individual who brought out these words, without being sure of the others' backing, would have risked a great deal. Nobody moved. . . . At last Molotov spoke. He said: "Stop it! Enough! You know you have the Party's confidence . . ." [7]

He certainly had Khrushchev's, and while the master faltered the servant throve. It was in the summer of this terrible year that he was promoted to be Second Secretary of the Moscow City

---

* Stalin actually demanded that Riutin should be executed, in defiance of Lenin's precept. It was Kirov, very soon to be assassinated himself, who persuaded the Politburo to resist Stalin's demand.

Committee and, as such, Kaganovich's deputy. This elevation, since all eyes were on Moscow, transformed him, as far as his Party comrades were concerned, from a local into a national figure. It meant to all who knew the signs that he was being groomed for very high office indeed. And he was exposed. For three more years he was to work with Kaganovich, but he was for all practical purposes more than Kaganovich's deputy: his immediate master was so much taken up with his duties as a member of the Politburo, as the boss of the whole of Moscow Region (not just the city), with overseeing many of the most important industrial projects in the land, that for long periods Khrushchev was virtually in charge of the city's life.

It was a turbulent life. Plans for the reconstruction of Moscow on a massive scale were already beginning to take shape, and with the feverish pulling down and rebuilding at ground level went the most grandiose project of all, the creation of the now celebrated Moscow Metro, the underground railway, or subway, conceived as the eighth wonder of the world and as a secular monument to the greater glory of the Soviet system, to surpass in splendour and magnificence the most splendid creations of past ages to the greater glory of God.

Although the whole system was called after Kaganovich, whose name was deeply incised in stone above the main entrance to each station, the man who was most directly responsible for the completion of the first stages of this masterpiece was our hero. From 1932 to 1934 he was subordinate to Kaganovich. In 1934 Kaganovich, while retaining the First Secretaryship of Moscow Province, appointed Khrushchev in his place as First Secretary of the Moscow City Committee. In that same year Khrushchev became a member of the all Union Central Committee, having far outstripped both Malenkov and Bulganin. In 1935 Kaganovich became People's Commissar for transport and devoted himself for a time above all to the radical reorganization of the railway system of the Soviet Union. Khrushchev stepped effortlessly into his shoes and was now the supreme boss of Moscow Region as well as Moscow City. He retained these positions until 1938, when he was made a candidate, or non-voting, member of the Politburo and was sent back to the Ukraine to purge the purgers and then to be Stalin's viceroy over 40 million souls, First Secretary of the Central Committee of the Ukrainian Communist Party. In 1939 he was made a full member of the Politburo. This was the summit.

Thus the final stages of Khrushchev's elevation coincided precisely with the darkest period of Soviet history. It was in 1934 that Kirov was assassinated in Leningrad, and this assassination was the signal for the start of that appalling process whereby Stalin killed off not only all those old Bolsheviks who had opposed him at any time but also all those, from senior functionaries to rank-and-file Party members, who had ever been associated with known members of the opposition or *their* associates, together with all those who might be suspected of harbouring critical thoughts, even though unspoken—and, for good measure, practically the whole of the higher command of the Red Army, together with tens of thousands of officers of field rank and above. To carry out this holocaust Stalin depended on the obedient and active support not only of his senior colleagues, the Molotovs and the Kaganoviches, but also of the Malenkovs, the Khrushchevs, the Zhdanovs, and the Bulganins, the new generation whom he had raised up to help him fight the old and who depended for their further promotion on the final liquidation of the old. Any who faltered, or who looked likely to falter, were killed. Khrushchev was high among those who did not falter, and he received his reward. From 1932 onwards the records allow us to watch him in action. What we shall see is very different from the picture painted by Khrushchev himself twenty years later in his formal denunciation of Stalin. It will also help to explain why the Russian people, whose memories are long, never welcomed Khrushchev the liberator to their bosoms and entertained a view of him strikingly different from that which the West came to hold. They knew too much.

CHAPTER EIGHT

"We Have a Beautiful Metro!"

BY THE BEGINNING OF 1932, when he became Kaganovich's deputy in Moscow, Khrushchev had proved himself in two distinct fields. With his cloth cap, his sloppy clothes, his brash, overbearing manner, and his ability to coax disgruntled workers and jolly them along as well as to bully them and lash them with his tongue, he was the practical man who knew how to get things done. High office and a host of sycophantic subordinates at his command had not changed him. As in his early days at Yuzovka, he still liked to get out into the field and face his problems on the ground instead of keeping his boots clean and operating from behind a barricade of paper. At the same time the talent for intrigue, for smelling out heresy, for paying out rope in the most calculated manner until his enemies stumbled and a short, sharp twitch of the halter broke their necks, put him in the front rank of Party hatchet-men. He could have made an outstanding career as an industrial overlord, a slave-driver that is, or as a Party watchdog. The combination of two characters in one made him unique and invaluable to Stalin. Ultimately it was to give him a critical advantage over Malenkov, who for too long had concentrated on Party infighting of the most savage kind, always close to the very seat of power, and over Kaganovich, the supreme slave-driver, who quite lacked his protégé's finesse when it came to back-room operations.

The two separate strands in Khrushchev's career were displayed most lucidly during his Moscow period. As a quasi-student in the Industrial Academy he had broken the anti-Stalin movement and heaved himself several steps up the ladder. As District Party Secretary, first in the Bauman District, then in Red Presnaya, he had continued the good work and received grateful acknowledgment from the Central Committee for his zeal and efficiency in pursuing and scattering what was left of the right-wing opposition. At the same time he had distinguished himself by introducing the new Stalinist discipline into the Moscow labour force. He was now to present himself as a prodigy of relentless drive on a positively Pharaoh-like scale, and soon as what can only be called an ideological terrorist of a savagery amounting to viciousness, the hammer of Trotskyites and Bukharinites, real and putative, and, without exception, the grossest flatterer of Stalin. Mikoyan was the runner-up. These two in the 1930s did more to forward the personality cult which, between them, they were later to define and indict than any of their colleagues.

This was the paradox, because these two also did more in their different ways to improve Soviet living conditions than all the rest of the Politburo put together. Khrushchev's great contribution did not come until after Stalin's death; but Mikoyan, the brilliant Armenian, who would have made a fortune in the West, was responsible for all those improvements in goods and services, all those alleviations of the bleakness of life under Stalin which, through the darkest years, gave the Russian people some hope for the future. It could be argued, and it would probably be true, that he and Khrushchev were outstanding in their flattery of Stalin because, unlike their colleagues, they shared a vision of better times for the common people and were determined at all costs to survive long enough at least to begin to realize this vision.

[2.]

Pharaoh operated above all in the tunnels of the Moscow Metro, and here—up to his knees in filthy water, giving pep-talks to the tunnellers, or in the chief engineer's office above ground—we have our first glimpses of him as he appeared to others. In 1935

an official account of the construction of the first section of the
Metro was published in Moscow.[1] Although Kaganovich is cited
throughout as the hero and inspiration of this tremendous feat,
N. S. Khrushchev is permitted a remarkable share of the build-
up too. Poor Bulganin is mentioned only as an afterthought.
The various sector chiefs and engineers who actually directed
and carried out the work are reduced to voices in a paean of
praise for the glorious leadership of Kaganovich and Khrushchev:

> Comrade Kaganovich's closest assistant in the subway construction
> was Comrade N. S. Khrushchev. All engineers, all brigadiers and
> shock-workers on the project know Nikita Sergeievich. They know
> him because he visits the construction sites each day, issues daily
> instructions, checks, criticizes, cheers on, and advises this or that
> shaft overseer, this or that Party organizer, on all specific and urgent
> problems.
> Comrade Khrushchev's office became indistinguishable from the
> project manager's office where Party organizers, shaft overseers, en-
> gineers, and individual brigade leaders work out the detailed plans
> required to fulfill the daring, urgent assignments of their proved
> leader, L. M. Kaganovich.

It is interesting to see, in this limited but extremely important theatre, the beginnings of a minor personality cult. The
deification of Stalin himself had only recently started in 1935,
and it is a little surprising to find that he was ready to permit the
public glorification not only of Kaganovich but also of Kaganovich's lieutenant. The authentic accents are most clearly heard
in the account (written in 1935, not twenty years later when
Khrushchev was supreme) of one of the tunnel engineers:

> In the life of every man there are especially memorable days. On
> days like this he suddenly begins to understand in a new way the
> simple things which he thought he knew all about long ago. On
> days like this he becomes inspired with love for things and phe-
> nomena which he had taken for granted before. Just such a day
> was the day when Comrade Khrushchev talked to me.

The task of tunnelling was a job after Khrushchev's heart: it
called for boldness amounting to recklessness, sacrificial toil, vast

operations based on insufficient forethought, a standing disregard of the limitations of human flesh and blood and the facts of nature. Speed was of the essence. Immense risks had to be taken to keep up to schedule: nobody knows how many died as a consequence of the inevitable catastrophes. The work was pressed through as though the very future of the Soviet Union depended upon its immediate fulfilment. But nothing except the *amour propre* of Stalin, Kaganovich, and Khrushchev depended on it. Moscow's immediate transportation problems could have been solved far more cheaply and quickly by the development of surface transport. The Metro was a dream and a boast. The first section had to be completed in time for the seventeenth anniversary of the Revolution in November 1934. It was a characteristically arbitrary date. It was characteristic, too, that, after all the sacrifices and risks and wild improvisations, the section was not after all completed in time. Nobody lost his head for this. . . .

Not everybody remembered Khrushchev's interventions with love and gratitude. Labour discipline came first. In a speech he made in 1933 he showed what he meant by labour discipline. Addressing the managers and foremen at construction sites, he told them not to rely on bureaucratic supervision but to get out among the workers and order them about directly:

The success of construction depends on the worker fulfilling his norm. If you are chief of a construction site, encourage the better worker, help him, let him earn more; but at the same time you must carry on a determined struggle against the self-seeker and the shirker, who comes to the construction site to snatch his wages and then run off. . . .

Under the influence of self-seekers who have wormed themselves into our construction sites, some workers have begun to think along the following lines: why don't we try to get our norms revised downwards? Pernicious and disorganizing aspirations of this kind must be severely put down. It is necessary to fight in a Bolshevik way, so that every bricklayer, plasterer, painter, fulfills his output norm. All kinds of opportunistic whisperers who talk of revising the norms must be rebuffed with total resolution: they reflect nothing but the pressure of the petty bourgeois element, sometimes even of the real kulak counterrevolutionary element. . . .[2]

Here, with Khrushchev in the van as usual, we see the beginnings of the system, soon to be accepted throughout the Soviet
Union, which equated demands for less work or higher pay with
a political offence against the state, to be punished as such.

If this was the spirit which moved Khrushchev as effective
master of the whole Moscow labour force, when it came to the
particular problems of the Moscow Metro we see in operation
another quality—the headlong way in which he threw himself
into grandiose schemes without adequate preparation, without
adequate data, without any initial small-scale experiment to
bring to light potential difficulties, and with no regard at all for
waste of energy and manpower. This was a quality which was to
become one of his distinctive marks when he could command
all the resources of his vast land—which was, indeed, to lead to
his eventual undoing. In the account of the building of the
Moscow underground we see this quality reflected in the narratives of the men on the job. Although the catastrophes and the
attendant loss of life are minimized and never totted up, time
and time again, in order to demonstrate the resolution, the boldness, the temerity of Kaganovich or Khrushchev, or both, to say
nothing of the heroism of the engineers, we are given glimpses
of disaster as well as an unusual insight into the almost total
disregard of the most elementary safety precautions so that the
work might be pushed on without a check.

During the construction of the underground we knew, of course,
that we were tunneling under a great city, that every disturbance
of existing foundations might lead to disaster; nevertheless, during
the first period of construction we did not show particular vigilance.[3]

Those are the words of one of the chief engineers. An example of this absence of "vigilance" is given by one of his colleagues. There had, he wrote, been no time to shore up buildings along the line of excavation. One day one of the houses
affected started to collapse. The inhabitants were evacuated and
a special commission of experts was convened to discuss the situation. The commission laid it down that excavation should stop
until the shoring up of buildings had been completed. Now it
was Khrushchev's turn. On his daily inspection he saw that work

had stopped. "What's the matter with you? Are you frightened of buildings?" he asked the engineer in charge, Stepanov. Stepanov explained the situation and went on to say that in spite of the findings of the experts and the doubts of his own colleagues on the site, he himself would be prepared to go on excavating and taking the risk. "Nikita Sergeievich's words definitely persuaded us to go ahead with the work along the entire line."

Here is another example of the mood, this time featuring Kaganovich himself. Kaganovich could drive every bit as hard as Khrushchev. He too was prepared to expose the Muscovites, below and above ground, to avoidable risks. One day he appeared on the scene and remarked, "You are now about to tunnel under a house which is full of Americans. For political reasons this house must not be permitted to fall down." Special measures were taken accordingly.

This sort of thing was going on in the very heart of Moscow. Years later the scars of collapsed houses and apartment buildings were still visible, until they became indistinguishable from the scars left by German bombs. And all the time Khrushchev drove. There were two tunnelling shields in operation, one English, one Soviet-made. English engineers who knew all about this kind of tunnelling gave an advance of three-quarters of a metre in twenty-four hours as the most the shields should be expected to achieve in safety. Khrushchev would have none of this. The English shield, he said, must complete three-quarters of a metre per shift, and the Soviet shield must "catch up with it" in a given time. Soon even that was not good enough. Each shield must now achieve a full metre per shift. And, of course, the brigade leaders vied with one another in "socialist" competition.

Nobody, least of all Khrushchev, had a clear idea of the soil conditions on the line of the tunnel. The engineers were always being taken by surprise. But they were never given time to sit down and think.

Comrade Khrushchev ceaselessly kept his eye on our work. Every day the surveyor marked on a chart in Khrushchev's office the movement of our shields. At the slightest slowing down Khrushchev would immediately call in Comrade Tyagnibeda or Suvorov and demand an explanation as to why the slowdown had taken place and what the difficulties were. This constant vigilance of Comrade Khrushchev always inspired the workers to work even better.

The nature of the difficulties and the conditions under which the workers (those who survived) were "inspired" to work even better are often graphically illustrated. Thus, on one occasion among many, the shield was suddenly flooded.

Immense torrents of water poured in from all sides, smashing the cross-timbers and sweeping workers off their feet.

On another:

The shield approached the silt—a brown, fluid mass. The caisson was working under an air pressure of 2.3 atmospheres. As each hour went by conditions became more difficult. Sometimes the silt resisted and unprecedented efforts had to be made to stop it, to save the tunnel, the machine, and, above all, the workers. Once a fire broke out in the caisson. In order to avoid the rapid spread of the fire in the compressed air, rich in oxygen, it was necessary to lower the air pressure. But this only opened the way for the silt, which poured in torrents into the shaft. . . .[4]

The tempo was frantic. In December 1933 Kaganovich himself made a speech to construction chiefs and shock-brigade leaders:

It must be said with the utmost sharpness that if we go on as we are going now the first section of the underground will not be completed by November 7 [of the following year]. The main task is to speed up the construction tempo. . . . We must increase the speed of excavating five times and the speed of tunnel-building from eight to nine times.[5]

In fact, as already remarked, the section was not finished after all in time for the seventeenth anniversary of the Revolution. It was not finished until May 1935. All over the Soviet Union arbitrary deadlines of this kind were being laid down, arbitrary increases in tempo and productivity demanded: if a factory managed to fulfil its norm, the norm was promptly increased. This did not "inspire" the workers or the managers. It worked the other way. Enterprises soon learned the technique of going slow, working all too easily within their powers, to avoid this inane and arbitrary progression. Khrushchev, as a shock leader to end all shock leaders, never learned this simple lesson. To the end of his career he kept on reverting to his old barnstorming ways, proclaiming grandiose programmes to be achieved regardless of cost—and regardless of the fact that they could never succeed. We shall see him at it twenty years later in the matter of the Virgin Lands. We shall see him at it in his absurd and meaningless boasting about "catching up" with America in no time at all in the production of this or that.

He trained his assistants well. "It was a difficult time," wrote the Party secretary in charge of one of the shafts.

Workers, even Communists, would come and ask to be released from work. Party candidate Kozlovski came and brought a doctor's certificate to say that it would be injurious for his health for him to continue working. I did not release him. . . . It is necessary to get used to the work. When you start working, of course you are soon fatigued. But you must not leave your post: weariness passes, and working inspiration begins. The medical commission does not know this, but we—the Party organization—know it well.

Inspiration was a fashionable word at that time. It was a euphemism for going on until you dropped. Either you had it or you were, in Kaganovich's phrase, a "hostile element," liable to be charged with wrecking and sabotage. Then you were dealt with by "administrative methods": this was (still is) the euphemism for GPU (now KGB) action.

For the Moscow underground a well known Chekist was appointed to this end, as Assistant Chief of Construction. Unlike Khrushchev, he did not "inspire"; he purged. He himself recounted how during his first major purge some of the unsatisfactory workers lacked personal papers; to escape being "sent away" the poor wretches tried to hide in the darkest recesses of the underground workings. But the gallant Chekist was too much for them. "My men descended into the shafts to hunt them out. Sometimes it was necessary literally to drag them up into the daylight." One can picture the scene, the beatings up in the darkness, the groaning and the yelling. How much better to be inspired by Comrade Khrushchev and do overtime for no pay.

In those early days of the Metro construction forced labour was not used. That came later, when the GPU had become the NKVD and Stalin's great purges produced an unlimited number of bodies of all kinds for the dirtiest and most dangerous tasks. To begin with, the unskilled work was largely carried out by members of the Komsomol, the Young Communist League, who either volunteered to toil away for practically nothing to the greater glory of the Soviet Union, or else were pressured into it by moral blackmail. The work also attracted the sweepings of the Moscow slums. But Khrushchev knew about forced labour at this time and took it in his stride. One of his special interests was the construction of the Moscow-Volga canal, which, like the White Sea Canal, was the product of nothing but forced labour —Yagoda's first drafts. Subsequent sections of the Moscow Metro were also built by forced labour—including, ironically, many foreign Communists who had sought refuge in the Soviet Union from the European dictatorships. One of the most distinguished of these, Valentín Gonzalez, the legendary anti-Franco general of the Spanish civil war, known as El Campesino, was sent to work in the Metro as a last chance to prove himself a genuine Bolshevik. "Good, faithful work and evidence of change of heart might lead to my rehabilitation," wrote El Campesino.

The Russians are extremely proud of the Moscow underground. It is their prize exhibit for foreign delegations, journalists, and tourists. They claim it as a masterpiece of construction, and they are quite right. Only they forget to explain that it is a monument not only to Soviet engineering but also to the slave labour that went into its construction.

Almost ninety per cent of the construction workers were in a position similar to mine. Many of them were old fighters, former military leaders, or even NKVD men. They had fallen into disgrace and had been allotted this sort of work, which offered them the faint—the very faint—hope that their efforts would in time restore them to their former position in the ruling class . . . the alternative to this work was Siberia, and so they did all they could to follow the faint ray of hope.[6]

El Campesino (who himself finished up in Siberia) was writing of a later period, on the eve of the war, when Khrushchev had gone back to the Ukraine to be Stalin's viceroy in Kiev; but, in spite of the industrial achievements of the Five Year plans, working conditions in the Moscow underground were then much the same as they had been in the early thirties. Soil still had to be shifted with wheelbarrows.

Lack of modern machinery and equipment made our work very difficult. Human muscles and effort had to replace the missing tools. I often worked in water up to my knees. After some time I noticed that I was always sent to the most dangerous spots when there had been a cave-in. An accident at work would have been a nice way of getting rid of me, I suppose. The Soviet propaganda would have turned me into a hero again.[7]

So much for the reality behind the famous "underground palaces," the stations of the Metro: great columned halls lined with multicoloured, highly polished marbles, porphyries, and all the rest.

The first section cost more then 500 million roubles (El Campesino was earning, though he regularly exceeded his norm, 300 roubles a month, "the basic wage of manual labourers in Moscow—a starvation wage," which came to barely 200 roubles when all deductions had been made).[8] The appropriation for 1934 alone was 350 million roubles. According to the report of the Seventeenth Party Congress in 1934, the Congress of the Victors, in the course of which Khrushchev was made a member of the Central Committee, the total investment in consumer goods for the whole of the Soviet Union under the first Five Year Plan had been 300 million roubles a year.

Over 70,000 square meters of marble were required for the stations of the first and second sections alone. This is one and a half times the amount used in all the palaces of Tsarist Russia during the fifty years preceding the Great October Socialist Revolution. . . . Lavish use was made of porphyry, granite, bronze, smalto, and ceramic, as well as glazed panels. Many of the interiors were adorned with gold leaf, statuary, bas-reliefs, and mosaics.[9]

It is impossible to tell what the Muscovites really thought about this splendour. Crammed together, two families to a room, in hovels, cellars, and crumbling apartment blocks; ill-shod, wretchedly clothed, undernourished, they swarmed and pushed and cursed their way into the magic trains which swept silently out of the darkness, came to rest in these halls of glittering splendour, and whisked the triumphant proletarians away to their miserable homes, to their bleak factories, or to queue for hours in front of barren shops for the simplest necessities of life —a box of matches, a needle and thread. We do not know what Khrushchev thought of these contrasts either. Later, much later, he was to condemn with great vehemence Stalin's mania for monumental building, for wedding-cake architecture, for extravagant ornamentation—all diverting and wasting millions of roubles that should have been spent on necessary housing.[10] But from 1932, first as deputy chief, then as supreme chief of Moscow, until 1938 he threw himself heart and soul into the great transformation of Moscow, which was never completed, and showed himself the best slave-driver of them all. For this he was duly rewarded.

Elected to the Central Committee in 1934, he became a candidate, or non-voting, member of the Politburo in 1938. By then he was earning Stalin's approbation in quite another way: this time for the qualities which had caused Kaganovich to single him out in his early days at Stalino. Nineteen thirty-four was a climacteric year for the Soviet Union as well as for Khrushchev. The second Five Year Plan was going well. Throughout the great land the chaos, the hunger, and the suffering produced by the collectivization and the first shocks of Stalin's "new style" in super-industrialization were beginning to give way to a slightly easier tempo and at least the promise of stability. All over Europe totalitarian dictatorships had established themselves, partly as a desperate response to what appeared to be the total collapse of the capitalist system: in England and America, where democracy still ruled, governments were helpless in face of near bankruptcy and chronic unemployment; the Soviet Union alone among nations was forging ahead with steady purpose, transforming a nation of illiterate peasants into an industrial society based on universal popular education. It was at this time, above all in 1933 and 1934, that Western visitors to Russia would return to a Europe scourged by dictators, to an England paralysed by a discredited fiscal and economic system, and proclaim that in the Soviet Union they had seen the future and that it worked. Confined to Moscow and Leningrad as they were, and not allowed to see below the newly shining surface of the privileged districts of both, they had no idea of the cost. They knew nothing of the great famine, man-induced, which had lately desolated the Ukraine. They knew nothing of the millions of so-called kulaks killed, deported to Siberia, sent to labour and die in the salt mines and the coal mines and the forests of the far North. The existence of great hardship they could see. There was no soap. There was considerable and, as it appeared to starry Western eyes, rather absurd pressure on intellectuals to toe the Party line: but obviously the government could not tolerate intellectual sabotage, and there were plenty of hostile counter-revolutionary survivals from the past who would all too quickly take advantage of any weakness on the part of central authority. Things would soon be better. They were getting better every day. Meanwhile, what mattered was the tremendous sense of purpose which filled the very young and, marching on, caught up the old and disillusioned in its train. How different from the state of the young under Baldwin and in America! How different, indeed. . . . At the very end of 1934, the glorious year in which Stalin had triumphed, confirmed, at the Congress of the Victors, the scattering of his enemies and the final defeat of counterrevolution, on the eve of 1935, which obviously would be the first year in which the hard-earned fruits of so much hardship, toil, and suffering would at last be harvested—on December 1, at exactly 4:30 in the dark winter afternoon, occurred the shooting of Sergei Mironovich Kirov, one of Stalin's right-hand men, a member of the Politburo, supreme chief of Leningrad city and Leningrad Region. This assassination, or murder, started off a chain reaction which was to blacken Stalin's name forever, turn the great land into a charnel house, and, as a by-product, elevate those who survived—Malenkov, Zhdanov, Bulganin, Beria, Khrushchev among them—to the most exalted positions, under Stalin, in the land.

CHAPTER NINE

The Great Purge: "Stalin Is Our Banner! Stalin Is Our Will!"

W E NOW have to take account of an entirely new element in our unravelling of Khrushchev's past. In later life Khrushchev was to say little or nothing about those years of swift promotion from 1926 to 1934, from the moment he left Stalin to the moment when he succeeded Kaganovich as the Moscow Party chieftain. In the secret speech of 1956 he had nothing at all to say against the manner in which Stalin seized and consolidated his power, nothing at all about the excesses of the collectivization and the super-industrialization programme, the smashing of all opposition, first from the left, then from the right, the elevation of the secret police to become virtually a state within a state. For Khrushchev, Stalin's crimes began only in 1934 with the murder of Kirov and the beginning of the "personality cult"—i.e., the deification of Stalin.

This was not, as some have suggested, because Khrushchev himself, as an ardent Stalinist, was actively involved in the construction of the Stalinist system, so that any criticism of Stalin's conduct and policies from 1926 to 1934 would inevitably have been self-criticism. On the contrary, all Khrushchev's colleagues in 1956 and all politically conscious Russians over the age of forty knew very well that the man who was now denouncing Stalin's crimes had, from 1935 onwards, not only profited by them directly but also most actively abetted them. The col-

leagues were in no position to point this out because they had all
been in the same boat. The citizens, unable to speak out, could
only remember and shrug their shoulders. The reason why
Khrushchev had nothing to say in criticism of the system which
Stalin had built up from 1926 to 1934 was that this system was
still in operation and was to be retained indefinitely. For the
same reason, in his denunciation of his late master, Khrushchev
limited himself to exposing Stalin's crimes against Communist
Party members and, to a lesser degree, against the Red Army
higher command. He had nothing at all to say about the oppression of the Soviet masses and the non-Communist intelligentsia;
and this was for the very good reason that he, Khrushchev, proposed to continue oppressing these. At no point did he ever
suggest that there was anything wrong with a system which had
bred such atrocity; this would have cut the ground completely
from under his own feet, since he intended to perpetuate the
system. Throughout, his attack was selective and arbitrary and
was concerned only with presenting Stalin as a great man gone
wrong and, in a sort of madness, perverting the noble system
which he had built up in the tradition of Lenin and which it
was his, Khrushchev's, mission to restore. This was not a project
calculated to please the Russians as a whole.

From the murder of Kirov onwards we are no longer confined
to the official records of Khrushchev's actions and speeches; we
can compare the record with Khrushchev's subsequent apologia.
The discrepancies here are very sharp indeed, so sharp that they
make it impossible to accept Khrushchev's unsupported word
for anything at all. More than this, they make it impossible to
believe the unsupported word of any of Khrushchev's colleagues, including the present leaders of the Soviet Union.
These have never yet challenged the Khrushchev version, which
they know to be false.

By 1934 Stalin, to all appearances, felt so sure of himself that
Moscow was once more full of his late enemies returned from
Siberia, such as Zinoviev and Kamenev, or actually employed as
Stalin's advisers or even officially as members of the government.
Bukharin, for example, who had just three years to live, was still
on the editorial board of the Great Soviet Encyclopædia, which

he had helped to launch in 1928. Soon, with other onetime opponents, he was to be a member of the commission appointed under Stalin to draft the new "liberal" constitution. It was a confusing time. For even while the most distinguished survivors of the Bolshevik old guard were making their final submission to Stalin and being variously rewarded, a savage and continuous purge was in progress among the rank and file of the Party and, still more, the Komsomol: a new generation was arising which had begun to question the validity of Stalin's growing tyranny and which was disgusted with the abject capitulation of the old oppositionists. But even as they raised their voices, these younger men were thrown out of the Party and the Komsomol and set to work in the forced-labour camps (inaugurated originally as "re-education" centres) of the new police chief, Yagoda.

Stalin himself seemed to be undecided as to what to do next. In one breath he amnestied large numbers of kulaks who still survived; abolished the GPU as an autonomous force and handed over its duties to the People's Commissariat for Internal Affairs, the NKVD; gave the Attorney General the power to supervise the activities of the NKVD and keep them within the law; invited members of the late opposition to cooperate in the drafting of a new constitution. In the next he would come out with some atrocious decree, such as the one which made a whole family responsible for any treasonable act committed by any one of its members: informing, even by children on their fathers, was thus made compulsory; failure to inform, even on husband or wife, was punished with great severity.[1]

How the old Bolsheviks reconciled their submission to Stalin with this sort of thing will never be known. They may have acted out of sheer moral and nervous exhaustion; or they may have believed they had reason to hope for a change if only they could hold on long enough. Whatever the reason, it helped them not at all: soon they were all to be dead at Stalin's hand.

There were, indeed, reasons to hope for a change. Stalin's Politburo was itself divided. And the issue was whether or not the time had come to ease the rule of force and invite the active cooperation of all who had been in opposition for the urgent task of building a strong, healthy, and united Soviet Union to meet the growing military threat from the outer world—from Nazi Germany, from Japan, from any of the Western powers who might join with either of these in a final effort to overthrow the Soviet government before the country was strong enough to be invulnerable.

[2.]

The chief among those who believed in the policy of reconciliation was Sergei Kirov, who had succeeded Zinoviev as the Party chieftain of Leningrad and was a member of the Politburo.

Kirov was not a sympathetic figure. His eyes were pale and cold. He was far and away the most able of Stalin's younger lieutenants and he had been as tough as anybody in the drives against the opposition and the peasants. To all appearance he was the very prototype of Pasternak's ruthless young commissars in their black leather jackets. But he was also highly intelligent, he had the born orator's feeling for the popular mood, and, tough though he was, harsh and cruel when he was convinced of the need for harshness and cruelty, he had not a vestige of Stalin's vengefulness, malevolence, and joy in cruelty. He wanted the revolution to succeed, and he believed the time had come for the new rulers to show their strength by accepting rebels and malcontents back into the fold.

In Leningrad, always the headquarters of particularism and rebelliousness, he had had more experience in dealing with difficult situations than any of his colleagues. And, amazingly, he was making himself respected and liked by the very people he had scourged. He had set himself up even against the excesses of the NKVD and was rapidly taking on the image of protector of the little man and champion of the aberrant who wished to live down their pasts and prove themselves useful citizens. And his fame had spread to Moscow.

At the Congress of the Victors in February 1934 he had made a dazzling appearance, applauded, some said, more warmly even than Stalin himself. At the end of the Congress his position was immensely strengthened: re-elected to the Politburo, he was also elected to the Orgburo and made a secretary of the Central

Committee; all the strings of power were now in his hand. This
meant that he would soon have to leave Leningrad and take up
residence in Moscow. But for some reason—it was said that his
presence in Leningrad was for the time being indispensable—the
call to Moscow was delayed. All through 1934 he went on taking
his own line in Leningrad. In November he attended a plenary
session of the Central Committee in Moscow, which he dominated completely, putting forward proposals for specific measures to hasten the movement towards amelioration. It was then
agreed that he must return to Moscow for good almost at once.
That was on November 28, 1934. On December 1 he was dead.

Western observers, above all the New York Menshevik circle,
writing in their Russian-language paper, which so often told the
truth about what was going on behind the scenes in Russia,[2]
believed from the start that there was more than met the eye in
the killing of Kirov. The actual shooting was done by a young
Communist called Nikolaev, who was allowed, armed with a
loaded revolver, to penetrate the security screen of the Leningrad City Soviet and kill Kirov in his own office. Nikolaev was
seized, tried *in camera,* and shot out of hand, together with fifteen other young Communists known to have been associated
with him. In the first convulsive reaction it was given out that
Nikolaev had been a "fascist agent" in the pay of a foreign
power; 104 unfortunates who had been sitting in prison since
long before the crime were dragged out and shot for good measure. Then, without a word of explanation, the "fascist agent"
story was abandoned. Now it was the Zinoviev–Kamenev opposition which was responsible. Leningrad was suddenly said to be
teeming with oppositionists—the whole country, for that matter,
but Leningrad, whose independent ways had long exasperated
Stalin, was the worst hit. Tens of thousands of individuals who,
often for the most ludicrous and trivial reasons, were regarded as
potentially untrustworthy, were rounded up and sent off in the
long, slow trains to labour camps in the East and the North.
Zinoviev and Kamenev were seized too, charged with responsibility for Kirov's murder, tried *in camera,* and sentenced to ten
and five years' penal servitude respectively. But Stalin had no
intention of making martyrs of these two wretched dead-beats.

He wanted to extract from them a confession of guilt which would enable him to smear with the Trotskyite brush anybody else he proposed to get rid of—Trotsky, still active in exile, still the man who was loudly and insistently telling the world about the realities of Stalin's Russia, being the symbol of all opposition and all things that were anathema. "What followed was a grotesque process of bargaining over a formula of recantation, bargaining that went on between Stalin's offices in the Kremlin and the prison cells of the Lubianka, where Zinoviev and Kamenev were held." [3] Zinoviev was choosy about the phrasing of this, his latest recantation in a long series. But it did not matter what he said. Zinoviev and Kamenev had become a comic turn. Not even their final trial and execution two years later could transform them into figures of tragedy. These two men in their time had helped to send many to their deaths; they were not even objects for pity.

Meanwhile, with the news of Kirov's death, and before even Nikolaev had been shot, an elaborate covering-up operation was set in motion. Stalin himself descended upon Leningrad, accompanied not only by Molotov and Voroshilov, as might have been expected, but also by the much younger Zhdanov (who was soon to be Kirov's successor in Leningrad) and none other than Nikita Khrushchev—functioning as a member of the commission to arrange Kirov's funeral and also as the representative of the workers of Moscow. This, as far as is known, was Khrushchev's first appearance on the national stage in immediate association with Stalin. Many years later, when he was seeking to disassociate himself from Stalin, it was to prove an unfortunate conjuncture. For some very strange things went on in Leningrad immediately after the murder. Khrushchev must have been privy to them. Twenty-two years later he was to confirm Western belief that Kirov's murder had been connived at, if not directly arranged, at the highest level. But, although later still he was to announce that a formal commission of inquiry was to sit on the case, he never went beyond vague accusations:

It must be asserted [he said in his secret 1956 speech] that to this day the circumstances surrounding Kirov's murder hide many things which are inexplicable and mysterious and demand a most careful examination. There are reasons for the suspicion that the killer of Kirov, Nikolaev, was assisted by someone from among the people whose duty it was to protect the person of Kirov.

A month and a half before the killing, Nikolaev was arrested on the grounds of suspicious behaviour, but he was released and not even searched. It is an unusually suspicious circumstance that when the Chekist assigned to protect Kirov was being brought for interrogation, on December 2, 1934, he was killed in a car "accident" in which no other occupants of the car were harmed. After the murder of Kirov top functionaries of the Leningrad NKVD were given very light sentences, but in 1937 they were shot. We can assume that they were shot in order to cover the traces of the organizers of Kirov's killing.[4]

Whom did Khrushchev have in mind as being responsible for Kirov's killing? He never said. Three years later it looked as though he was about to say more, when he announced to the Twenty-first Party Congress that by an extraordinary chance the chauffeur of the car in which the responsible Chekist had been killed had been discovered still alive in Siberia and was being questioned. The matter then died.

If Khrushchev meant Stalin, why did he not say so? In that same speech he was accusing his late master of crimes no less atrocious. The same applies to Yagoda, head of the NKVD at the time of the murder. If Khrushchev had wanted to accuse Yagoda there was nothing in the world to stop him from doing so. He did not. And in any case, by 1937, when the Leningrad NKVD chiefs were finally shot, Yagoda himself was under arrest and being prepared by his successor, Yezhov, for his own trial and execution.

Who then? Why was it necessary first to make a most disturbing and damaging accusation and then to wrap that accusation up in mystery?

The time was February 1956. The occasion, the Twentieth Party Congress, marked Khrushchev's final bid for supremacy over all his colleagues by setting himself up, with the help of Mikoyan and others, as the man who could dethrone Stalin and turn the Soviet Union to happier paths. On the platform with him were, among others, Molotov, Kaganovich, Malenkov. It was known that Molotov and Kaganovich had been most zealous in that critical year of 1934 in persuading Stalin to stick to the hard line of terror as opposed to Kirov's soft line of reconciliation. Malenkov, of course, was not yet on this high level, any more than Khrushchev himself; nevertheless, he was already very much of an insider. After his years on Stalin's personal secretariat and his experience as a member of the Moscow Party Committee, where he had worked closely with Kaganovich, Khrushchev, and Yezhov, he was posted in 1934 to a full-time appointment in the newly created Department of Leading Party Organs (ORPO), which superseded the Party's Department of Higher Personnel. Here he was second-in-command to Nikolai Yezhov at the time of the Kirov murder. Yezhov was the dreadful little psychopath who in the early autumn of 1935 was to take over the NKVD from Yagoda and carry the great purge to almost unbelievable lengths. Kaganovich, as head of the Party Control Commission from February 1934, was Yezhov's immediate boss until Yezhov succeeded him in 1935, leaving Malenkov to run ORPO.

We thus discover a new combination: just as in 1932 Moscow was being run by Kaganovich, Khrushchev, Yezhov, and Malenkov—with Bulganin on the side—so, in 1934, the Control Commission of the Party, with its subsidiary, ORPO, was in the hands of Kaganovich, Yezhov, and Malenkov—with Khrushchev on the periphery as Kaganovich's confidant and as the working colleague of the other two. The Control Commission was uniquely in charge of Party discipline and higher Party appointments. When the great purge was running wild under Yezhov it was Malenkov's task, as chief of ORPO, to supply him with dossiers of all Party members it was thought desirable by Stalin or any of his colleagues, or by Malenkov or Yezhov themselves, to eliminate. This was their heyday. Less than a year before Yezhov was himself destroyed by Stalin and replaced by Beria, Malenkov wrote of his master in *Party Construction:*

The Soviet people love their intelligence service, because it defends the vital interests of the people and it is their flesh and blood.

. . . The faithful guardians of Socialism—the NKVD men—under the leadership of their Stalinist People's Commissar, Comrade Yezhov, will continue in the future to crush and root out the enemies of the people—the vile Trotskyite, Bukharinite, bourgeois-nationalist, and other agents of fascism. Let the spies and traitors tremble! The punishing hand of the Soviet people—the NKVD—will annihilate them! Our ardent Bolshevik greetings to the Stalinist People's Commissar of Internal Affairs, Nikolai Ivanovich Yezhov.[5]

This paean to the terrorist-in-chief was composed at the very height of the terror, at the very moment when Yezhov was preparing by blackmail and torture the last of the three great treason trials which were to end with the annihilation of the whole of the Bolshevik old guard.

The point to be made is that Yezhov was Kaganovich's man, and Malenkov was Yezhov's man. It was well known that Yezhov, the most unpopular man in the Party, filled with bitter resentments and jealousies towards his more presentable comrades, had set himself the task of making a career through backstairs intrigue. As he rose, he contrived to establish for himself a private network of dependable lieutenants, bound to him by mutual advantage: he thus had his men in all the Party organs, in the armed services, and in the NKVD, which he was soon to command. There is no doubt at all that Kaganovich feared Kirov as a strong rival under Stalin; Molotov too. There is equally no doubt that the younger Party leaders, including Malenkov, Zhdanov, and Khrushchev, feared for their very jobs, which depended utterly on Stalin's tough course: so long as he ruled by terror, they helping him, so long as all the most able of the old Bolsheviks and their protégés were kept down, they were safe. But if ever Stalin decided to adopt Kirov's policy of reconciliation, bringing back into high office men who had once been in opposition, the newcomers who had climbed into their shoes were finished. The whole Party machine, headed now by Kaganovich, typified by the Malenkovs and the Khrushchevs, thus had the strongest possible interest in Kirov's demise. Kaganovich could have given the order; Yezhov (whose second-in-command was Malenkov) could have arranged for it to be carried out. And this is almost certainly what happened.

But could this have been done without Stalin's consent, or at least his tacit assent? It could not. According to contemporary accounts, Stalin was filled with rage and grief by Kirov's assassination. Eulogies and obituaries of the dead man filled the Communist press for days. The magnificence of the state funeral was without precedent. Stalin was himself in Leningrad, and the crude tampering with the evidence indicated twenty-two years later by Khrushchev could not possibly have been carried out without his knowledge. Even if Stalin had done nothing more than curse Kirov in the presence of Kaganovich ("Will nobody rid me of that turbulent pretender?"), he was ready to cover up for the men who had carried out the crime.

Why, then, did Khrushchev balk at naming him?

Later, in the same speech, he had this to say of Yezhov and his relations with Stalin:

We are justly accusing Yezhov of the degenerate practices of 1937. But we have to answer these questions:

Could Yezhov have arrested Kossior [the Ukrainian leader], for instance, without the knowledge of Stalin? Was there an exchange of opinions or a Politburo decision concerning this?

No, there was not, as there was none regarding other cases of this type.

Could Yezhov have decided such important matters as the fate of such eminent Party figures?

No, it would be a display of naïveté to consider this the work of Yezhov alone. It is clear that these matters were decided by Stalin, and that without his orders and his sanction Yezhov could not have done this.[6]

Why was Khrushchev so ready to incriminate both Stalin and Yezhov for the liquidation of Kossior (and many others), while making a mystery of the Kirov case?

The answer is not very difficult. In making his secret speech in 1956 Khrushchev was working with two main objects in view, one apparent to all, one apparent only to those with an intimate knowledge of Kremlin politics from 1934 onwards. The first was to disassociate himself from Stalin's crimes; the second was to hint very strongly at the guilty knowledge of certain of his fellow members and rivals in the famous collective government—

above all Kaganovich, Malenkov, and Molotov. Responsibility for the liquidation of the great Ukrainian leaders had to be pinned very firmly and directly on Yezhov and Stalin, for the simple reason that, as we shall see, Khrushchev himself was to profit most directly from their liquidation. When it came to the Kirov murder, on the other hand, although Khrushchev must have had first-hand knowledge of what had actually happened, and although he may have approved it, he cannot have been an active agent in the murder plot. He was thus free to twist the facts or make a mystery of them; short of directly accusing Kaganovich, Malenkov, perhaps Molotov, all seated on the platform with him, of the murder, he did what he could to smear them by implication. None of these could clear themselves without admitting to guilty knowledge. But none of them, it will be remembered, followed Khrushchev and Mikoyan and joined in their condemnation of Stalin. Instead they had to sit silent, listening to Khrushchev twisting other facts in his favour—as when he pretended that the Central Committee Plenum of 1938, at which he had been elected a candidate member of the Politburo, had condemned the terror, when in fact, having queried certain "incorrect" expulsions from the Party, it had praised Yezhov for the "integrity" of the purge.[7]

In a word, the secret speech cannot be understood unless it is realized that Khrushchev was striking his first major blow at those rivals who within a year were to combine against him—and at the eleventh hour be beaten by him and disgraced. Khrushchev was sailing very close to the wind, but at least he was sailing. His colleagues were far more guilty, and they could say nothing against Khrushchev because of this.

There was a good deal to be said. Khrushchev was largely covered from accusations of active complicity in Stalin's crimes, which had been connived at or instigated by those who were in 1956 his senior colleagues—Molotov, Kaganovich, Voroshilov, Mikoyan too, all Politburo members at the height of the purges. Malenkov, like Khrushchev, was not then a member of the Politburo, but everybody knew that as head of ORPO he had worked hand in glove with Yezhov. Yet all these men, had they not themselves been so vulnerable through their own guilt,

could have turned round then and there and demonstrated con-
clusively that, even if Khrushchev had not participated actively
in these crimes, he had supported them up to the hilt. They
were in no position to cite from Khrushchev's own speeches during the 1930s and compare what he said then about Stalin and
Stalin-worship with what he was saying in 1956. Let us do it for
them.

In his secret speech Khrushchev violently assailed the flattery
accorded Stalin, above all by Beria, and Stalin's own self-
glorification. He instanced in particular the *Short Biography*
published in 1948, written by Beria and, said Khrushchev,
amended by Stalin in his own hand: "This book is an expression
of the most dissolute flattery, an example of making a man into a
godhead, of transforming him into an infallible sage, 'the greatest leader, sublime strategist of all times and nations.' " [8]

All this is very true, but Khrushchev was the last man to
throw stones in this particular glass house. Listen to him in August 1936 as he spoke in Moscow, trying to stir his listeners to a
furious hatred of Kamenev, Zinoviev, and others who were then
being tried for their lives—but not yet found guilty:

They pulled the strings of this bloody plot and directed a blow
at the heart of the Revolution, at thee, our Stalin, and at thy closest
disciples. Damned fascist degenerates! They lifted their hands against
one whose name millions of toilers pronounce every day, every hour,
with pride and boundless love. . . . They lifted their hands against
the greatest of all men . . . our dear friend, our wise *vozhd*, Comrade Stalin.[9]

And again, during the second great show trial, five months
later, he addressed a mass meeting in Moscow in these terms:

These murderers aimed at the heart and brain of our Party. They
raised their villainous hands against Comrade Stalin.

By raising their hands against Comrade Stalin they raised them
against all of us, against the working class, against the toiling people!
By raising their hands against Comrade Stalin they raised them
against the teaching of Marx, Engels, and Lenin.

By raising their hands against Comrade Stalin they raised them
against everything that is best in the possession of humanity. For

Stalin is hope; he is expectation; he is the beacon that guides all progressive mankind. Stalin is our banner! Stalin is our will! Stalin is our victory! [10]

Two hundred thousand Muscovites were said by *Pravda* to have listened to that speech in Red Square in January 1937. Quite a number of these must have survived until 1956 to hear Khrushchev denounce the cult of personality. All Khrushchev's colleagues in the Presidium must have remembered that speech and many others like it. They must have known too that Khrushchev and Kaganovich had been the first men to speak of Stalin as *vozhd*, or leader in the absolute sense. "Our great genius, our beloved Stalin," he later said; "our great leader of the peoples, our friend and father, the greatest man of our epoch"; "the greatest genius of humanity, teacher and captain, who leads us towards communism, our very own Stalin." [11]

The interesting thing is that neither Molotov nor Malenkov ever permitted himself to speak of Stalin in such fulsome terms; but they had to sit on the platform listening to Khrushchev by implication accuse them of fostering Stalin-worship, which had in fact been carried by him to its dizziest heights.

There were yet other aspects of the secret speech which Khrushchev's senior colleagues could have contradicted had they been in a position to expose themselves. In one of the apparently most wise, tolerant, and reasonable passages of all, Khrushchev attacked Stalin for his use of the term "enemy of the people":

Stalin originated the concept "enemy of the people." This term automatically rendered it unnecessary for the ideological errors of individuals or groups standing on controversial positions to be proved. This term gave the green light to repression of the cruellest kind, violating every norm of revolutionary legality, against anyone who in any way disagreed with Stalin, against all those who were only suspected of hostile intention, against all those whose reputations were not crystal clear. This concept, "enemy of the people," in fact, eliminated the possibility of any kind of ideological argument or the expression of personal views on any issues, even quite practical issues.

It has to be said that in regard to those persons who in their time came to oppose the Party line there was no sufficiently serious reason for their physical annihilation. The formula "enemy of the people" was specifically introduced for the purpose of physically annihilating such individuals.[12]

That is all fine and true. The trouble was that Khrushchev himself was as free as anyone in his use of the term. Thus, the senior soldiers in his armies must have remembered how in 1937, at the height of the Yezhov terror, when, in Khrushchev's own words "mass arrests and deportations of many thousands of people, execution without trial and without normal investigation created conditions of insecurity, fear, and even desperation," he went out of his way to denounce General Garmanik as an "enemy of the people" and a "traitor to the Motherland." [13] Garmanik, a hero of the civil war, was Deputy People's Commissar for the Army and Navy (under Voroshilov) and chief of the Army's political administration. He committed suicide just a week before Marshal Tukhachevsky and eight other marshals of the Soviet Union were publicly accused of spying for a foreign power and high treason. For years he had been a member of Khrushchev's own Moscow city Party committee, to which he was re-elected, with Khrushchev's approval, three days before he killed himself.

In the secret speech of 1956 there was another passage of sweet reasonableness:

Now, after a sufficiently long historical period, we can speak of the fight against the Trotskyites with perfect calm and can analyse this matter with sufficient objectivity. After all, there were around Trotsky people whose origins could not by any means be traced to a bourgeois society. Some of them belonged to the Party intelligentsia, some were recruited from among the workers. We can name many individuals who at one time and another joined the Trotskyites; nevertheless, these same individuals also played an active part in the workers' movement before the Revolution, during the Socialist October Revolution itself, and also in the consolidation of the victory of this greatest of revolutions. Many of them broke with Trotskyism and returned to Leninist positions. Was it necessary to annihilate such people? We are deeply convinced that, had Lenin lived, such an extreme method would not have been used against many of them.[14]

Emotion recollected in tranquillity . . . Here is Khrushchev on the Trotskyites in November 1936 after the execution of a number of alleged Trotskyites at Kemerovo:

The working people of Moscow city and province . . . fervently approve the fair sentences published today . . . on the enemies of the people, the foul gang of counterrevolutionary Trotskyites. We draw our proletarian sword to chop off the heads of these loathsome creatures, double-dealers and murderers, agents of fascism. . . . The mad beast must be finished off.[15]

And here, for good measure, are further passages from the speech to the 200,000 in January 1937. He is glorying in the outcome of the second great show trial, which ended in the execution of many of his other colleagues:

Comrade workers, men and women, engineers, employees, scientists, artists, and all working people of our country! We are gathered here in Red Square to raise our proletarian voice in complete support of the sentence passed by the Military Collegium of the Supreme Court on the enemies of the people, the traitors of the Motherland, the betrayers of the workers' cause, the spies, the diversionists, agents of fascism, the vile, despicable Trotskyites.

Here, in Red Square, before all the peoples of the Soviet land, before the workers of the whole world, we approve this sentence and declare that whatever enemy tries to obstruct our victorious movement forward to a Communist society will be crushed by us and annihilated! [stormy applause] . . .

Judas-Trotsky and his gang intended to turn over the Ukraine, the Maritime Provinces, and the Amur Region to the German and Japanese imperialists, and to transform our blossoming Motherland into a colony of German and Japanese imperialism. And they wanted to reduce Russian, Ukrainian, Byelorussian, Georgian, and all other peoples of the Soviet Union to the ranks of "inferior races" to be ruled over by the "superior race" of German Fascist bandits.

Like their bosses, the Trotskyite serfs counted only on the defeat of the USSR in a war with the German and Japanese imperialists;

they strove to hasten that war and to prepare for the defeat of the USSR. They set off explosions in factories; they spied for the fascist secret service. They killed and poisoned workers and Red Army men, children as well as grown-ups. They wrecked train-loads of our glorious Red Army men and they disrupted transport, being paid for this by the Japanese secret service. The Trotskyite murderers trafficked with the blood of the fighters of our valiant Red Army! . . .

There rises a stink of carrion from the vile, base, Trotskyite degenerates.

The despicable ringleaders and the members of the Trotskyite gang have received their deserved punishment for their black betrayal of the Motherland. The loathsome Trotskyite creature has been crushed in the Soviet Union. But this must not dull our vigilance; on the contrary, we should become more vigilant and increase still further our work in all fields of socialist construction in order to finish off and wipe out all remnants of these vile murderers, fascist agents, Trotskyites, Zinovievites, and their right-wing accomplices.[16]

We have enough to indicate the public line Khrushchev was taking in the middle 1930s. It is established out of his own mouth not only that he acquiesced in the great terror and in Stalin-worship, but that he was active in abetting both. His speeches are the speeches of the born agitator, calculated deliberately to lash his audiences into a frenzy of hate. Nor was he content to string along behind Stalin, dutifully slandering those who were already down and could no longer be helped. It has often been said, without any evidence to support such statements, that even though Khrushchev had to echo the official condemnation of the "opposition" or himself die, he was active behind the scenes in saving many individuals from the attentions of the secret police. On the contrary, he was loudest in urging all good Communists not to rest for a moment in the urgent task of ferreting out concealed enemies, in keeping at white heat the atmosphere of suspicion and hatred:

Sometimes a man sits, and enemies crawl round him, almost stepping on his feet. But he does not notice them and puffs himself up: "Among the personnel under my jurisdiction there are no wreckers and aliens." He says this not because there are in fact no enemies, but because of his deafness and political blindness caused by the idiotic disease—heedlessness.[17]

And again:

. . . the enemy may foully disguise himself and carry on his subversive activity in the deep underground. . . . But let these enemies know that no matter how deep down they may sit in their burrows, we will uncover and annihilate them, and reduce to dust every last one of them, and scatter them to the four winds so that not even a trace will remain of these damned betrayers of the socialist Motherland.[18]

CHAPTER TEN

Viceroy of the Ukraine

IN THE SPEECHES he made at the time of the great purge we become aware for the first time that, with all his other qualities, Khrushchev was also a most accomplished actor. As with all born actors, it is the hardest thing in the world to separate genuine feeling from histrionics, and later on in his career we shall be confronted time and time again with this very problem—most spectacularly perhaps in his extraordinary diatribe against the West after the breakdown of the Paris summit conference in the summer of 1960, but also in a hundred lesser episodes. As he reveals himself increasingly in his activities on the international stage it will become clear that he in fact had an extremely ugly temper, but also that, on occasion, he was clever at appearing to lose his temper when he was calculating to a nicety the intended effect of this or that demonstration.

Calculation was very much a part of his quite sickening demagogy over the corpses of his late comrades in the middle 1930s. He knew, none better, that the charges brought against the old Bolsheviks—charges repeated by him in his speech to the 200,000 and on many other occasions—were false to the point of high fantasy; he knew, further, that their so-called confessions were elicited by torture and moral blackmail in the Lubianka prison, a few blocks away from his Moscow Party headquarters. Later, in his secret speech of 1956 and thereafter, he was to retail, with the air of a man outraged by the sudden revelation of evil, a few very carefully selected instances of false witness and physical torture. But, like every other Russian, he knew very well what was going on at the time. He acquiesced in it; as we have seen, he actively connived at it. More than this, once again he put himself a jump ahead of Stalin. It will be remembered that in the last sentence of the extract from the speech to the 200,000 he spoke of the need to "finish off and wipe out all remnants of these vile murderers, fascist agents, Trotskyites, Zinovievites, and their right-wing accomplices." That was in January 1937, immediately after the second great treason trial, which, like the first, had concerned itself with alleged Trotskyite conspiracy. The third great trial, which featured Bukharin and other "rightists" and retrospectively associated them with the Trotskyites, was not mounted until March 1938—fourteen months after Khrushchev, none other, had prepared the way by publicly accusing them of being Trotsky's "accomplices." He was still running true to type, pointing the way, as he had done in Stalino in his very early days, which Stalin was later going to take. He knew that Bukharin and his associates had never been accomplices of Trotsky just as well, as he knew that Radek and Sokolnikov had not planned with Germany and Japan the overthrow of the Soviet Union and that Trotsky himself had not planned the restoration of capitalism. But his voice as he proclaimed these lies, and many more besides, quivered with outrage and indignation.

He was making an important career, a career that had been jeopardized by the rise of Kirov, now safely murdered in his prime. It was a career which depended utterly on Stalin, who could make him or break him. What had he to offer Stalin? Not a powerful and subtle brain like Malenkov, not a keen understanding of finance and administration like Bulganin: he had to offer his total subservience, his remarkable gifts as an agitator (a transmission belt between Stalin and the workers), and his capacity for intrigue in the interests of Stalin—and himself. Molotov, Kaganovich, Mikoyan, Voroshilov, and a handful of others could, certainly at this stage, argue with Stalin. Malenkov, at a lower level, could produce useful and constructive ideas. Khrushchev could act only through agitation and command. He had no justification except as Stalin's instrument, and he had to go to very great lengths to demonstrate that he was nothing but Stalin's instrument.

What he thought about the atrocities in which he was required to assist, we do not know. The born actor is necessarily a man who can think himself into a part until he becomes that part. It is fairly safe to say that the demagogue in the high flush of his oratory believes for the moment what he is trying to make others believe: as we say, he becomes carried away by his own eloquence. He is also conditioned, of course, by the phrases which are the common currency of his time. Our own "free world" contains some rather nasty dictatorships; the phrases "Western value," or "Christian values" are used by Western politicians to characterize the TV or Coca-Cola culture; in America "Commie" is sometimes a term of abuse for anyone who stands to the left of Mr. Joseph Kennedy; in Britain the "affluent society" contains the slums of Glasgow and Dundee. In Khrushchev's Russia "sabotage" and "wrecking" came to stand for ignorance or carelessness, "fascist agent," "Trotskyite," "degenerate," or "filthy spy," for anyone who had ever queried any of Stalin's policies.

In between his bursts of public eloquence, nevertheless, Khrushchev knew that he was lying, and from 1938 onwards he himself was not merely an abettor and instigator of terror but also an important part of the terror machine. Violence, though not the violence of malevolence and spite, came very naturally to him. We must remember that long before Stalin broke into violence Khrushchev was demanding the immediate application of "repressive measures." And long after Stalin was dead, his image shattered, Khrushchev was to turn to violence in Hungary; still later he was to tell rebellious Soviet writers that the Hungarian revolt would never have taken place had there been a little preliminary shooting of the Hungarian intellectuals. There was to be no nonsense of that kind in Russia, he declared at that famous and macabre garden party in the summer of 1957; if it came to the crunch, "my hand would not tremble!"

Now, in 1938, he was about to instigate a reign of terror of his own. He was sent back to the Ukraine as Stalin's viceroy over 40 million souls, having left for Moscow as a quasi-student of the Industrial Academy just ten years before.

He was forty-four, the father of three children in their teens and another aged nine. His second wife had stuck with him during all this decade of climbing ever upwards over the corpses of late comrades. She must have seen something in him invisible then to those around him, but to become apparent to the whole world in years to come. When we ask ourselves how the Khrushchev who had clawed and manœuvred his way upwards, stepping again and again into the shoes of colleagues disgraced or liquidated, managed to retain more than a spark of common humanity, the answer must be, can only be, that he was married to Nina Petrovna. The life story of this remarkable woman, if it could be told, would help us to understand Russian reality better than any account of the activities of her husband. But Russian reality, with its extraordinary mingling of violence and gentleness, treacheries and loyalties, ruthlessness and warmth, still remains hidden behind the ugly barrier of Soviet propaganda and Soviet government action.

Khrushchev's return to the Ukraine, his escape from the hysterical viciousness of political existence in Moscow, must have been a very great relief to Nina Petrovna as well as to him. It was also the luckiest promotion imaginable. In all he was to spend twelve years away from Moscow, four of them in war, unremarked by the outer world with its gaze fixed on the Kremlin, and increasingly detached from the ceaseless infighting among those who believed that the sure way to power and glory was to attach themselves as closely as possible to Stalin's person. These were wrong; Malenkov above all was wrong. The man who in 1953 was ready to exercise supreme power was the man who had for many years been practising the use of power as virtual dictator of a great province of the empire, a whole country of 40 million, with its own language, its own history, its own proud traditions. Many believed that by staying away from Moscow for so long Khrushchev had put himself out of the running for the succession. He knew better; he had learned how to govern, while his more spectacular colleagues had learned only to intrigue and to survive. He had learned how to handle men, while his colleagues in the Kremlin had learned only how to command them, to intrigue against them, and to kill them. He had learned a great deal about the way people lived, while his colleagues deliberately barricaded themselves against the people, confining their contact with the common man to the reading of police reports on one hand and the lies of corrupt statisticians on the other. By the time he came back permanently to Moscow in December 1949 he had matured into an independent force, an almost unique phenomenon in Stalin's Russia.

But he did not start off like that. On the contrary, to begin with he had to justify his promotion by carrying to Kiev Stalin's message of ill-will.

[2.]

The Ukraine, with its separatist ambitions and its tendency to despise the Great Russians, had suffered more deeply than any other part of the Soviet Union from Stalin's policies since 1928. It was a land of vital importance to the Soviet leadership. Although in area it amounted to only 3 per cent of the Soviet Union, it held 20 per cent of the Soviet population—and the most advanced 20 per cent, at that. With its infinitely rich black earth, it had long been the granary of Russia, and before the development of the Urals it was also the supreme workshop of Russia. Resistance to collectivization had been stronger and more bitter there than in any part of the Soviet Union, and the great famine which desolated the country as a result of the killing of livestock, the burning of crops, and the seizure of what was left by the police and the military, was above all a Ukrainian famine. In Moscow and Leningrad people went hungry; in Kharkov and Kiev they starved to death in tens of thousands.

After the departure of Kaganovich to Moscow in 1929, Party leaders of the Ukraine were chosen for their toughness. But toughness could not save the ablest among them. There were suicides and liquidations. Finally, two men who owed everything to Stalin and exerted themselves to carry out his most malignant commands, Postychev and Kossior, were themselves arrested and shot.

Khrushchev in his secret speech had a good deal to say about these men—and he had good reason for this. He had stepped immediately into their shoes. He tried to turn them into martyrs, passive victims of Stalin's homicidal mania. They were not martyrs. The fate they suffered was the fate they themselves had prepared and consummated for untold thousands. The best account of the Ukrainian variation of the Yagoda–Yezhov terror, presided over by Postychev and Kossior, is contained in one of the most remarkable prison narratives ever written, the story of his imprisonment and torture and interrogation in Kharkov by the German scientist Alex Weissberg.[1] This is a classic account of the atrocities with which we are all now familiar (if only through Khrushchev's own story of them!), written by a man of such remarkable character that he could look back on his experiences as a bad joke. The bad joke took place under Postychev and Kossior. Postychev himself was then already on the way out. He had offended Stalin, as Khrushchev himself was to tell us much later, by querying the validity of some of the *vozhd*'s accusations against some of his Ukrainian colleagues. After a period of obscurity, during which he was almost certainly under arrest, he was formally expelled from the Moscow Politburo in January 1938, and the man who moved up into his place as a candidate member was Khrushchev. In that month Kossior, who had succeeded Postychev in Kiev, was demoted, and Khrushchev took his place as First Secretary of the Ukrainian Party. A few months later Kossior was arrested. This left another vacant place in the Moscow Politburo, and in 1939 Khrushchev moved up to full member.

By now he had become the scourge of the Ukraine. His first job was to purge the Ukrainian Party of all sympathizers with, or associates of, the arrested leaders. In the words of D. S. Korotchenko, then Chairman of the Ukrainian Council of People's Commissars, later to be advanced by Khrushchev, Comrade Khrushchev, "the best son of our people, the excellent Bolshevik, the Donets miner," had been sent to Kiev by Stalin to pull the faltering Party together and "to deal the final blow to the whole Trotskyite, Bukharinite, bourgeois-nationalist gang in the Ukraine." [2]

Deal with it he did. By 1938 the industrialization of the Soviet Union was beginning, on the surface, to show. Food production had very far from recovered from the collectivization; consumer goods were still in very short supply. The surface was so thin that even after another three years of accumulation, when the Germans came crashing in, it took only six weeks of war to bring the whole country down to starvation level and empty the shops of goods of all conceivable kinds for the duration and much longer. But Khrushchev and his colleagues were part of the surface. In Kiev, as in all great cities, there were special shops and special restaurants reserved exclusively for the highly privileged: above all, senior Party officials, political police officers, officers of the Red Army, ballet dancers, actors and writers, senior scientists and engineers. Access to these shops secured for the privileged luxuries undreamed of by all but some scores of thousands. And over this remarkable elite presided the Party secretaries.

I have called the First Secretary of the Ukrainian Communist Party Stalin's viceroy. Khrushchev was precisely this, and he lived in viceregal splendour. Polo ponies and elephants he lacked, polo never having been a Russian game and elephants not being indigenous to the Ukraine. He had everything else, as Stalin had everything else in his palatial villas outside Moscow, at Sochi on the Black Sea, and elsewhere: hosts of servants, an army of bodyguards, a fleet of sleek black motor-cars, some of them bulletproof, furs and jewels, women, food and drink of the richest and grossest kind. All over the Soviet Union senior Party secretaries, flanked by the local garrison commanders and chiefs of police, lived like alien and barbaric conquerors in and off a hostile land: in the Ukraine, as also in the Caucasus and Russian Turkestan, they were in fact precisely this, often ruling through native henchmen at all levels, of the kind known in other circumstances as collaborationists. Korotchenko, a born Ukrainian, might celebrate Khrushchev as "the best son of our people"; but Khrushchev was not a Ukrainian at all, and his job, surrounded as he was in his palace by his court, was first to kill off all Party members who might be suspected of thinking of themselves as Ukrainians,* then to Russify with all possible speed, and with the sort of roughness which came so naturally to him, his dominion of 40 million souls.

With the first he began moving at once. "I pledge myself to spare no efforts in seizing and annihilating all agents of fascism, Trotskyites, Bukharinites, and all those despicable bourgeois nationalists on our free Ukrainian soil." [3] This pledge is taken from Khrushchev's election address in May 1938. How insipid, by contrast, the speeches of even the most rancorous Republicans and Democrats, conservatives and socialists, to say nothing of liberals, in our own effete society! What is more, here was a politician who fulfilled his election pledges. Soon the survivors of his purge were offering glowing testimonials. Thus, in July, the Ukrainian Party organ declared:

> The merciless uprooting of the enemies of the people—the Trotskyites, Bukharinites, bourgeois nationalists, and all other spying filth—began only after the Central Committee of the All-Union Communist Party sent the unswerving Bolshevik and Stalinist, Nikita Sergeievich Khrushchev, to the Ukraine to lead the Central Committee of the Ukrainian Communist Party.[4]

Here is an even more valuable testimonial from none other than Comrade Uspensky, chief of the NKVD in the Ukraine, the uppermost authority in all that land on the techniques of oppression:

> I consider myself a pupil of Nikolai Ivanovich Yezhov. Comrade Yezhov teaches us to fight the enemies of the people, to purge our country, our Motherland, of its enemies. I pledge to follow Comrade Yezhov, the militant leader of the NKVD, in every respect. . . .
> Only after the faithful Stalinist, Nikita Sergeievich Khrushchev, arrived in the Ukraine did the smashing of the enemies of the people begin in earnest. . . . [5]

---

* The term of abuse for all Ukrainians—and all other Soviet minorities—who attempted to maintain their national identities once Stalin had reversed his earlier policies and decided to Russify at all costs, was "bourgeois nationalist." The Ukrainian situation was complicated by the fact that part of the Ukraine was under the sovereignty of Poland.

That was in June 1938. Kirov had been dead three and a half years. For two and a half years the great purge had raged throughout the Soviet Union, very much including the Ukraine. Early in 1937 Yagoda, the original horror, had been superseded by Yezhov, whose "degenerate practices" Khrushchev was later to condemn so picturesquely. For eighteen months he had run amuck over the Soviet Union like a rabid dog. Yet after all this Khrushchev and Uspensky still found work to do. Yezhov in fact had only another few months to go at the time of Uspensky's tribute. Beria was to take over effectively almost at once as a result of a sudden panic action by Stalin when it was borne in on him that the country, above all its heavy industry and its armed forces, was being choked to death by Yezhov. In December 1938 this unspeakable creature finally disappeared forever, liquidated by his successor, Beria—and with him, among thousands of other senior police officers (who had only been carrying out the instructions of the master murderer, Stalin, as best they knew how), went poor Uspensky, his faithful pupil, for such a short time the right-hand man and impassioned admirer of Khrushchev in the Ukraine.

Beria, brought in to abate the terror, soon got into his stride as the head of a terror machine which was to act a good deal more discreetly but no less bloodily than the Yezhov machine. The difference was that Yagoda and Yezhov had been primarily concerned with ridding the Party, the Army, and other institutions of all those who did not owe everything to Stalin and could not be relied on to hang or swim with him; Beria was more concerned with terrorizing the masses, which he did in fine style, at the same time rounding up hundreds of thousands, indeed millions, of unpolitical unfortunates to keep going the vast and expanding network of GULAG, the forced-labour administration, which performed the very useful task (in a land where food and clothing were short) of providing immense contingents of expendable unskilled labour for mining or development work in the more inclement regions of an extremely inclement land.[6] Beria himself, who was not a subtle man in spite of his scholastic appearance when sober,[7] would have been hard put to it to say whether his primary task was to keep 180 million people subdued and obedient by police terror or to provide an immense pool of labour which did not have to be paid and could be exploited and worked to death without any questions asked. In the end, of course, it was discovered that even Russia could not go on squandering manpower in this way and was being brought to a standstill as Yezhov had all but brought it to a standstill in 1938. But that was not until after Stalin was dead. Until that time, from 1939 until 1953, Beria and Khrushchev were associated in the closest manner in Stalin's Politburo.

[3.]

Figures of the purged are hard to come by. We know from Khrushchev himself that 98 of the 139 full and candidate members of the All Union Central Committee elected in 1934 were shot.[8]

The 1934 Central Committee was elected at the notorious Seventeenth Party Congress. It was known as the Congress of the Victors, because in the course of it Stalin formally celebrated his victory over the opposition. By the time the Eighteenth Party Congress met in 1939, 70 per cent of the "victors" had been killed.

The Ukrainian Central Committee reflected this general pattern. By the time Khrushchev arrived in Kiev in January 1938, 69 per cent of the Central Committee elected at the Thirteenth Ukrainian Party Congress *only six months earlier* in June 1937 had been liquidated, and yet Uspensky could declare that "the smashing of the enemies of the people" started seriously only after Khrushchev's arrival. Could Khrushchev do better than this? Indeed he could! At the Fourteenth Ukrainian Party Congress, held six months after his advent, only 3 of the 166 members and candidate members of the 1937 Committee were left. And the purge went on: at the Fifteenth Congress, in 1940, over half the members of the 1938 Committee, elected under Khrushchev's aegis, were re-elected. In a word, as far as the destruction of higher Party functionaries was concerned, Khrushchev in Kiev did as well as, if not better than, Stalin in Moscow. By 1940 he had an instrument exactly suited to his will.

It will have been noticed that in their Kiev speeches Khrushchev and his admirers made frequent references not only to the usual Trotskyite-Bukharinite-fascist-spying filth but also to a new enemy, "bourgeois nationalism." This was, in fact, the main enemy from 1938 onwards: it was the Stalinist term for local patriotism, whether in the Caucasus or in Soviet Turkestan or in the Ukraine, but above all in the Ukraine. It was Khrushchev's main task in the years that remained to him before the Germans came trampling in (to be received at first by many Ukrainians with bread and salt as heaven-sent liberators from Stalin—and Khrushchev) to smash the Ukrainian national consciousness, which had flared up in 1917 (when the Ukraine proclaimed itself a sovereign state, only to be crushed by Lenin and Trotsky) and again in the great fight against collectivization in 1929. Beaten again into submission, the Ukrainians had nevertheless clung to their language and their national customs. These were now to be stamped out.

A vivid idea of the strength and tenacity of Ukrainian patriotism, its dislike of the Moscow government in general and of the Moscow Bolshevik government in particular, can be obtained from an instruction of Trotsky's to a Communist agitation squad dispatched to the Ukraine when it was struggling to maintain its independence under the Hetman Petloura immediately after the Revolution. Not only is this instruction a first-class example of Bolshevik infiltration techniques; it is also an indication of what Lenin and Trotsky were up against in the Ukraine (they had to go very carefully indeed, operating what was in effect a major deception plan or confidence trick). It is also, incidentally, a pleasure to be able to show that Trotsky, like many other old Bolsheviks whom Stalin was to kill, was in some respects no better than his murderers.

The arguments [wrote Trotsky] we discuss here in Russia with perfect frankness can only be whispered in the Ukraine. . . . It will therefore be your duty to observe the following precepts:

1. Do not force Communism upon the Ukrainian peasants until our power is stabilized in the Ukraine.

2. Set about the cautious introduction of Communism on the old estates in the guise of cooperative associations.

3. Do your best to make people believe that Russia is not really Communist at all.

4. To take the wind out of Petloura's sails, insist that Russia is all for the independence of the Ukraine, provided that she agrees to set up a Soviet government.

5. Only a fool would go about shouting from the housetops that the Soviet government is fighting Petloura. Sometimes it will be advisable even to start rumours to the effect that we are in alliance with Petloura, at any rate until Dennikin is finally liquidated.[9]

Here is a perfect example of Leninism in practice offered by a man who spent his declining years indicting Stalin for brutal and unscrupulous behaviour. Lenin and Trotsky won. The Ukraine was subdued. It was Khrushchev's task in 1938 to give it the knock-out blow.

Here is what Lenin said he believed about the nationalities problem, formulated in a resolution adopted at the Seventh Conference of the Bolshevik Party in April 1917, after the overthrow of the Tsar, but six months before the Bolsheviks' seizure of power:

The right of all nations forming part of Russia freely to secede and form independent states shall be recognized. To deny this right or to omit measures which will guarantee its realization in practice would be equivalent to advocating a policy of seizure and annexation.[10]

The moment he obtained power, Lenin changed his mind. Not content with the seizure of the Ukraine and the tsarist colonies in the Caucasus, he made a spirited attempt to take Poland.

In 1923, after the civil war, which brought more ruin to the rich Ukrainian lands than to any other part of the Soviet Union, great promises were made about recognizing the equality of the Ukrainian language with Russian, the Ukrainization of Party and administrative machines, the autonomy of Ukrainian literature and Ukrainian culture generally. Ten years later these promises were forgotten. Those who reminded Stalin of them were destroyed. Their destroyers, above all Postychev and Kossior, were then themselves destroyed, and now it was Khrushchev's turn. To defend Ukrainian culture was now high treason. All those who had stood up for the Ukrainian language and for Ukrainian culture, such a short time before officially recognized by Moscow, were now branded as "fascist degenerates" and "bourgeois nationalists." Khrushchev himself accused "fascist-Polish gangs" of doing everything they could "to detach the Ukraine from the Great Soviet Union, from the heart of our Motherland—Moscow." [11] The school curricula were changed to drive out the native language and memories of the native traditions. Ukrainian spelling was changed. Ukrainian history was rewritten so that national heroes became renegades and traitors. The schoolteachers themselves had to be taken off work in large numbers to be given shock courses in the Russian language. To assist him in this good work, Khrushchev was pleased to exalt certain Ukrainian writers and intellectuals who were prepared to sell themselves, renounce their own birthright, and assist in the oppression of their own people in return for Stalin's blessing. Chief among these was the writer Alexander Korneichuk, who was to make a brilliant career first by denouncing his own countrymen, then by advancing as the liberator of Ukrainian culture with Timoshenko's troops as they occupied first the Polish Ukraine (after the Molotov-Ribbentrop pact) and then Bessarabia, finally, with his Polish renegade wife, the novelist Wanda Wasilewska, as an integral part of Stalin's notorious peace offensives. As far as the record goes, Korneichuk was Khrushchev's first acquaintance in the world of culture, which he had not encountered until he was elevated to the rank of viceroy, disposing of all the patronage associated with great princes, in 1938.

CHAPTER ELEVEN

1939: Invader of Poland

WITH HIS PROMOTION to full membership in the Politburo in March 1939, Khrushchev received Stalin's formal acknowledgment that he had done all that had been expected of him in the Ukraine. Although he was still based in Kiev, as Zhdanov, Kirov's successor, was based in Leningrad, and was to remain there until the Germans came two and a half years later, he was now a voting member of the highest council in the land, one of the handful of men who assisted Stalin in the making of policy and who would, if they survived, be in the running for the succession when Stalin died.

It is time to glance at these men who, with two or three others, formed the group which dominated the Eighteenth Party Congress in 1939. Kalinin was to die naturally in 1946, Zhdanov in dubious circumstances in 1948, but the rest were to stick together, reinforced from time to time with new blood, until the end of the Stalin period. All the senior old Bolsheviks had been killed; all the Stalinists too who had ever questioned the absolute rightness of any of Stalin's decisions had been killed with them. The men who were left either owed their positions entirely to Stalin or had in effect been created by him.

Stalin himself was now fifty-nine. His only contemporaries were Marshal Voroshilov, fifty-eight, who controlled the Red Army, and Kalinin, sixty-one, a colourless individual who, as Chairman of the Presidium of the Supreme Soviet, was titular head of State.

Then came four men whose Bolshevik pasts went back before the Revolution, whose ideas had thus been formed under Lenin, but who had been insignificant figures compared with scores, with hundreds, even, of their murdered comrades; but who had firmly attached themselves to Stalin in the early days of his struggle with Trotsky. By far the most distinguished of these was Molotov, now forty-nine, who as a very young man had indeed played an important role in Petrograd in 1917. With his wooden appearance and his stammer, it was he who had been dismissed by Lenin as "the best filing clerk in Petrograd." But Lenin was not perceptive about people: he never understood that it had been Molotov who had kept the Bolshevik Party on the rails until his arrival at the Finland Station in April 1917;* and he certainly never realized that this unprepossessing young man was acting as Stalin's confidant and chief-of-staff in the highly successful operation to create and capture the Party apparatus while Lenin was still alive. Afterwards, and until the death of Stalin, Molotov was to figure without a break as Stalin's Bolshevik conscience, steadfast, wholly loyal, and wholly bloody, doing more than any man to strengthen the will and purpose of his master when he wavered.

A little younger than Molotov, and also prerevolutionary Bolsheviks, were Kaganovich, forty-six, whom we have already met, Andreyev, forty-four, a dour and devoted apparatus man, and Mikoyan, also forty-four, both of whom we shall encounter hereafter.

Khrushchev himself, now forty-five, also belonged to this age group; but, as we have seen, he had not joined the Party until after the Revolution. And at this time he was overshadowed by Zhdanov, two years his junior, whose rise had been spectacular and swift: after serving for twelve years far from Moscow at Nizhni Novgorod, where he did brilliantly well, in 1934, at the age of thirty-eight, he was made in one great sweep a member of the Party Secretariat and a candidate member of the Politburo;

---

* Molotov, then only twenty-seven, had held the Petrograd Bolshevik Party together while Stalin and Kamenev were still exiled, and after their return strove to prevent them from compromising Bolshevik exclusiveness by cooperating with other revolutionary parties until Lenin's arrival from Switzerland.

then, after Kirov's murder, he was sent to Leningrad in his place. Zhdanov was an extraordinarily interesting and able figure. Had he lived, it is unlikely that either Malenkov or Khrushchev would have achieved the dizzy summits: by virtue of his personality and his ability he was Stalin's natural heir. Because he was known above all to the West for his heavy-handed conduct towards Tito's Yugoslavia and for the postwar persecution of writers, musicians, and painters known as the *Zhdanovschina,* his full character has never been understood outside Russia. In fact he was the only Stalinist in the same street with Kirov. Tough and intransigent to a degree in getting his way, actively hostile to the West, ruthless in his insistence on obedience to certain principles (but he was the only man in Stalin's entourage who had any principles)—within this harsh framework he was alert, interested, intelligent, amusing, and good-tempered in a coarse and cynical way. He subdued Nizhni Novgorod on behalf of Stalin, as later he subdued Leningrad; but he managed to spike his opponents with a minimum of violence and often to win them to his side. How this was done he was to show after the war when he was Stalin's representative in Finland: the Finns had every reason to hate him, since it was he above all who had urged Stalin to invade in 1939; but in 1945 he managed to get on remarkably well with his victims, putting the Soviet demands for reparations and the surrender of territory with perfect clarity, but, once these were accepted, conducting himself like a civilized and amiable human being.

After Zhdanov and Khrushchev came Malenkov, thirty-eight, and Beria, forty. Neither of these was yet a member of the Politburo, but both were very strong, Beria by virtue of his command of the police, Malenkov because of his control, in Stalin's name, of the Party apparatus. The great drama of the succession was to be played out, while Zhdanov was still alive, between Zhdanov and Malenkov; after Zhdanov's death, between Malenkov, Beria, and Khrushchev.

Zhdanov, Malenkov, and Khrushchev all allowed themselves a certain independence of mind; Zhdanov and Malenkov achieved also a certain independence of speech which was denied to Khrushchev: Zhdanov because he was an outstandingly strong

character with ideas of his own, Malenkov because his finger was
continually on Stalin's pulse and he knew from day to day, from
year to year, just how far he could go. Khrushchev was dictator
of the Ukraine, but it was not until much later that he felt
strong enough to take a line of his own.

He was lucky in his new job. As a member of the Politburo he
would be called to Moscow for important meetings or when his
own particular province was under consideration. But he was
not one of the inner council who met nearly ever day under
Stalin's chairmanship. In 1939 the problems facing this council
were grave and pressing and of a kind with which Khrushchev
had had little experience. The purges were over. Beria, while
quietly inaugurating his own particular brand of terror and
building up the forces of the political police into an army organized on military lines, with its own heavy weapons, tanks, and
aircraft, was at the same time engaged in reversing a large number of sentences on Party members and Army officers of outstanding value who had not been shot but only imprisoned. Stalin and Molotov and Voroshilov were above all now concerned
with foreign policy, with nothing less than the issue of war and
peace. In May 1939, eight months after Munich, two months
after the invasion and dismemberment of Czechoslovakia, Stalin
replaced his Foreign Secretary, Litvinov, with Molotov, the clearest of signals that propaganda for collective security in face of
Hitler was to be dropped and that the Soviet Union was no
longer going to pretend that it was concerned with anything but
its own survival. In June it fell to Zhdanov, who for some time
had been concerning himself with foreign affairs, to give the
first unmistakable clue as to Stalin's new direction. In a signed
article in *Izvestia* he wrote:

I permit myself to express a personal opinion . . . although my
friends do not share it. They still think that in beginning negotiations on a pact for mutual assistance with the USSR, the British and
French governments had the serious intention of creating a powerful barrier against aggression in Europe. I believe that the British
and French governments have no wish for an equal treaty with
the USSR. . . . It seems to me that the British and French desire
not a real treaty acceptable to the USSR but only talks about a

treaty in order to play upon public opinion in their countries about the supposedly unyielding attitude of the USSR and thus to make it easier for themselves to make a deal with the aggressors.[1]

This was the first official hint of the Soviet pact with Germany. Zhdanov, of course, was not acting on his own initiative. He was flying a kite on behalf of Stalin and Molotov; just as Khrushchev had several times been used to prepare the way for new phases in Stalin's domestic policy, so Zhdanov was now being used to prepare for a new initiative in foreign policy.

There is no evidence at all that in these days Khrushchev took an active interest in foreign affairs. His whole background, training, and adult preoccupations with the purely practical problems of survival, advancement, and helping to make the Soviet Union work would only have confirmed a native insularity. Stalin saw himself as a strong man manœuvring among strong men on the international stage, with Molotov as his chief of staff. Mikoyan had been to America to study foreign business and manufacturing methods and thus had a clearer picture than any of his colleagues of the real nature of the outer world. Kaganovich with his responsibilities for heavy industry and then for reconstructing the whole of the Soviet transport system—to say nothing of his work on the great Dnieper dam, involving cooperation with foreign engineers—was highly conscious of America, Germany, France, and Britain as great industrial powers. Zhdanov, as the master of Leningrad, Russia's exposed outpost immediately vulnerable to Western attack, had thought a great deal about the European power balance. Malenkov made it his business, sitting hard against the centre of power, to acquaint himself with all the problems of his master, and his mind was strong and supple enough to master them. Compared with all these, Khrushchev's interests were wholly parochial, but his parish, nominally the Ukraine and large enough, was extended in his mind to comprehend the whole of the Soviet Union. He cast his vote at such critical meetings of the Politburo as called for a vote. But while his colleagues, with Stalin, manœuvred between Germany on one hand and Britain and France on the other, he, characteristically, had an immediately practical job to do.

One very important aspect of his final purge of the Ukraine was, as we have observed, to transform a dubious, partly alien borderland into an integral part of the Soviet Union, fit to bear the first impact of invasion from the West. With the signing of the notorious nonaggression pact with Germany, he had to be ready for a further move: he was responsible for extending the government of the Soviet Union to eastern Poland.

When the Red Army moved into Poland on September 17, 1939, stabbing in the back the proud and difficult nation still fighting forlornly against the weight and savagery of the first German *Blitzkrieg,* the Soviet commander-in-chief was Timoshenko, commander of the Kiev Special Military District. Khrushchev was his civilian counterpart, and, with Timoshenko, he signed the proclamation informing the Red Army divisions that they were marching into the "western Ukraine" (i.e., Poland) "not as conquerors but as liberators of our Ukrainian and Byelorussian brothers." [2] To be on the safe side, however, the troops were instructed to "wipe from the surface of the earth anyone and everyone who seeks to obstruct the realization of this great historical cause of the emancipation of our brothers." It was a great moment for our hero, who no doubt believed that the Polish masses would indeed rejoice to be freed from the rule of "landlords and capitalists." To make sure that this was so, as the Party boss of the Ukraine (to which the new territories were added) and as Stalin's Politburo nominee, he was supported by the whole propaganda machine of the Ukrainian Party and by the Ukrainian NKVD under a very young and boundlessly promising professional thug, Ivan Alexandrovich Serov. This was the beginning of an extremely sinister friendship.

After Yezhov, Serov, with his charm and physical courage, must have seemed the height of presentability. In fact he turned out to be Beria's cruellest and most ruthless agent: he did not scream at the top of his voice like Yezhov; he was not driven by personal resentments and hatreds, nor was he, like both Yezhov and Beria, politically ambitious. He was quite simply good at his work and happy in it, one of the few Russian villains with a sunny nature through and through. After an Army training he was switched to the NKVD and at thirty-four found himself promoted to be Deputy Commissar for State Security. In this job he was responsible for drafting and signing the atrocious Order No. 001223, dated October 11, 1939, which detailed the procedure and the categories for the proposed deportations from the Baltic States—which he himself was to have the honour of supervising eight months later.* Immediately after this came his appointment to the Ukraine and the beginning of his long and fruitful association with Khrushchev. The work in which he was so happy consisted, above all, in the mass deportation of foreigners to the Soviet far North and the deep interior of Siberia; it made a splendid change from deporting Russians.

Nobody knows how many Poles he deported, operating under Khrushchev's wing, during the first occupation of the Polish Ukraine, which lasted from September 1939 until June 1941. They numbered well into a million—above all members of the socialist parties, Jews, priests, petty-bourgeois shopkeepers, bourgeois businessmen, and all conceivable "enemies of the people." Nobody knows what proportion of the hundreds of thousands of Polish soldiers who had retreated into eastern Poland in face of the Germans, only to be captured by the Russians, fell to the NKVD as distinct from the Red Army. But these prisoners, each and every one, owed their fate either to Timoshenko or to Serov and always to Khrushchev as the chief civilian administrator, who presided over the sovietization of the unfortunate lands. Among them were the many thousands who, decimated by starvation and typhus, made their painful way southwards towards Kuibyshev to join General Anders' army after the amnesty settled by the Stalin-Sikorski agreement of 1941. Among them were the 10,000 Polish army officers shot by the NKVD, most of them in the Katyn Woods near Smolensk as the Germans approached, an incident which was to have such a dire effect on subsequent Soviet-Polish relations.³ Besides these, and most particularly Khrushchev's concern, were the remnants

---

* The occupation of the Baltic States and the subsequent deportations were supervised by Andrei Zhdanov.

of the Polish Communist Party, which had been "abolished" by Stalin in 1938, after its senior leaders had been summoned to Moscow "for consultations," there to be arrested and shot by Yezhov's men as part of Stalin's deliberate plan to destroy all those foreign Communists (above all Germans and Poles and Spaniards) whose survival might embarrass him in his long-range political manœuvres.

It was not all destruction. Stalin and Khrushchev wished to take over their part of Poland in working order, so a great number of Poles had to be left alive and at work. Khrushchev's job was to see that these were properly sovietized. He threw himself into this task with characteristic zeal. And, as usual, he went out among his people.

A man of his responsibilities might have been forgiven for following his master's example and conducting his campaign of deportation, expropriation, extermination, and terror at long range from his splendid office in Kiev. But this was not good enough for Khrushchev, the man who in the old days at Yuzovka used to wrap himself up in sheepskins against the cold and travel on a sledge the length and breadth of his tiny realm, the man who later got out among the workers in the filthy shafts and tunnels of the Moscow underground. His boundless energy, his increasing delight in publicity, drove him out once more into the field, this time the foreign field. As the Red Army moved into Poland with scarcely a check from the bewildered Poles, who hardly knew what was hitting them, Khrushchev was there, just behind the "front-line" troops. As the Soviet tanks moved into town after town, Khrushchev was just behind them to receive the submission of the civil governments. Quite a drama was made of his investing and seizure of the great city of Lvov, capital of the Polish Ukraine, which in fact surrendered (it had no choice) with scarcely a shot fired. His private propaganda army sent back lunatic reports to the Moscow papers about the heroism of the Soviet troops in general and Comrade Khrushchev in particular: he was represented as being received as a liberating angel with flowers and tears of gratitude and joy. The whole occupation was presented as one glorious fiesta, or jamboree, of thanksgiving. And Khrushchev did his best to lend colour to these reports by organizing a mass importation of representatives of Soviet culture to entertain and elevate their liberated brothers: ballet dancers from Kiev and Moscow, theatre companies, opera singers, poets, and film-makers flooded the seized territories to show the Poles what they had been missing through being sundered from paternal Russia.[4]

To prepare for the inevitable rigged elections, Khrushchev's very first elections, the country was flooded with portrait-posters of the Soviet leaders—800,000 of these in one week—and leaflets and brochures by the million, explaining the joys of life in the Soviet Union and the millennium that awaited the peasantry and the workers reunited with their Russian brothers, whom they had last seen under the tsars. The elections were a great success. The Soviet invasion started on September 17; the elections for the new People's Assembly took place on October 22. Khrushchev in person was here, there, and everywhere, and as a result of his labours over 90 per cent of the liberated brethren voted the Party ticket.

There were plenty, of course, who did not vote. They could not vote because they were in the process of deportation as enemies of the people. The election campaign, short as it was, provided Khrushchev, Serov, and the NKVD with a splendid opportunity to sort out in advance the sheep from the goats: any individual who showed signs of reluctance to vote as Khrushchev told him to vote instantly qualified as an enemy of the people and as such was transferred to the next slow train of cattle cars heading for the Soviet far North.

Later there were further elections, this time to the Supreme Soviet in Moscow. The Polish Ukraine had come of age. It had also become very Russian: there was a vote of nearly 100 per cent for the Party ticket. That was in March 1940. The last round of elections was for the local soviets, and these took much longer to prepare. It was one thing to find 113 collaborators to install as deputies to the Supreme Soviet of the USSR and the Supreme Soviet of the Ukraine; it was quite another to find enough loyal brethren to fill the 79,000 seats in the local soviets drawn up on the Russian model—a task made no easier by the previous destruction of the Polish Communist Party. But Khrushchev did it, even though it meant importing a considerable number of hard cases from the Soviet Ukraine.

It was made no easier, too, by the process of sovietization in industry and agriculture. The liberated brethren soon found that life under the Russians was not all ballet and superfilms. They were called almost immediately to follow in the footsteps of their more fortunate brothers from the Motherland. In the shortest possible time the factories and shops were taken over by the state and the peasants were collectivized. By the winter of 1940 the peace of the grave had descended on the land. Khrushchev was back in Kiev, lord now of an additional 8 million people who had been forcibly and, by Russian standards, highly efficiently *gleichgeschaltet* and absorbed, body and soul, into the pattern of Soviet life. It was a formidable satrapy—a population almost as great as the population of France, the best part of Soviet industry, the best part of Soviet food production. The magnitude of this aggrandizement, and the suffering it caused, was concealed from the West by the fog of war. We had no thought for anyone but Hitler and the terrible things the Germans were doing to the Poles. We watched, sick at heart and outraged, the Soviet invasion of Finland in the winter of 1939 (Zhdanov's new province), but we saw nothing, beyond the bare fact of Soviet occupation, of what was going on in eastern Poland. Had the view been clear, the name of Khrushchev would have become a household word fifteen years sooner than it did. This was his background, this the nature of his rise, this his early achievement. And this was the man who, with an air of bland innocence, was to ask his diplomatic guests, years later in Moscow, how it was that he managed to make rings round them, although they had been to better schools.

This, also, was a man who could later say that he had no responsibility for Stalin's crimes. It depends what one means by a crime. The invasion of Poland and the deportation in atrocious circumstances of over a million Poles were not among the crimes he listed. Nor was Serov's next operation, the mass deportation of hundreds of thousands of Lithuanians, Esthonians, Latvians, and Bessarabians when Russia took their countries by agreement with the Germans. Nor was the collectivization, first of Russia, then of Eastern Poland. Nor was the killing of the real opposition leaders. Nor, for that matter, was the normal rule (as distinct from the Yezhov terror and certain selected acts of Beria) of the secret police.

CHAPTER TWELVE

The Great Patriotic War

IN JUNE 1941 the Germans, who for months past had been massing their crack troops, armoured divisions, and air-force formations along the frontiers of Russian-occupied Europe—eastern Poland and the Baltic States—launched their greatest *Blitzkrieg* of all, striking in a single night of flame and terror deep into Khrushchev's new empire, then, cutting through the Soviet armies, carving them up and enveloping them with terrifying ease, far into Byelorussia and the Russian Ukraine. "Do you believe that we deserved this?" stammered Molotov to the German Ambassador in Moscow at midnight on June 21, when the tanks were already over the border and the *Luftwaffe* was pounding railway stations, airfields, and troop concentrations far behind the lines.[1] For once this tight little man was thinking as a Russian, not as the spokesman of a gangster tyranny. In the end it was the Russians, paradoxically, who were to save him and his fellow gangsters from the destruction which they had brought on Russia.

At some stage in this terrible war Khrushchev, who was the first among the Soviet leaders to feel the direct impact of it, and who was never to be far from the front line and the desolation of the threatened areas, underwent a change of heart. It is impossible to tell just when and how; it was a thing he never mentioned.[2] But the Khrushchev who emerged from the war in 1945 was not at all the same man as the Khrushchev who was all but overwhelmed and swept away by it in the summer of 1941. Russia, much later, was to profit from this change.

This is not to say that he had a sudden revelation and turned into a saint. Far from it. He remained to the end the consummate career politician, the opportunist, the actor, and the natural bully. But whereas before the war, as we have seen, he had come to identify himself wholly with the tiny boss class, a sycophant, a bootlicker, a most accomplished hypocrite in the service of his master, the conscienceless intriguer against all potential rivals and the scourge of those above whom he was set in authority, afterwards he showed that he had remembered what it was to be a human being—and a Russian. More than any of his colleagues, with the single exception of Zhdanov, who organized and lived through the defence of Leningrad, where 600,000 civilians starved to death, Khrushchev saw at first hand the whole story of the people's reaction to the German invasion,[3] and it is not fantastic to suppose that long before it was all over he had reached the conclusion that violence and coercion were not enough, that Russia was more than the precious Communist Party. Judging by what we know of his behaviour immediately after the war, he was then closer to the great mass of his fellow Russians, who believed that they had earned with their suffering and blood trust and consideration from their government, than to Stalin, Beria, Molotov, and Kaganovich—Malenkov too, who seized the first opportunity to blight the newly blossoming national consciousness which, though necessary for defeating the Germans, could be nothing but a threat to the established tyranny.

Khrushchev's war record is impossible to unravel, so many contradictory reports have been put out in official publications. It is to his credit that he was never one of the inner council, the State Defence Committee, established under Stalin's chairmanship to supervise the conduct of the war. Molotov was vicechairman, and the other members of the original council were Voroshilov, Malenkov, and Beria. This was the remote body which controlled the military conduct of the war, presiding in the first two years over the complete breakdown of the great Soviet war machine which Stalin had created, then in 1938 wrecked, then in 1941 deployed in the most lunatic manner, which could not have helped Hitler more had he been in Hitler's pay. Time and time again this unpleasant gang of unrepresentative thugs, at first huddled together in despondency, later, as things began to go better, recovering their native arrogance, were saved by the Zhukovs, the Vatutins, the Rokossovskis (Rokossovski straight from one of Beria's own prisons; Zhukov to be disgraced the moment his services were no longer needed; Vatutin, one of the ablest of them all, killed in an ambush by Ukrainian rebels), were saved above all by the volunteers and conscripts from all the nations of the Soviet Union, whom they had oppressed for so long and whom they were soon to oppress again.

Khrushchev was not among them. He was out in the field. Later, in 1944, after Stalingrad, after the tremendous tank battle for the Kursk salient in the high summer of 1943, with more than 3000 tanks meeting each other head on in the steppe (the forgotten battle that finally tore the heart of the *Reichswehr*), the State Defence Committee was enlarged to include members whose experience was going to be needed in reorganizing, in subduing, the reconquered territories: Mikoyan, Kaganovich, Bulganin, and the brilliant young economist Voznessensky, who was later to be shot out of hand for venturing to disagree with Stalin.[4] But Khrushchev was still not included. He was kept at the job of working actively with the soldiers so long as they fought on Russian or Ukrainian soil, and it was Malenkov, not Khrushchev, who was first sent out to the Ukraine to begin, while the fighting was still going on, the rehabilitation of the Ukrainian economy.

Khrushchev, throughout the war, was in uniform. In the words of Oleg Penkovskiy, whose hatred of him was pathological, "his uniform fitted him as a saddle fits a cow." [5] He was not, of course, a front-line soldier. He was, in effect, the supreme political commissar, master of all the Army, corps, regimental and battalion commissars, and, as such, a highly suspect character with the troops. As the civilian chief on the military councils of a variety of fronts, including the Stalingrad front, he had the main tasks of ensuring that the Kremlin's orders were carried out, of watching over the loyalty and obedience of the generals, of operating with the NKVD troops (Beria's Specials) in standing between the front-line troops and retreat. (At certain stages of the great campaign, those who retreated were shot down by the machine guns of the NKVD, and special punishment battalions were organized, driven on from behind, to make paths through minefields with their own shattered bodies, or to storm, by sheer weight of numbers, at no matter what cost, impregnable positions.) He had also to watch over the loyalty of Party members.

Later on in the war Party membership was conferred as an honour on all soldiers who had done well; but in the early days, the days of shame and chaos, the Party men belonged, one and all, to the ruling elite and were hated as such. The Germans were under standing orders to shoot them at sight;[6] if they sought succour from the enemy with the Russian peasants, these were scarcely more merciful. In the confusion of retreat tens of thousands of Party members were tempted to tear up their Party cards and throw them away. If they survived and sought to make contact with their own units in the rear, they were either shot or reduced to the ranks. Konstantin Simonov's monumental war novel, *Victims and Heroes,* written after the de-Stalinization, gives the most vivid picture yet (though still understated) of the fearful confusion of the retreats and the encirclements in the early months of the war, and the looting of Moscow in November 1941 when the police had fled to the back areas and the Germans were just down the road. The personal drama of this book is supplied by the injustices suffered by Simonov's hero, who, wounded and caught behind the German lines, loses, through no fault of his own, his Party card. Khrushchev was the man responsible for the restoration of iron discipline after the terrible late summer months when dazed and bewildered troops, betrayed by inefficient commanders at the front and by Stalin's inadequacy in the rear, found themselves caught between the German tanks and Stukas and a hostile peasantry, which all too often welcomed the Germans as deliverers from oppression.

Khrushchev is supposed to have done other things. He is supposed, for example, to have been responsible for the destruction in the Ukraine of all crops, buildings, and immovable engineering works which might be useful to the enemy, and for the evacuation of whole factories, machinery and workers, from the mines and factories of the Donbas to the safety of the Urals. A great legend has been built up and elaborated about the ruthless execution of Stalin's scorched-earth policy and the miraculous transfer of machinery. In fact it was not like that at all. After the war the earth was scorched indeed, but this work was largely the work of the Germans.

By far the greater part of the destruction occurred either during the active fighting or later in the course of the German retreat. For example, we heard a great deal of the blowing up of Kaganovich's great Dnieper dam, Dneprostroy, the showpiece of the thirties, by retreating Red Army troops. But at the time it was not critically damaged, and it went on manufacturing electricity for the Germans. It was the Germans who blew it up before they left—as they blew up everything, with a patient, meticulous exactitude wholly foreign to the Russians. To travel, painfully slowly, by train on the newly opened railway from Moscow to the new frontier at Brest-Litovsk in the days after the war was a nightmare experience. For hundreds of miles, for thousands, there was not a standing or a living object to be seen. Every town was flat, every city. There were no barns. There was no machinery. There were no stations, no water-towers. There was not a solitary telegraph pole left standing in all that vast landscape, and broad swathes of forest had been cut down all along the line as a protection against ambushes by partisans. All along the line lay the twisted rails pulled up by the Germans, who had worked with special trains fitted with great drag-hooks as they moved west. In the fields, unkempt, nobody but women, children, very old men could be seen, and these worked only with hand tools. In winter it was even more uncanny. Then the blanket of snow quite concealed what tiny vestiges of life remained. Mozhaisk, Borodino, Gzhatsk, Viasma—nothing could be seen of these famous towns that were but the brick chimney stacks, relics of wooden houses, sticking up above the snow like surrealist graveyards. Smolensk stood, a ruin, on its hill. Minsk, the great capital of Byelorussia, simply was not there—only a plain of snow, broken by meaningless hummocks. As it was for White Russia so it was for the Ukraine.

Certainly immense efforts were made to evacuate machinery factory by factory to the East, and Khrushchev, among other, more urgent responsibilities concerned with trying desperately to hold the line, was technically responsible for this. But his overseer was Malenkov, in charge of war production, and for every factory whose machinery was moved many were left intact. The workers, more often than not, were got away, but in the Urals they had to build new factories and new machines. At the height of the German threat to Moscow, when the city was all but surrounded, the train carrying the diplomatic corps and military missions away from danger took five days to cover the six hundred miles from Moscow to Kuibyshev. Most of that time was spent in sidings. And my most vivid memory is of the endless trains moving west from Siberia, carrying up fresh troops, fresh guns, fresh equipment, to fight under Zhukov in that last desperate battle for Moscow, quite blocking the lines to the east. While all along the line, in sidings, or tumbled into fields, were trainloads of machinery, rusting under the snow, machinery which had been wrenched from concrete beds, breaking the mountings which bolted it down, scattered uselessly and aimlessly all over that desolate landscape under the first early snow, and regiment after regiment of derelict and rusting locomotives, brought thus far from the west and left standing idle for want of men to drive them and to service them, for want of tracks to move them farther east.

Even then, when the lines were jammed with troops being brought up from the rear, when every machine that could be got to the east was urgently needed, the State Defence Committee (Beria's special branch of it) could think of nothing better to do than to clutter the lines still further with trains of deportees, including inoffensive Volga Germans from the trim and immemorial colonies below Saratov, being conveyed by heaven knew what roundabout routes, and dying on the way as they waited in their cattle cars, unwarmed, unfed, on their interminable way to the deep Siberian interior. And with the deportees were political prisoners of all kinds picked up by Beria's men—because they had lost their identity cards in the flight from burning villages, because somebody had denounced them, because Beria's men in their smart and plushy uniforms, the only well-fed, well-clothed men in that vast suffering country on the edge of disintegration, still had their quota of arrests to fulfil.

Khrushchev was away from all this, though still very much part of the machine.

He is also officially said to have been the prime organizer of partisan warfare behind the German lines. He must, by virtue of his position, certainly have had something to do with this; but the great centre of partisan warfare, which was the scourge and terror of the German soldiery hanging on in those immense and brooding forests a thousand miles away from home, was not in the Ukraine but in Byelorussia to the north, and it was organized from the civilian point of view above all by Pantaleimon Ponoromenko, Khrushchev's opposite number in Minsk, who was to rise high and then be reduced by Khrushchev in 1955. It is inconceivable that Khrushchev, spending all his time at the headquarters of fronts and armies, could have given more than the broadest overseeing to the raising and training of partisan units and their dispatch to join the resistance workers in German-occupied territory.

There were not many resistance workers in the Ukraine, and the open steppe was no place for guerrilla warfare; there Khrushchev's main concern was with collaborators, who swarmed, and, with Red Army deserters, went over to the Germans in organized units, never properly employed, under the supreme command of General Vlassov, one of the heroes of the defence of Moscow, who, despairing of equity and justice for the Russian people, tried in vain to get the Germans to use him intelligently with the sole object of overthrowing Russian leadership.

Nevertheless, Khrushchev must have been very much aware of the heroism of the partisans, as of the detestation of the regime on the part of the majority of his own Ukrainian flock. For just as hundreds of thousands of Ukrainians seized the opportunity of the war to revolt against their own regime, and hundreds of thousands more all over the fighting area refused even elementary cooperation with their own troops, so there were millions who fought to the death for Russia, their own people, and their own soil. Because they needed a symbol, and because Stalin in November 1941, when one and all believed that he had fled from Moscow with his government and the police, had delivered from the Mayakovsky underground station his great rallying speech, calling the Russian people his brothers and sisters, and because he had allowed the churches to reopen and had enlisted God, or at least the Orthodox hierarchy, on his side, and because he now talked about Russia and patriotism instead of Lenin and Bolshevism, and because increasingly he was presented as a hero figure, stern, remote, but loving and wise, they died with the words *"za Stalinu!"* on their lips, invoking the man who had been their scourge for so long and who, without turning a hair, as soon as the war was over and victory won was to become once again the scourge of the survivors.

The partisans, quite often desperately young, quite often girls in their teens equipped, like men, with grenades and pistols and tommyguns, trained in back areas and then brought forward to infiltrate through the dark forests behind the enemy lines, were everything that legend says they were. A British general, upstanding and tough, on one of the rare occasions when a representative of the Western Allies was allowed anywhere near the front, was asked to inspect a detachment of partisans who had just finished their final training at a divisional headquarters and were due to go over into no man's land, and beyond, that very night. Among these ranks of young and solemn faces, standing rigidly to attention, there were three or four girls in their teens, their hair cut short, loaded down with lethal ironmongery. They saluted with the rest, answering questions in clipped and formal tones; the Englishman, remembering his own daughters, had to turn away and weep.[7]

Khrushchev, for all his preoccupation with the higher strategy and the higher discipline, was deeply involved in these scenes. He knew that his people were fighting for Russia, not for Communism. For the first time he was not going among them to bully them; he was there to bless them and encourage them—fighting as they were, incidentally, to save him, and for Russia, which he also loved. He saw, too, the way in which the able commanders were being muddled by orders from Moscow, and the way in which the sycophantic and inefficient commanders were being rewarded with decorations for their subservience to Stalin —to whom he had been utterly subservient for so long. He saw at first hand the heroism of Stalingrad.[8]

He also carried out unspeakable actions, forcing commanders to persist in attacks against their professional judgment, so that they committed suicide when they failed. We need not believe all his self-praising anecdotes in the secret speech: he was denigrating Stalin, smearing Malenkov, exalting himself. But a modicum we may believe. It is the likeliest thing in the world that at the time of the ill-conceived and luckless Kharkov offensive in 1942 he did in fact telephone the Kremlin for permission to call the operation off before it led to a major encirclement of the attacking Red Army. No doubt Stalin did say, either in person or, as Khrushchev insisted, through Malenkov, "Let things stand as they are."[9] Khrushchev somehow implies that he fought against this decision, but there is nothing in his actual words to show that he did anything of the kind, and it would have been improbable. In those days Khrushchev still touched his cap to Stalin and did what he was told. The only point to be made here is that Khrushchev would have had to be an emotionless monster to live through the experiences he undoubtedly shared without asking himself whether Stalin, whether he as Stalin's loyal agent, had been on the right course. He was the representative of the Politburo on the critical fronts. He was directly responsible for every political commissar throughout the vast commands which operated within his territories. More than any other man he must have been aware of the suspicion, the detestation, of the fighting troops for these men who could, at will and without understanding either strategy or tactics or the simplest logistics, interfere with their commander's orders in obedience to their rule-of-thumb understanding of general directives from the Kremlin. It is inconceivable that he did not vow to himself to order things better if ever he got the chance.

He got the chance in 1944. The Ukraine was free of Germans. Stalin at once reappointed him First Secretary of the Ukraine, and more besides: he was made Chairman of the Ukrainian Council of Commissars into the bargain, thus duplicating Stalin's own dual position as head of the Party and head of the administration of the Soviet Union. It was an extraordinary accumulation of power, unprecedented under Stalin. It meant that although Khrushchev had been excluded from the Defence Council, the inner cabinet, and although he had not been promoted beyond lieutenant general (not bad for a civilian, but Zhdanov was a colonel general), Stalin had been impressed by his practical performance in the field and was convinced of his total loyalty.

It also meant jealousy among his colleagues. It was not a question of their asking who this jumped-up Khrushchev was, with his absolute power over the richest land of the Soviet Union: they knew just who he was, overbearing, loud, boastful, and yet cunning. And this man had been turned into a miniature Stalin, free, as none of them were, to run in his own way the affairs of a vast territory with a population almost as large as that of France.

But not quite free. Apart from Stalin, who was now far more concerned with his international activities, with shining as a world statesman, than with what went on at home, there were two other men who had a lively and practical interest in what Khrushchev was doing, both dedicated to cutting him down to size. One was Malenkov, the other Andreyev. Malenkov had by now made his name as the drive behind Soviet war production. He was still only a candidate member of the Politburo, but his membership in the State Defence Committee from the beginning had marked him out as a special case. In 1944 he was put in charge of the rehabilitation of the liberated areas; the greatest and most important liberated area was Khrushchev's Ukraine. Andreyev, the dim but tough administrator, a member not only of the Politburo but also of the Secretariat, had been in charge of agriculture since 1943; the richest agricultural area in the whole of the Soviet Union was Khrushchev's Ukraine. Thus both these men could legitimately concern themselves with Khrushchev's activities, could keep Stalin informed about him in detail, and were in an ideal position for conspiring against him. At first things were too desperate to permit indulgence in the usual power-game of intrigue and counter-intrigue: the liberated areas had to be put into running order, and jealous comrades were compelled by the sheer weight of events to work together in harness. But before long Khrushchev's rivals were to get their chance.

CHAPTER THIRTEEN

Reconstruction, Russification

THE REASON why for some years after the war the whole of western Russia, Byelorussia, and the Ukraine seemed empty of people in winter was that, the houses all being gone, the people were living in dugouts, pits dug into the earth and roofed over with fir branches, wattle, and earth; as a rule a length of stovepipe stuck out of the humped roof scarcely lifted above the ground. Hundreds of thousands, perhaps millions, lived like this, not only all over the countryside but also amid the ruins of the great cities, Minsk, Stalingrad, Kiev. Not only were the people without houses, they were dressed in rags: for four years, from 1941 until 1945, there had been no clothes of any description to be bought throughout the length and breadth of the Soviet Union. There were no boots or shoes. The peasants went about barefoot or in bast shoes, or, if they were very lucky indeed, in winter, in the traditional felt *valenky*, worn to almost nothing. Men and women could not go to work in the factories for lack of boots or shoes; children, for the same reason, had to be kept from school. There was very little food: the starvation years of 1941 and 1942 were over, but nearly everyone was hungry. Cattle in immense numbers had been slaughtered or had died of hunger while being moved back ahead of the advancing Germans. Crops were unsown. The whole country, apart from the tremendous new war industries in the East, was derelict and at a standstill. The Ukraine was ravaged, burned, and blasted too.[1]

This was Khrushchev's inheritance. The first job was to get the factories rebuilt, the mines pumped dry, the land under the plough. But there were no ploughs, let alone tractors. Instead of appealing to the world for help, Stalin had made his great decision to conceal Russia's wounds and exploit the might and success of the Soviet Army in order effectively to annex a great part of Eastern and Central Europe. It was a game of blackmail and bluff. It was called exploiting the revolutionary situation. The Russian people were the ones who had to pay. No rest for them, no thanks, no rewards. For the first time since 1914 the Russian peoples were united and ready to salute their government. The greatest of all Stalin's crimes was to throw away, apparently with perfect disdain, this unique chance, to ignore this miraculous conjuncture, and to revert at once to his prewar tyranny, to exploiting the Russian people to the limit and beyond in the interests of Muscovite imperialism: Russians in their millions had to suffer and die in order that the hammer and sickle should fly over Warsaw, Prague, Sofia, Bucharest, and East Berlin.

In the early stages it was all done by bluff and blackmail. The Soviet Union was exhausted, the great Red Army extended to breaking point. Ten million soldiers had died—ten million of the strongest and most able-bodied. At least ten million civilians had died, massacred by the Germans, worn out in German slave camps, starved to death throughout the Soviet Union. Russia had shot her bolt. But the bluff was not called. The Western Allies disarmed. Stalin's Five Year Plan for reconstruction got under way. As the Allies grew weaker, Russia grew stronger and Stalin gained in confidence—until, by pushing too far, he roused the West against him in a vast rearmament drive. Rearmament now included immense expenditure on nuclear weapons, which Stalin had at first neglected. The Russians had to go hungry again while Stalin concentrated all their best brains, all their energies, all their treasure on the fabrication of atom and hydrogen bombs and rockets. Until the country which did not know how to feed itself (though once Russia had been one of the world's greatest exporters of grain), the country which could not support a single public filling station throughout its vastness —which had no roads for motor-cars, anyway—the country which, ten years after the war, still had not shod all its people, was the first to put a man in space.

Khrushchev, in his list of Stalin's crimes, had nothing to say about his deliberate crushing of the Soviet people in his lust for territorial gain—territorial gain so soon to be made useless by the developments of modern weapons. He could not denounce this, because he was up to his neck in it.

To begin with, in Kiev he had not only to assist in the reconstruction of his devastated empire, not only to re-establish Party rule and Soviet institutions, but also to cope with insurrection on a very large scale indeed. The rebels were quite distinct from the collaborationists, whose rounding-up and execution were also his responsibility. Those who recall the vicious witch-hunts which went on all over German-occupied Europe, above all in France, when the Germans were pushed back, can all too easily imagine the atmosphere of hysterical vindictiveness in which, in the Ukraine, all those who had come to any sort of terms whatsoever with the Germans were pursued. Individuals paid off old scores; the malicious and malevolent rejoiced in the role of informer; the frustrated and covetous saw the way to better jobs by denouncing their superiors. It was a situation very much after the hearts of the NKVD, which, under the wing of the Ukrainian First Secretary and Prime Minister, took full advantage of it. They had not only the collaborators, actual and imaginary, on the spot to deal with: all those Russians, men, women, children in their teens, who had been shipped off to Germany to work in the war factories, and who survived to make their way home, were treated in principle as traitors and deserters—just as escaped prisoners of war were treated as deserters—unless they could bring the firmest proof to the contrary. At a time when the Soviet Union was desperately short of manpower, when Stalin, by a single imaginative act of grace, could have transformed his people into eager followers, he chose instead to organize another blood-bath, to shoot or deport hundreds of thousands of potentially loyal citizens.

And this, of course, played into the hands of the real rebels I have referred to. The Ukrainians overrun by the German armies fell into four categories: those who got on with life as best they could, thus laying themselves open to being treated as collaborators; those who joined the partisans, more or less organized, cooperating with the Soviet armies; those who formed nationalist partisan bands, fighting for their own land, the Ukraine, impartially against the Red Army and the Germans (a very large number); and those (mainly soldiers taken prisoner or cut off from their units, or deserters) who volunteered to fight for the Germans against the Red Army under General Vlassov. Many of these, in due course, were sent back to Russia by the Western Allies to meet a certain death. Some, together with prisoners of war, managed to escape, and these joined the independent partisan bands, who, with the Germans out of the war, now concentrated on fighting the Russians for their own survival.

There were many of these bands operating in the western Ukraine, but they were gradually mopped up by Beria's NKVD troops (who had aircraft, river gunboats, heavy artillery, as well as rifles and machine guns). Those who were left, some scores of thousands, coalesced in the foothills of the Carpathians under a legendary leader, whether brigand or patriot it is impossible to tell, called Stepan Bandera. On occasion Soviet Army formations had to be called out to reinforce the para-military police in major pitched battles. In due course Bandera was killed. But several years went by before the whole of the Ukraine was pacified.

This was the chaotic background against which Khrushchev had to establish his authority. This authority had to be established not only in the old Russian Ukraine, but still more in the Polish Ukraine, which had been overrun by the Germans less than two years after its seizure by the Russians. The whole cruel business of sovietization had to be gone through a second time, including the recollectivization of the land.

[2.]

It was not only the very freshly formed collectives in Russian-occupied Poland that had fallen apart under the German occupation. Throughout vast areas of the Soviet Union where no

Germans had penetrated the collectives had dwindled to nothing, for lack of police and Party power. When Khrushchev's colleague in the Politburo, Andreyev, took on the task of redisciplining the peasants, he found that in thousands of collectives all but the feeblest members had virtually contracted out, as often as not with the active connivance of the farm managers, who, in return for a consideration, would let individuals off their "work-days" on the collective land and would even sell them parcels of that land.

In the Ukraine matters were far worse than elsewhere, and Khrushchev, as master of the Ukraine, had to use an iron fist or abdicate. There seems to me no doubt at all that his wartime experiences had indeed opened his eyes to some, at least, of the evils of Stalinist rule; but he was caught in a trap, the prisoner of his own past—a situation to be repeated time and time again during the years to come, right up to his downfall. Stalin in Moscow had no other thought than to restore the status quo and to rebuild heavy industry in the shortest possible time by the uninhibited employment of violence and terror. This did not happen immediately. At first it seemed that he too, touched by the sacrificial heroism of the Soviet peoples during the war, was to reward them with his confidence, withdrawing them, as it were, behind a curtain of iron to lick their wounds and gather new strength. But by the start of 1946 all that was over. Germany was defeated and lay prostrate, but the Russians were told that they must prepare for yet another war; they could not rest until prewar output had been trebled:

We must achieve a situation whereby our industry is able to produce each year up to 50 million tons of pig iron, up to 60 million tons of steel, up to 500 million tons of coal, and up to 60 million tons of oil. Only under such conditions can we regard our country as guaranteed against any accidents. This, I think, will require perhaps three more Five Year Plans, if not more.[2]

Very soon after that, through his obdurate and criminal challenge to the West, Stalin had succeeded in provoking the United States—to say nothing of Britain and Europe, including West Germany—into such a mighty rate of material growth as to make nonsense of these heroic figures.

They were to be achieved by the old, old way: by slave labour, by the rigid implementation of the draconian labour laws of 1933, by Party threats and naggings backed by the force of the NKVD. Slave labour was vastly augmented by the arrest of hundreds of thousands of "deserters" and "collaborators," above all from the Ukraine, and by the extraordinary action—extraordinary even for Stalin—of obliterating from the map of the Soviet Union a number of complete nationalities. In the words of Khrushchev, who was telling the unadorned truth, "the mass deportations from their native places of whole nations, together with all Communists and Komsomols without any exception; those deportations were not dictated by any military considerations." [3]

The peoples in question, as listed by Khrushchev, were the Karachi, the whole population of the Autonomous Kalmuk Republic; the whole population of the Chechen-Ingush Autonomous Republic; all the Balkars from the Kabardino Autonomous Republic. These events took place in 1943 and 1944. These unfortunates were deported because some of them had exhibited disloyalty to the Soviet Union while under German occupation. "The Ukrainians," added Khrushchev "escaped this fate only because there were too many of them and there was no place to which to deport them. Otherwise he would have deported them also."

Khrushchev did not say that these deportations had been supervised by his favourite policeman, Serov, whose men had surrounded village after village in the night and marched away the inhabitants at the point of the gun, separating men, women, and children and shooting those who resisted or tried to escape. Nor did he mention that at this time Stalin had also deported the Tartars from the Crimea, abolishing their own Autonomous Republic, which later became a part of the Ukraine, a part of Khrushchev's own empire. It goes without saying that he had nothing to say about his own deportations of innumerable Poles from the Polish Ukraine or the deportation in 1940 of hundreds of thousands of Latvians, Esthonians, Lithuanians, also by Serov (this time working under Zhdanov), when Russia occupied the Baltic States.

Later still, of course, it was the turn of the Jews—such as had survived the German occupation and returned to their homeland. Curiously, quite a number of Jews from eastern Poland and the Baltic States owed their lives to Khrushchev, Zhdanov, and Serov, who had sent them to Siberia (where, also, many died) before the Germans could get at them and murder them. Khrushchev showed himself to be a fairly crude anti-Semite in later years; violent anti-Semitism was also endemic in the Ukraine: there were many Ukrainians, Balts too, among the rank and file of the notorious *Einsatzgruppen,* special formations belonging to Heydrich's *Sicherheitsdienst,* which were responsible for the rounding-up and extermination of the Jews in occupied Russia. The gas chambers of Auschwitz, Madjanek, Treblinka, and elsewhere were fed mainly with Jews deported by the Germans from Western Europe, including Germany itself. In Russia the usual procedure was for the *Einsatzgruppen* to round up all the Jews found in a given area or a city, march them out to a selected spot, force them to dig a great trench, then to undress and stand on the edge of the trench to be sprayed with machine-gun fire. One of the largest of these massacres took place immediately outside Khrushchev's own city, Kiev, in a ravine known as Babi Yar, on September 29 and 30, 1941, where 33,771 Jews, men, women, and children, were killed in two days, the shooting clearly audible in the centre of the city.[4] As the Soviet Army approached Kiev to retake it in 1943 the Germans took fright and decided to dig up the corpses and burn them. A certain SS Colonel Blobel, a failed architect in civilian life, who had supervised the shooting, had since fallen into disfavour and was himself forced by Heydrich to conduct the exhumation and the burning.

But the Germans need not have worried. The four *Einsatzgruppen,* according to their own official returns to Heydrich, killed more than a million human beings in this manner, mostly Jews, in the course of two years, very largely in Khrushchev's Ukraine.[5] The Russians, naturally enough, had a great deal to say about German atrocities in general, but they never made the Jews an issue. For years after the war, during all Khrushchev's time and later still, Kiev was a forbidden city: the only foreigners allowed to go there were a handful of UNRRA officials. But I remember very well, when I was first allowed to go there in 1955, asking the local director of Intourist to direct me to Babi Yar. At first he pretended he had never heard of Babi Yar. But when I insisted he said, "Why do you want to go and look at a lot of dead Jews? If you're interested in Jews you'll see more than enough live ones on the streets!"

There was no monument at Babi Yar—or, for that matter, at any other places where the Jews had been massacred. There was nothing to show that anything out of the way had ever happened there. Babi Yar remained a forbidden word until the young poet Yevtushenko in 1963 incurred Khrushchev's intense displeasure by writing his celebrated poem, "Babi Yar," in which, as a Russian, he proclaimed his share of the guilt. It will be remembered that Shostakovich set the Babi Yar poem for voices and orchestra in the last movement of his Thirteenth Symphony, performance of which was forbidden at the last moment.[6]

[3.]

It may well be that these last pages have a planless and inconsequent appearance. This is intended. It is impossible to make a neat pattern of the complex violence that drove Nikita Khrushchev and haunted him and hemmed him in when, after living through the fearful sufferings of the war and the German occupation with his own people—his eldest son was killed at Stalingrad—he sought to turn himself into their benevolent and respected father under Stalin. It was then that he let his shaven hair grow for a short period: it was an elegant silver-gray, and the portraits of him at this period show a gentle, modest father figure, beautifully turned out. He fostered a minor personality cult of his own. Whereas all over Russia the official portraits, hung in every office, in every factory, in every shop—and on holidays plastered over every building, ten times life size—showed always Stalin, usually Lenin, sometimes on holidays the other members of the Politburo, in the Ukraine, above all in Kiev and Kharkov, the portrait of Khrushchev alone would appear alongside Stalin's. There were poems, too. In 1944 Khrushchev caused a collective of thirteen Ukrainian writers to compose a long poem to the glory of Stalin. It was called "To the Great Stalin from the Ukrainian People," and it started:

> Today and forever, oh, Stalin be praised
> For the light that the plants and the fields do emit!
> Thou art the heart of the people, the truth and the faith!
> We give Thee our thanks for the sun Thou has lit!

The poem was submitted to Stalin together with an immense roll containing 9,316,973 signatures. In this unique memorial Khrushchev caused a niche for himself to be carved:

> We're united and solid, and no one will dare
> To touch our young land which is clean as first love.
> As fresh and as young with his silver-grey hair
> Is Stalin's companion, Nikita Khrushchev.[7]

But Stalin's companion was beginning to build up trouble for himself. As I have already observed, he was not quite alone in the Ukraine. Malenkov had business there as chairman of the committee for the rehabilitation of the liberated lands; Andreyev, dour and unsympathetic, had business there as agricultural overlord of the Soviet Union. Both these men watched Khrushchev's ascendancy with jealous eyes. It is inconceivable that either of them, above all Malenkov with his special relationship with Stalin, omitted to report unfavourably on this viceroy who was getting too big for his boots and starting to behave as though he, not Stalin, were the ruler of the Ukraine. And it is clear that for some time Stalin, who could put a stop to any nonsense when he cared to, had his own reasons for tolerating Khrushchev so long as he was useful, as he was. Khrushchev knew his Ukraine and was getting results. It would have amused Stalin, too, to watch Malenkov and Andreyev showing jealousy. Andreyev was a bore and humourless; Malenkov, with his needle-sharp brain, his eyes everywhere, his tremendous natural gifts, his unrivalled inside knowledge of everyone who counted in the Party—unrivalled except for Beria's—was indispensable; but he was also young and a little too ready to presume on his gifts: it would do him no harm to think of Nikita Sergeievich as a rival to be watched. And no matter what sort of empire Khrushchev was able to hammer out of the Ukraine with his tight group of devoted lieutenants headed by Demyan Korotchenko, the whole thing could be blotted out in a moment if need be.

Everything depended on Khrushchev's continuing to do well and keeping in his place. Suddenly, in 1947, something went wrong. It could have been the famine of 1946. Just as Khrushchev was beginning to get agriculture moving, the Ukraine was smitten by one of its classic droughts. Not a word was said about this in the Soviet press, and I remember how, when I wrote about it early in 1947 and shortly afterwards visited the Soviet Union, I was almost violently set upon not only by Soviet officials but also by British and American correspondents. What did I mean by making up stories about a famine in the Ukraine? Things had never been better. But the story was not made up. There had been in fact a most appalling famine: the Ukraine was virtually sealed off. And at the end of 1947, shortly before his own death, Zhdanov spoke in Moscow and announced that there had indeed been a setback to food production, which had postponed the end of bread rationing. In 1946 the Ukraine, he said, had suffered the worst drought since 1890. Once more Kiev was starving.

In February 1947 Andreyev, not referring to the drought, announced to the Central Committee in Moscow that there had been serious failures in Ukrainian agriculture, caused mainly by the omission over a number of years to sow spring wheat. Immediately after this Kaganovich was sent to Kiev to take over the Ukrainian Party from Khrushchev, ostensibly because it was expedient and desirable that the posts of First Party Secretary and Prime Minister should be separated. This was the sort of blow which in the past had been the certain presage of a Party functionary's imminent extinction. To Khrushchev it must have seemed the end of the world, the first disastrous step in a process which would swiftly lead to his being stripped of all important offices, then moved to a derisory post, and then to his final liquidation. It had happened to so many of the individuals he himself had supplanted on his way to the top. It was inevitable and natural and deserved.

But it had nothing to do with the failure of Ukrainian agriculture: that, as Zhdanov was to admit much later, was due to the drought. And the talk about spring wheat was almost insolently absurd. What it had to do with was certainly Khrushchev's getting too big for his boots in the eyes of his rivals, almost certainly his failure to resovietize with sufficient conviction and speed the Polish Ukraine, which he had subdued so swiftly and masterfully in 1939 and 1940. From October 1944, when the Polish Ukraine was reoccupied by the Soviet Army, until March 1947, when Kaganovich came from Moscow to take over from Khrushchev, only 504 collective farms had been set up. In the next ten months, under Kaganovich's aegis, the tempo was accelerated in a really startling way: another 1150 collectives were set up. At the same time the NKVD was strengthened and given its head in the business of putting down the insurgent armies or bands. During the greater part of 1947, which was precisely the period during which Stalin was starting up the Cold War in earnest and needed to re-establish absolute discipline in his western borderlands, the western Ukraine was virtually in a state of siege. By the time Kaganovich was recalled to Moscow in January 1948, resistance was finally broken, and the resovietization, the collectivization continued virtually unopposed, until, a year later, the new First Secretary could announce that the collectives had been increased by another 3500, making over 5000 all told.

The new First Secretary was none other than N. S. Khrushchev.

It was a queer episode. For over six months Khrushchev had simply disappeared from sight. The Ukrainian press, his own press, had no word to say about him. He had relinquished the First Secretaryship to Kaganovich in the first week of March. In the second week of March he bobbed up in a special session of the Ukrainian Central Committee and, admitting the Ukraine's agricultural shortcomings, blamed them on his own Minister of Agriculture. Ten days later he took a further downward plunge, being relieved "at his own request" of the secretaryship of the Kiev Regional Party Committee. Two days after that, on March 24, he lost his secretaryship of the Kiev City Party Committee. It looked like the end. In June 1947 he did not even appear at the plenary session of the Ukrainian Central Committee. Yet throughout this period of eclipse he nominally retained the premiership of the Ukraine and at no time was he formally dropped from the Moscow Politburo.

That Malenkov had a great deal to do with this train of events was demonstrated when one of his own Moscow protégés, Nikolai Semonovich Patolichev, who at thirty-eight had served under him on the Orgburo in Moscow and had been promoted to the All Union Party Secretariat, was sent to Kiev to be Second Secretary of the Ukrainian Party under Kaganovich: since Kaganovich clearly would not stay in Kiev forever, it was a natural assumption that Patolichev would take over the First Secretaryship in due course—a consummation which would, in effect, have made Malenkov master of the Ukraine.

But Khrushchev fought back, and Kaganovich, instead of finishing him off, almost certainly helped him, to such effect that in December 1947, when Kaganovich went back to Moscow, Khrushchev resumed his old position as Ukrainian viceroy. He then threw out Malenkov's Patolichev and sent him off into the wilderness to be Party boss of Rostov-on-Don, and appointed as Prime Minister his own most faithful henchman, Demyan Korotchenko, who had been his shadow since early Moscow days. He was so strong now that not only could he resume packing the Ukrainian Party with his own supporters, who were later to serve as the base of his own position in the successful bid for supreme power, but he also, a year later, on the occasion of the Ukrainian Sixteenth Party Congress, was accorded special praise by *Pravda,* in an editorial quite remarkably (even by *Pravda's* standards) full of lies, for all sorts of wholly imaginary achievements in agriculture and industry. That was in January 1949. At the end of that year, in December, Khrushchev finally said farewell to his Ukraine. He was called to Moscow, this time for good, once more to take over the Moscow Region and city organizations, but also, more important, to be a secretary of the All Union Central Committee. Almost at once he started to make himself felt as a new force in the land.

CHAPTER FOURTEEN

Overture to the Struggle for Supremacy

WE ARE NOW moving into the edge of the pattern, the acute and long-drawn-out conflict of forces, which was to produce what we think of as the Khrushchev era. From now on Khrushchev was to use the conflicts of others, as in the past he had used the misfortunes of others, as a means of self-advancement which was to culminate in his supremacy. The key event which made this pattern possible was the death of Zhdanov in August 1948.

Zhdanov had been more actively bound up with the development of Stalinism in its final phase than any other individual. Compared with this remarkable creature, still only fifty-two when he died, the fellow members of the Politburo, including in their different ways Molotov, Beria, and Malenkov, were instruments in the hands of Stalin: Zhdanov was a creative force. Plainly he could function as such only because his ideas were in the closest possible accord with the ideas of Stalin himself at that critical time. But he could express those ideas, as Stalin could not, and he was characterized by a personal dynamism and energy of conviction which were unique in the Soviet Union (Khrushchev had dynamism, but not, at that time, noticeably the conviction).

Zhdanov passionately believed that the Soviet people had to be saved from the corruption of the West, to which far too many innocent citizens, in the shape of the soldiery, had been and still were exposed as the result of their eruption into Europe (returned soldiers had to be virtually quarantined when they got back to Russia for fear—well justified—that they would infect their friends and relatives with their tales of what they had seen in the way of material wealth even in war-ravaged Eastern and Central Europe). He passionately believed that there must be a fight to the finish with the United States over the still largely prostrate body of Europe, and all his actions were informed by a savage rejection of Western influence and by an equally savage belief in Russian messianism expressed in Marxist terms. He was the best-educated man in the Politburo, and he passed as the great intellectual at the court of Stalin because his interests ranged far and wide, because he neither drank himself silly every night nor shared the bottomless coarseness of Molotov, Beria, Andreyev, Voroshilov—or Stalin himself. "Despite his well-known narrowness and dogmatism," wrote Djilas, who had had to deal with him, "I would say that his knowledge was not inconsiderable. Although he had some knowledge of nearly everything, even music, I would not say that there was a single field he knew thoroughly—a typical intellectual who became acquainted with and picked up knowledge of other fields through Marxist literature." He liked to present himself, whether to the Finns, whose country he bestrode, or to the writers and musicians and painters broken by his decrees, as the stern but magnanimous patron-prince.[1]

This was the man who, at Stalin's right hand, set the tone of the Soviet attitude towards the outer world from 1946 to 1948. While at home he took it upon himself to organize and prosecute the great purge of the arts, the struggle against "cosmopolitanism" and for "socialist realism"; abroad he set up as an anti-Western crusader. It was he who in Warsaw in September 1947 presided over the creation of the Cominform, a direct response to the Marshall Plan, and in his speech on that occasion branded America, so recently Russia's ally in her life-and-death struggle with Germany, as the active enemy. It was he who disciplined most rigidly Russia's new satellites in Eastern and Central Europe. It was he who encouraged Dmitrov of Bulgaria in what *Pravda* was soon to call his "problematic and fantastic federations and confederations" and customs unions. It was he, a little later, in the summer of 1948, who advised Stalin to cast Marshal Tito into the outer darkness, unable to understand that the Yugoslav Communist Party might dare to rally round their own excommunicated leader and defy the might of Russia. It was undoubtedly his intolerant dynamism which brought Stalin to try conclusions with the Western Allies by trying to starve them out of Berlin. He was the dynamo of the Cold War and the scourge of the satellites and foreign Communist Parties.

During all the time that Khrushchev was in the Ukraine, watched jealously by his close colleagues in Moscow (including Zhdanov, who must have had nothing but contempt for what he would regard as the oafish and servile ways, the low cunning, of the peasant from Kalinovka), the real battle for influence over Stalin was being fought out between Zhdanov and Malenkov, both of whom had arrived in the Politburo after Khrushchev. Early in 1948, after Khrushchev's rehabilitation at Stalin's hands, Malenkov appeared to be winning, his cautious, chess-playing, unemotional skill at manœuvre and organization wearing down his talkative and energetic rival. Zhdanov certainly had begun to lose favour in January 1948, when *Pravda* attacked the federation plans for southeastern Europe which he had been sponsoring behind the scenes. His reputation took a heavy fall when Yugoslavia rallied behind Tito in defiance of Stalin. It was not helped when the inauguration of the Allied airlift began to make nonsense of the blockade of Berlin. In July 1948 he was dead. He may have been poisoned—not by the Kremlin doctors, as Stalin later insisted, but by agents of Malenkov. But it was known that he had a bad heart, and it is far more likely that he died of heart failure after a stormy scene with his master.

At any rate, he died, and Malenkov exploited his death up to the hilt, purging the Soviet Union of all his supporters and protégés, above all in Leningrad but also in Moscow and elsewhere, and so fixing things that a number of the most important of these were shot (this was the mysterious "Leningrad affair" which Khrushchev, in his secret speech, used as a point of attack against Stalin, but the attack was really directed at Malenkov). It was certainly as an immediate result of Zhdanov's death that Stalin, in December 1949, brought Khrushchev up to Moscow as a counterweight to Malenkov's too formidable concentration of power.

And it is likely that Malenkov, far from opposing this move, actively welcomed it. Khrushchev in the Ukraine was a power in his own right; in Moscow, where Malenkov held all the Party strings, he was a newcomer. Furthermore, the actual occasion of Khrushchev's advent was the relegation of Andreyev from his position as agricultural overlord. Khrushchev, Andreyev's victim in the Ukraine, now assumed responsibility for agriculture throughout the Soviet Union.

In 1949, four years after the war, food production in the Soviet Union, which had been scandalously low ever since the collectivization twenty years before, was in as bad a state as it had ever been. Even in 1940, on the eve of the German invasion, production was still lower than it had been in 1928, on the eve of the collectivization, and this in spite of a large increase of population throughout the Soviet Union and the addition of rich new lands in the West (part of Poland, the Baltic States, and Bessarabia).

What had been scandalous in 1940 became catastrophic with the German invasion. After the war, with the reconstruction of heavy industry once more Stalin's obsession, no attempt was made to re-equip the farms, let alone improve them. The shortage of able-bodied and intelligent manpower went hand in hand with an almost incredibly wasteful use of the women and children and idiots and old men who still remained on the farms. Andreyev's only achievement, with the help of the NKVD, was to get the collectives organized again and to see that the state got more than its share of the collective produce at absurdly low prices, thus pauperizing the farms and ensuring that the peasants spent all their energies on cultivating their own small private plots, off which they lived and the surplus produce of which they could sell at high prices on the open market, a kind of official black market.

[2.]

The actual issue which led to the relegation of Andreyev was a sudden reversal of a ten-year-old policy: since the Eighteenth Party Congress the collectives had been worked on what was known as the link system; small gangs of peasants under a leader were responsible for certain cultivations, assisted by what machinery there was, which was centralized in Machine Tractor Stations, the members of which lived apart and were used by Party and police as unofficial overseers and informers; sharing no common life with the villagers, the mechanics of the MTS regarded themselves as belonging to a superior class (as indeed they did), and it was one of their duties, in return for certain privileges, to know which peasants were slacking and which families were concealing hoarded grain. The advantage of the link system was that small groups of peasants were at least given the feeling of limited responsibility for the land they worked. The main disadvantage was that this system militated against the development of large-scale mechanical cultivations; but since machines were few and far between and most of the work in the forties was still being done by hand, except on the so-called millionaire collectives in the rich grain areas of the Ukraine, this was no great disadvantage. Primitive it was, but the whole agricultural economy was also primitive.

Nevertheless, during his last years in the Ukraine, Khrushchev had been preaching, and in a very limited way putting into effect, a different system. Instead of being worked by small groups, the land was to be cultivated by large and comparatively impersonal brigades under a "brigadier," and since the attack on Andreyev, when it came, took the form of an attack on the link system and a glorification of the brigade system, which had been denounced by Andreyev, with the approval of the Party in full congress, in 1939, it was obvious that big changes were expected. And the reason why Khrushchev's rivals, above all Malenkov, no doubt welcomed his return to Moscow was that they all knew very well that the surest path to ruin for any ambitious individual was to be associated with agriculture, which under Stalin was bound to fail and go on failing.

Khrushchev himself must have known this as well as anyone. Not only did he take the job on; he at once began to make a great noise about it, the sort of noise that no subordinate of Stalin's had dared make about anything in all the long years of Stalin's rule. Instead of hedging his bets he started to gamble very heavily indeed in this most vulnerable and hopeless of all fields.

Ironically, all those who congratulated themselves in the conviction that by accepting public responsibility for agriculture Khrushchev was riding for a fall were, in principle, correct. It was in their timing that they showed how disastrously they had underestimated this extraordinary man. In the end, fourteen years later, one of the main elements in Khrushchev's downfall was to be precisely his agricultural failure. But by that time Malenkov and others had all been put down—and, for the fun of it, Malenkov himself was made to confess that he had shown his incompetence largely by the failure of his agricultural policies: Malenkov never had anything to do with agriculture; the policies for whose failure he apologized were Khrushchev's.

In the early 1950s things looked very different. Another of Khrushchev's Ukrainian schemes had been to increase the size of the collectives by amalgamating a number of small ones to make larger units. And his great dream was the abolition of the traditional Russian village in favour of large and up-to-date settlements to be called agro-towns. This amalgamation scheme he was now to apply to the whole of the Soviet Union; the agro-town dream was to be advanced as practical policy. It was this that got him into serious trouble only a little more than a year after his noisy return to Moscow. This, also, was the first of those nationwide "hare-brained" schemes which were, for better or for worse, to become the distinguishing feature of the Khrushchev era. He was launched firmly on the Khrushchevite road even while Stalin was still alive.

[3.]

But Stalin, while still very much alive in 1950, was already senile. The mood in the Kremlin had deteriorated beyond all measure since the proud last days of the war, when Stalin had been able to impose his character and will in, as it were, hand-to-hand personal combat with the champions of the West. Now he avoided all personal confrontations, and, since the death of Zhdanov in 1948, even his foreign policies had been wholly negative. His last great initiative was the Korean War, beginning in June 1950, unprepared for, ill considered, hopelessly misguided, which raised against him the embattled might of the United States and forced him into a stalemate. As far back as 1948 Milovan Djilas, still an ardent Communist, still a Stalin-worshipper, had been unpleasantly impressed by the swift decay of Stalin's faculties. Here he is on a high state occasion:

The dinner began with someone—I think it was Stalin himself—proposing that everyone guess how many degrees below zero it was, and that everyone be punished by being made to drink as many glasses of vodka as the number of degrees he guessed wrong. . . . I remember that Beria missed by three and remarked that he had done so on purpose so that he might drink more glasses of vodka.

Such a beginning to a dinner forced upon me a heretical thought: These men shut up in their narrow circle might well go on inventing even more senseless reasons for drinking vodka—the length of the dining-room in feet, or of the table in inches. And, who knows, perhaps that's what they do! At any rate, this allocation of glasses of vodka according to the temperature reading suddenly made me clearly aware of the confinement, the inanity and senselessness of the life these Soviet leaders were living gathered about their superannuated chief even as they played a role that was decisive for the human race. . . .

There was something both tragic and ugly in his senility. The tragic was invisible. . . . The ugly kept cropping up all the time. Though he had always enjoyed eating well, Stalin was now quite gluttonous, as though he feared that there would not be enough of the food he wanted left for him. On the other hand, he drank less and more cautiously, as though measuring every drop—to avoid ill effects.

His intellect was in even more apparent decline. He liked to recall incidents from his youth—his exile in Siberia, his childhood in the Caucasus; and he would compare everything recent with something that had happened long ago: "Yes, I remember, the same thing. . . ."

In one thing, though, he was still the Stalin of old: stubborn, sharp, suspicious whenever anyone disagreed with him. He even cut Molotov, and one could feel the tension between them. Everyone paid court to him, avoiding any expression of opinion before he expressed his, and then hastening to agree with him.[2]

Khrushchev was not there in 1948. He was well out of it, still in the Ukraine. The men who mattered when Djilas last met Stalin were Zhdanov, to be dead within six months; Voznessensky, the young planning genius, who impressed Djilas above all others, and whom Stalin was to have shot out of hand a year later for venturing to disagree with him; Molotov; Beria; Malenkov; and Mikoyan. Kaganovich was still a power, but losing ground; Andreyev was soon to lose it. Voroshilov was not much more than Stalin's old drinking companion, senile too.

[4.]

When, two years after that dinner, Khrushchev came to Moscow, the men who mattered, under Stalin, were only Molotov, Beria, and Malenkov—with Mikoyan in the wings. Khrushchev was junior to half a dozen others, including Andreyev, and Kaganovich. But the men he had to reckon with were, above all, Malenkov and Beria, who ran the Party and the police on behalf of Stalin, each therefore being a potentate in his own right, disposing of vast forces answerable directly to him. Beria's forces had the guns and the prisons, but Malenkov's ran the government and Party machine. Molotov was all-important to Stalin, though he was bullied outrageously, and had become a national figure in his own right; but he was nothing without Stalin. Kaganovich was still used as a gifted and tough organizer, the man to get things done. Mikoyan, the Armenian with the mind of a great man of business, his understanding of Western ways, his invaluable detachment, had his very specialized uses. Bulganin was moving up as a useful stooge and organizer.

These and other members of the Politburo and the Secretariat could combine and counter-combine among themselves against each other—never against Stalin. But with Zhdanov gone, the only two individual powers were Malenkov and Beria, working now with, now against, each other, and regarding the new arrival, Nikita Sergeievich, as easy game and not in their class at all.

Khrushchev had nothing behind him in the way of forces, except the elaborate Party apparatus he had built up in the Ukraine, the friendship of a number of military commanders whom he had worked with and helped to get promoted during the war, Stalin's personal favour, and his unique experience of governing a huge and rich territory for a great many years as effective dictator. On the face of it, Malenkov as the supreme Party manager under Stalin should have been able to wreck the apparatus Khrushchev left behind him in the Ukraine by purging Khrushchev's men and substituting his own. Beria, for his part, could have conducted his own purge. But things did not work out like that. In 1950, just three years before Stalin's death, the men who were jockeying for position with an eye to the succession might, and did, intrigue against each other, but they dared not go too far; they were also compelled to maintain some sort of common front against Stalin—just as later, for a time, they were compelled to maintain a common front against the Soviet people—and each was above all interested in curtailing the power of the others while, at the same time, maintaining a certain solidarity. For all were vulnerable.

Molotov was Stalin's indispensable chief of staff, counsellor, technical adviser on foreign affairs, and formal spokesman for the Soviet Union to the outside world, a man of considerable personal dignity, though coarse and sly when unbuttoned, who had won the respect of the Soviet people by his public demeanour; but he was also Stalin's butt and bottle-washer, and he had to suffer uncomplainingly the arrest and imprisonment of his own extremely gifted and ambitious wife.

Malenkov looked after the Party for Stalin, manipulated the great apparatus of rule in the immediate interest of his master and with an eye to his own advancement, worked hand in glove with the police in purge after purge. He was, after Zhdanov, the best-informed man in the Politburo; after Voznessensky the keenest brain; beyond all question, behind the rolls of fat, the most cultivated as well as the most deadly.

Beria, with the immense power of the police apparatus at his back, the ruler of a state within a state, disposing not only of millions in his labour camps but also of hundreds of thousands of the finest brains and craftsmen, a great proportion of them German, in the precision enterprises, ranging from the development of atomic energy to the manufacturing of cameras (the celebrated Dynamo football team was an NKVD enterprise), held his post only by flattering Stalin outrageously. This man, with his pince-nez, his cold blue eyes, the compressed lips in the square mouth, the Kremlin pallor, who shared with so many secret-police chiefs, Communist and anti-Communist, the look of a dedicated schoolmaster, held in his possession dossiers not only of every Party member but also of each of his own colleagues, which could have led to the downfall of each and all of them. But he himself, like all the others, was subject to a higher power in the shape of a certain General Poskrebyshev, Stalin's personal and confidential secretary, about whom nobody knew anything, the commander of Stalin's personal guard, on whom the master could call with no fuss at all if, for example, he decided to have Beria shot between tea and dinner.

"You are blind like little kittens," Stalin once chided his closest colleagues when they were not, he thought, conscious enough of certain threats to the security of the government.[3] They might have retorted, "We are as helpless as blind kittens, so long as Comrade Poskrebyshev still lives." On the night that Stalin died Poskrebyshev disappeared from view and was never heard of again. So they held together, and Khrushchev, though Malenkov and no doubt others did their level best to undermine his growing influence, was part of the cement. We can see him with his far-away look, his air of calm detachment to the fore, balancing among the murderous forces and calculating, behind all his noisy talk about revolutions in agriculture, the next step and who was needed on his side to make it possible for him to take it.

By now, in 1950, at fifty-six, he was very much the man the world was soon to know, drunken and coarse and alternately savage and jolly in his moments of relaxation, alternating between bullying and cajolery and jeering towards his own subordinates, ever watchful among his equals, a compulsive talker, a compulsive schemer, a compulsive worker. He was highly presentable. In the Ukraine he had enjoyed being king and he had started grooming himself to look the part.

Marshall MacDuffie, the head of the UNRRA mission to the Ukraine at the time of the 1946 famine, was one of the first foreigners ever to meet Khrushchev—perhaps, indeed, the very first American Khrushchev had ever met. They met again in 1953, and MacDuffie reported that during those seven years there had been no visible change in the man. Only he was more used to foreigners. Of Khrushchev in 1946, MacDuffie reported: "He stared at me quizzically and with great curiosity, like a man studying a bug on a rock." [4] But he had not been at a loss. He had not been afraid to display his personal sense of humour. He made the sort of impromptu jokes, teasing his own entourage and MacDuffie too, which were to become so familiar later on. He had talked with perfect authority. And he was individual enough to do what no Soviet leader had done for decades: when it was time for the UNRRA mission to leave he gave a farewell party at a country villa outside Kiev for the mission members and their wives, and after the party "sat on the porch with them until long past midnight, discussing their personal lives and plans." [5]

Here was the man, recognizably, who later, at the height of his power, would spend innumerable hours stolen from the working days of one of the busiest men in the world to chatter discursively to foreigners who had gone unprepared for anything but a brief and formal audience—the man who talked with Mr. Walter Lippmann for hours on end, the man who was deeply and dangerously affronted when, at his first exploratory meeting with the young Kennedy in Vienna, the brand-new American President made the serious mistake of approaching him in a brisk and businesslike manner, unthinkingly holding this rambling conversationalist so very much his senior to the sort of time-schedule which would have suited the head of an American corporation.

In other words, by 1950, when Khrushchev moved in to work with the Molotovs, the Berias, the Malenkovs, he was very recognizably the Khrushchev we soon came to know. Between 1938, when he had left Moscow for Kiev, and 1950, when he returned, he had been transformed from the outstandingly able boss of a closed apparatus, the Moscow apparatus, taking his cue from a tyrant whom he abased himself to glorify, into a personality in his own right who was prepared to take risks of a strictly calculated kind in order to impress that personality on a far wider public than any of his colleagues dared appeal to. It is not too much, I think, to say that at this stage he understood that the man who had the best chance of succeeding Stalin was the man who could establish himself as a human being of a certain boldness and a certain independence of mind, a man who had broken out of the tight, self-regarding circle of the higher Party leadership and could go among the people and show a certain awareness of the country's needs.

Malenkov was also a personality in his own right and he too possessed some awareness of the country's needs, as was shown by his behaviour immediately after Stalin's death. But, though possessed of a keener mind than Khrushchev, he made what we can now see to be the mistake of relying absolutely on his control of the levers of power within the closed circle of the ruling class—which, admittedly, he sought to extend beyond the professional Party apparatus by his patronage of the new industrial and managerial bureaucracy, exemplified by the leading figures, technocrats before they were Party members, of the great centralized production ministries. In a word, he sought to base his ascendancy on a continuation of precisely the sort of conspiratorial manœuvring which had brought him to the top under Stalin (and which had brought Khrushchev himself very close to the top in Moscow before 1938), not perceiving that there were other forces at work throughout the Soviet Union as a whole which would be bound to make themselves felt decisively once Stalin was removed from the scene.

These other forces, in very broad terms, were the product of a widespread and growing dissatisfaction on the part of all the ablest men in the land—industrialists, technocrats, soldiers, managers, the more intelligent Party functionaries, scientists, engineers, and the broader intelligentsia—with the pass to which Stalin had brought the country since 1945. The whole immense machine was in imminent danger of running itself into the ground. By brute force the Five Year Plan for national reconstruction was succeeding: the Soviet Union was being rebuilt. Nothing else was succeeding. Stalin, in decay, had not only lost all creative force; he was persecuting with paranoiac savagery all those who in their work and their ideas dared show the least glimmer of creative force.

The Soviet people, having come of age in the crucible of war, were being treated as prisoners in a vast slave camp, and Beria, Stalin's agent, was the chief warder. Repression and arbitrary violence carried to lunatic lengths had worked—though at the cost of great suffering, great inefficiency, great waste, great distortions of the fabric of society—while the Soviet Union had been intent on creating at all costs the crude foundations of her industrial and military might, very much as the cruelties and savagery of the English industrial revolution had worked a hundred years before in the era of the enclosures, child labour, starvation wages, and the "dark satanic mills." They could work no longer. The very machine which Stalin in his brutal way had fashioned required for its servicing and development a labour force reasonably intelligent, reasonably nourished, reasonably hopeful, organized by ambitious, able, and skilful men who could put their hearts into their work and use their initiative and brains without the almost certain knowledge that they would be shot, or at least sent to Siberia, as a result of the least exercise of individual judgment.

Malenkov saw this and Khrushchev saw it; but Malenkov decided to base his concealed appeal too narrowly, to the men in industry and technology who had already reached the top and, as such, were themselves suspect. He was now beginning to favour them at the expense of the Party functionaries, corrupt and useless, whom he thought he held, as their master, in the hollow of his hand. Let the Party bureaucracy do what it was told and go on being corrupt; the industrialists, the engineers, given their heads, would provide the required dynamic when the time came to release it.

Khrushchev, wrinkling his little eyes and seeing into the future in his queer instinctive way, knew that this was not enough. Like Malenkov, like all his colleagues from Molotov and Beria downwards, he knew very well that there could be no immediate appeal to the Russian people as such, whose traditional alienation from their government, an alienation which also appealed to their deepest instincts of self-preservation, had been sharpened immeasurably by Stalin's personal methods of rule. But, unlike Malenkov, he understood that between the official managers entrenched in their swollen ministries and the mass of the Russian people there was in the making a vast new class of some millions who were seeking forms of self-fulfilment. These, under Stalin, occupied a sort of limbo, but they themselves by the nature of their work (let us call them for short a new bourgeoisie) were no less cut off from the people than their masters and would thus be driven, willy-nilly, to cooperating with any government which permitted itself to invite their cooperation.

Khrushchev's first dramatic flourish in the dangerous field of agriculture was intended to call the attention of all these to the existence of a man who could generate practical ideas of his own, a dynamic figure standing out miraculously from the faceless chieftains united in a defensive and offensive conspiracy against the people over whom they ruled.

CHAPTER FIFTEEN

Stalin's End; Malenkov's Challenge

KHRUSHCHEV'S choice of agriculture as his first field of operations was, as we have seen, a risky one; but risks had to be accepted. His plan for agriculture was, in the circumstances, inspired. Stalin was driving the industrial economy to destruction. He had succeeded, in return for little concrete gain, in raising the outside world in arms against him. He had reduced the Soviet people to the level of prisoners in one vast labour camp. The only exceptions were those engineers and physicists working on nuclear physics and the problems of rocket-propulsion, and these, paradoxically, forming highly privileged enclaves living comfortably and given their heads in a scientific world otherwise dominated by Lysenko figures, were the personal responsibility of—of all people—Beria. Stalin doodled dreams of immense and grandiose schemes to transform nature by diverting great rivers, by planting millions of acres of forest belts in the arid steppe, by inaugurating irrigation schemes calculated to pay off in fifty years if they did not bankrupt the country first—all at a time when the existing farmlands, neglected and decayed, could not produce enough bread to carry Russia through from day to day. But he was aware, even though he never left Moscow except in armoured cars or armoured trains, that agriculture was, to put it mildly, stagnant, and he was ready to try for a breakthrough, provided it did not cost money. Khrushchev provided the plan for just such a breakthrough, which had about it the sort of megalomaniac grandeur which was calculated to appeal to Stalin as the man who could transform nature. And it cost nothing at all.

The first part of the plan, which was carried through, was the amalgamation of thousands of small collectives to make fewer large ones. This was a logical extension of the change-over from Andreyev's system of cultivations by small groups, or "links," to the more impersonal "brigade system," already tried in the Ukraine. The campaign was conducted and publicized by Khrushchev personally in a manner unprecedented. By June 1950 he triumphantly announced that the number of collectives in Moscow province, where he started operations, had been reduced from 6069 to 1668, and the process spread throughout the length and breadth of the Soviet Union.

This was a reasonable movement, except that, as always thereafter, Khrushchev went too far. Except on the rich black earth of the Ukraine, many of the collectives had indeed been too small to produce the best results in the most economical manner. Khrushchev himself gave some extremely revealing figures about the size of the farms in Moscow province. Over a quarter of the collectives, he said, owned less than 250 acres; 40 per cent had between 250 and 500 acres. Only 16 per cent had more than 750 acres. Even more startling and to the point, in the course of his argument he let fall the remark that on the smallest collective farms (i.e., below the 250 acres) there were "not more than 10 to 15 able-bodied workers." [1] This is one of the key figures to an appreciation of Soviet agriculture: in England a 250-acre farm, producing four or five times more per acre than one in the Soviet Union, would be run by the farmer himself and 2 able-bodied workers, 3 at most. The smallest collective in the USSR in 1950 was run by a "chairman," who did no field-work at all, helped by an accountant, also chairborne. Besides these there would be 10 to 15 workers. Even then, what machinery there was would be worked and serviced by tractor-drivers and mechanics from the neighbouring Machine Tractor Station. There was indeed room for rationalization.

A digression about Soviet farming is necessary if only because in years to come Khrushchev was to stake his reputation on a revolution in Soviet farming methods: in the days of his ascendancy he was to make more speeches to farmers and about farmers than about all other interests put together. Year in, year out, he was to instruct the peasants with obsessional detail—and to bully and harry and break the responsible officials, from the highest to the lowest, without cease. He started off in 1950 by taking the first step towards rationalization that had been taken by anybody since the collectivization twenty years earlier.

The important point about the collectivization was that it did nothing to bring Soviet agriculture into the twentieth century. Propaganda in the thirties, particularly films showing deliriously happy peasants careering about in their new tractors over the vast rolling fields of the black-earth zone, produced the impression in the West that the ordinary collective farm was a balanced, highly mechanized unit worked in the names of Lenin and Stalin by a peasantry which had miraculously freed itself from its immemorial bondage to the earth. Reality was very different.

Before the Revolution, and after the liberation of the serfs in 1861, the big estates of the landowners—some enlightened and experimental, most not—had produced the bulk of the cash crops, the food for the towns. The peasants themselves, grouped together in their primitive villages, either hired themselves out as labourers to the great landowners or to their more enterprising or grasping neighbours, or worked their own inadequate holdings for a meagre subsistence—as Khrushchev's father had worked. It was part of Lenin's programme that these same peasants should seize the possessions of the landlords and divide them up among themselves. This was to ensure that the peasantry, in 1917 four-fifths of the total population, would range themselves on the side of the Bolsheviks, until such time as Lenin and his friends were ready to bring them under control. They got on so well that by 1928 the Soviet Union was producing more food than Tsarist Russia had produced before 1914.

The collectivization, when it came, in no way altered the physical appearance of the countryside. The most able, enterprising, or grasping peasants, as we have seen, were forcibly dispossessed and shot or deported to Siberia. In the more prosperous areas innumerable villages were burned out and left derelict. But in those villages that remained, the feebler and poorer peasants went on living as they had always lived, in their wooden or mud houses lining both sides of a long, very broad, deeply rutted village street. But now the land they had won in 1917 was taken from them, pooled, assumed by the state, and given back on statutory conditions as a block to the inhabitants of the village as a block, to be worked by them as a block, under a chairman, or manager, appointed by the state. Each householder, each member of the collective, was granted a small plot of land, usually adjoining his dwelling, which he might in his spare time cultivate for his own sustenance. The size of the plot varied from time to time, as did the number of cows or pigs the individual might keep, as did the conditions under which he might sell the surplus produce on the open market at free prices. Spare time was time over and above the obligatory norm of "work-days" spent on the collective land. As for the produce from the collective land, the state had first claim, demanding for artificially low prices a quota of grain and other produce, which usually swallowed up, often exceeded, the whole produce of the collective. The three fundamental points were that there was no magic about a collective farm: except in the richest regions it consisted of a street of huts, with the land which had once belonged to the individual owners of those huts. The land was worked collectively under a chairman, or manager. And compulsory deliveries to the state at less than cost made it impossible for the average farm to make enough either to reward its members adequately or to build up funds for investment in farm buildings, livestock, fertilizers, and so on.

When in 1950 Khrushchev undertook to enlarge the collectives by amalgamation he was doing a number of things simultaneously. He was breaking up the old village societies by throwing a number of villages together to work a single farm. He was reducing the number of chairmen, or managers, and seeking to create a situation in which one efficient manager could do the work of half a dozen or a dozen inferior ones. He was throwing fields together so that they could be more conveniently worked by modern machinery—but there was next to no modern machinery, except on the great Ukrainian farms and in the cotton fields of Soviet Central Asia. He was creating units large enough to support trained technical advisers, agronomists and so on. All this was splendid in theory, but the units, having been too small, were now too large. Six thousand acres as a unit is too large to be managed in detail by any individual, unless in the simplest style of prairie farming; in England, on the big farms of East Anglia and Lincolnshire, it is customary to break up a 5000-acre holding into separate 1000-acre blocks for management purposes; and there the managers are highly trained, with a long tradition of first-class farming behind them. The Russians who could efficiently manage 1000 acres were few and far between. Six thousand acres were altogether beyond their powers. They had also to deal with a backward, hostile, obscurantist, illiterate, drunken, and superstitious peasantry.[2]

Khrushchev knew about the peasantry, none better. He was born one of them. He had lived among them in his early days as a district Party secretary. And they had not much changed since then—unless for the worse. For the worse, because the best of them had been wiped out during the collectivization, and the best of the survivors and their children had been either drawn into the towns or killed in war. Those that remained—and it was the able-bodied women who still, in 1950, bore the brunt of the work—had no incentive to work for the collective and, unless they lived within fifty miles of a town, no incentive to work even on their private plots to produce a surplus. They had to be educated and they had to be ordered about. It was hard either to educate them or to order them about when they were scattered in small and primitive village groups.

The real Khrushchev dream was the *agrogorod,* the agro-town. In the Soviet illustrated magazines highly coloured drawings appeared showing smiling garden cities, like model towns, blossoming in the illimitable steppe. These cities had everything —swimming pools, cinemas, theatres, lecture halls, schools, restaurants, municipal offices, and modestly splendid apartment blocks, set among trees. These cities were to house the peasants of the future, and the peasants of the future were not to be peasants at all, they were to be skilled agrarian workers, no different in mentality from their cousins in the factories, forming a new agrarian working class which simply worked in the fields instead of at the bench. They would be conveyed to the fields in public transport, do their stint in highly organized brigades, and return at dusk to take off their muddy boots, wash themselves down, put on clean shirts, and pass the evening watching television, attending evening classes, cinemas, amateur dramatics, and so on— enjoying, in a word, the sort of civilized evening which was not then available even to the most favoured factory hands. These agro-towns dotting the steppes and the forest had, as presented in *Ogonyek* and other publications, the air of a Wellsian Utopia. It was impossible for the outsider to imagine what Khrushchev was up to, for the agro-towns were presented as Khrushchev's, not Stalin's, personal conception; none of Stalin's closest colleagues had ever been allowed to publicize a personal dream before. Today, knowing far more about Khrushchev than we knew then, it is possible to see what he was up to.

He was flattering Stalin and getting in his good books by dreaming up the sort of wholly unreal scheme that Stalin himself in those days was personally fathering. He was also appealing to Stalin's obsession with regimentation: the factory workers had always been easier to control than the peasants, if only because they were concentrated under the eyes of strong forces of police and Party functionaries and depended wholly on the state for their wages and means of subsistence. The uprooting of the peasants from their immemorial villages and their concentration in agro-towns, where there would be no question of their retaining their private plots, their two acres and a cow, where family and village ties would be destroyed forever, would achieve the same effect. The industrialization of farming techniques would, given adequate investment in machines, farm buildings, stock-breeding, and fertilizers, lead to efficiency in the production of food. All this would have gone down well with Stalin in those closing years of his life. He knew, as Khrushchev knew, that the descriptions and "artist's projections" were nothing but the blueprints of a utopian dream. There was no conceivable possibility of achieving anything faintly resembling the agro-town scheme to replace the rotting and broken-down villages of the great Russian plain. But as far as Khrushchev was concerned it made a splendid talking-point, and it publicized Khrushchev as a man of far horizons to millions who had never heard of him, to hundreds of thousands of able officials frustrated by the negatives of Stalin. Malenkov, no doubt, gladly permitted this publicity: Comrade Khrushchev was sticking his neck out; soon he was due for a fall. But, by some rare instinct, Khrushchev knew what Malenkov and his colleagues did not know: that any publicity is better in the long run than no publicity. He had established himself as the only man in the country besides Stalin who could act, apparently, on his own initiative and get away with it. He had also sown the seed of an idea, which was to recur again and again after his enlargement and flower briefly in the spectacular opening of the Virgin Lands in 1954.

The agro-town scheme, of course, soon came to grief. All through the summer of 1950 Khrushchev hammered away at it. In June he demanded the start of a pilot scheme in Moscow province. But the pilot scheme had no relation to the tuppence-coloured dream. By the spring of 1951, he said, collective farmers must themselves "take the necessary measures" to move from their small villages to quite new sites where "large, comfortable houses will be gradually constructed later." [3] He did not say how the uprooted families, their traditional homes abandoned, were to live on their bare new sites until these new houses were "gradually constructed later." In fact there were a few trials, and what happened was that the unfortunate guinea pigs were expected to pay for their own moves and put up temporary huts for themselves, using their own labour, their own resources, and their own material.

This experiment produced a predictable reaction. Early in 1951 there appeared an article in *Izvestia* signed by the chairman of one of the guinea-pig collectives, who bitterly complained of the hardships caused by the Khrushchev new deal. What this amounted to in practice, he said, was that 112 households were uprooted from 4 villages and moved, at their own cost, to a fifth, where they had to build their own huts—nothing else.[4] The same sort of thing had been going on elsewhere, but the *Izvestia* article was a signal for high-level attack. A month later *Pravda*, over which Khrushchev had some control as a

Party secretary, *Socialist Agriculture,* which, as agricultural
overlord, he could control, and *Moscow Pravda,* which was effectively his own organ, as he was the Moscow Party chieftain, published a definitive article signed by Khrushchev "On Construction and Organization of Public Services on Collective
Farms." [5] Next day all three papers carried an "Editor's Note,"
saying that there should have been a footnote beneath Comrade
Khrushchev's article explaining that his schemes were "open for
discussion." After that there was no more mention in any newspaper of the whole affair. But soon it was under public attack
from certain lesser Party functionaries, and at the end of 1952,
at the Nineteenth Party Congress, Malenkov himself sharply denounced the whole conception. But that was part of another
struggle. In the interval Khrushchev had changed his employment. No announcement was made, but he faded out of the agricultural picture and began to emerge as a Party organizer. A
very interesting situation indeed was in the making.

[2.]

Stalin's main objects during the last three years of his life, until
in December 1952 he finally went off his head, were to curb
Malenkov while nevertheless presenting him as his most obvious
successor—up to a point—and also to reduce the enormous personal power wielded by Beria, without wrecking his indispensable police apparatus. Both Malenkov and Khrushchev had to be
strengthened *vis à vis* Beria, and Khrushchev was used at the
same time as the counterweight to Malenkov. Another man who
had his part to play in this complicated manoeuvre was Bulganin, nominally responsible for the armed forces and brought
forward into unexpected prominence in November 1950, when
he delivered the annual "State of the Union" address in the Bol-
shoi Theatre on the eve of the thirty-third anniversary of the
Bolshevik Revolution. Beria was being quietly undermined by
the purging of certain of his key men, notably Abakumov, Minister of State Security, who was replaced in 1951 by S. D. Ignatiev.

Malenkov's situation was more complicated. For a long time

he had run the Party more or less as he liked. As a member of the Politburo and the Party Secretariat and as Chairman of the Org-buro he was strategically placed to control everything that went on. But although he had packed the Party with his yes-men he had neglected it as a living force. For a long time he had shown a dangerous contempt for the Party bureaucracy, which consisted too largely of corrupt place-seekers and doctrinaire dead-beats. He had been showing an ever-growing interest instead in quite a new set of people, the gifted industrial managers and techno-crats on whom the economy of the country depended, and whose contempt for the Party *apparatchiki* was absolute. Most of these, of course, were nominal Communists; they had to be for the sake of their careers; but they were like those Western Chris-tians who maintain their stake in the next world by attending Church at Christmas and Easter and having their infants bap-tized. Malenkov saw that the future belonged to these men, and, in general, he was right. As Deputy Prime Minister concerned with production ministries, while running the ordinary Party bureaucracy with one hand, he worked hard with the other to bring into the higher councils of the Central Committee some of these apolitical figures, each of whom was worth a thousand Party functionaries. What he was doing, in effect, was manœu-vring to regenerate the highest level of the Party, while using the bulk of the Party—for which he was right to feel contempt —as a docile instrument.

Did he blame himself for the degeneration of the Party? He should have done so. It had become corrupt and horrible be-cause Stalin with his endless purges had killed so many of the decent individuals in it; but he, Malenkov, working with the political police, had acted as Stalin's main instrument.

Now in 1951 and 1952 Khrushchev—almost certainly in alli-ance with Mikoyan, who was interested only in efficiency, and the comparative newcomer to the Party Secretariat, Mikhail Sus-lov (who really believed in the Party, in which he had laboured more or less obscurely for decades, as an ideological force), and with Bulganin as well, who knew all about the hatred and con-tempt of the military higher command for the Party, which sim-ply got in its way—managed to persuade Stalin that something had to be done. The Party, Malenkov's special preserve, had to be sorted out, purified, rejuvenated, reorganized, and he, Khrushchev, with his healthy Ukrainian background, uncontaminated by the Moscow rat-race, was the man to do it. From now on it was war to the knife with Malenkov, who had to cooperate with Khrushchev and pretend to like it. It was also a very nasty blow at Malenkov, who could not escape responsibility for the scandalous state of affairs—all the more because he himself had rather demonstratively on more than one occasion spoken out against Party corruption, declaring that there were better Bolsheviks outside the Party than many who were in it. What had he done, besides sponsoring half a dozen outstandingly able operators in industry, to ensure that these "better Bolsheviks," non-Party men, were brought into the fold and the corrupt and inefficient thrown out?

All through 1952, with very little personal display on Khrushchev's part (he was now at the core of the machine and did not need display), the preparations for a major Party purge went on. And in October 1952, at the Nineteenth Party Congress, delayed for so many years (there should have been a Congress every three or four years; Stalin had preferred to rule without calling one since 1939), he appeared publicly on a level with Malenkov, as the key figure. Malenkov delivered the formal report; Khrushchev gave a special report on the Party reorganization. The struggle between the two men, one a most familiar figure, the other only recently emerged from the obscurity of the Ukraine, blunt and comparatively uncouth, was now conducted on the platform under the gaze of the whole world, which did not understand what it saw. Even as he had to welcome Khrushchev as the man who was rejuvenating the Party which he had controlled for so long, even as he had to join in Khrushchev's violent attacks on corruption, idleness, nepotism, and general decay, Malenkov managed to get in a vicious jab at his dear colleague by condemning out of hand those agricultural policies sponsored by "certain of our leading officials" which were Khrushchev's own: "The mistake these comrades made was that they overlooked the major task of the collective farms—the business of production." [6]

Stalin was amusing himself. The Nineteenth Party Congress was physically dominated by Malenkov, generally thought of as the heir presumptive, and Khrushchev, for the first time publicly presented as the counterweight to Malenkov. But from the beginning Stalin himself overshadowed the stage, and at the end he produced a *coup de théâtre* of a formidable and sinister kind.

Everybody now knew that he was old and was not up to the strain of speaking at length. He did speak, but briefly and perfunctorily. His great contribution was a document of imposing size which had been presented to the Congress delegates for consideration on the eve of the Congress: a long theoretical disquisition which was, in effect, a progress report on the advance towards Communism, on the Soviet Union's relations with the capitalist world, and on methods to be used on the last stages of the journey from socialism to Communism. Stalin's "Economic Theses," as the document was called, were to form the basis of the thinking of the Congress, and they did in fact contain a few new ideas—enough to show that Stalin himself was at last beginning to acknowledge the facts of life in the new technological and nuclear age. His most important contribution, which the world never acknowledged, because the "Theses" were almost immediately overshadowed by more spectacular happenings, was the tortuously arrived at, tortuously expressed, pedantically qualified sidestepping of Lenin's cheerful notion that so long as capitalism existed wars were inevitable and to be welcomed, since only as a result of wars could the proper conditions for the spread of world revolution be created. This had been a fundamental part of the Leninist canon, to which Stalin had clung stubbornly eight years after the advent of the atomic bomb had made nonsense of it—with unhappy consequences to the Soviet economy and to Soviet strategy in Europe. Stalin would not abandon it wholly even now: wars were still inevitable, he declared, but with good luck and good judgment the Soviet Union would be able to keep out of them, leaving the capitalist powers to tear each other to pieces in their fight for markets.

On the last day of the Congress everything Stalin had said in his famous "Theses" was overlaid and forgotten in the excitement, speculation, and alarm produced by a dramatic reshaping

Nikita S. Khrushchev.

(For photo credits see the list of illustrations, page vi.)

Above: Stalin and Khrushchev in 1936. *Below:* May Day, 1937. Left to right: Shvernik, Khrushchev, Dmitrov, Stalin, Molotov, Mikoyan.

Above: Khrushchev talking with young miners from Donbas at a Stakhano-vite rally near Moscow in 1936.

Above: General Timoshenko and Khrushchev at a Party rally in Kiev in 1938.
Below: As leader of the Ukraine Communist Party, Khrushchev visits construction workers in Moscow in 1938.

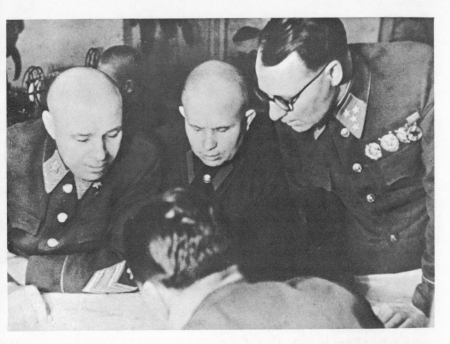

Above: Khrushchev with Marshal Timoshenko (at left) and another Red Army general at headquarters of the South-Western front in 1942. *Below:* With a woman who had been bombed out at Stalingrad in 1942.

Above: Khrushchev talking with the liberated people of Kiev in November 1943. *Below:* Conferring with Marshal Konev (at left) at a command post on the Ukraine front in June 1944.

Above: Khrushchev with Prime Minister Malenkov (at left) at the Lenin memorial meeting in 1954. *Below:* With Prime Minister Bulganin, who replaced Malenkov, during the visit to England in 1956.

Khrushchev with Marshal Tito on his first visit to Belgrade, in 1955.

Geneva, 1955. Khrushchev, Zhukov, and Bulganin.

Above: May Day, 1957. Left to right: Zhukov, Khrushchev, Bulganin, Kaganovich, Malenkov, Molotov, Mikoyan. *Below:* Khrushchev with Mao Tse-tung at the Kremlin in 1957.

Below, left: Khrushchev with novelist Mikhail A. Sholokhov. *Below, right:* Greeting British Prime Minister Harold Macmillan on his arrival in Moscow in February 1959.

United Nations, 1960. Khrushchev, Gromyko, and Zorin pound the table in disapproval.

Above: Khrushchev with General Charles de Gaulle in Paris in 1960. *Below:* With Cuban President Fidel Castro at the United Nations in 1960.

Khrushchev with President John F. Kennedy at Vienna in 1961.

Above: Madame Nina Khrushchev. *Below:* Khrushchev at a collective farm in 1963.

Khrushchev in Yugoslavia in 1963. *Above:* At play (Marshal Tito in dark glasses). *Below:* With shipyard workers at Split.

of the superior echelons of the Soviet Communist Party—no longer to be called Bolshevik. At the very moment when Malenkov and Khrushchev were enjoying their disputed triumph, both were reduced in a most extraordinary way.

For decades, as we know, the Soviet Party had been ruled by Stalin, operating through the small Politburo and the Party Secretariat, consisting of about a dozen and half a dozen men respectively. These men loomed very large, so large that some of them at times seemed to wield scarcely less power than Stalin himself; and, because in recent years the effective Politburo had been even smaller than the official list suggested, the obvious deduction was that Stalin had been engaged in short-listing his possible successors. Suddenly all this was changed. The Politburo, renamed the Party Presidium, was suddenly enlarged from a total of eleven to twenty-five full members and eleven candidates. The Secretariat was pushed up from five to ten members. What had been a tiny ruling body with most of its members very close to Stalin was transformed overnight into an unwieldy and absurd committee of thirty-six, named, under Stalin, in alphabetical order, so that untried newcomers found themselves elevated to stand, to all appearances, on a level with the most senior Party chieftains in the land. The only comfort for Malenkov was that his own protégés formed the majority of the new intake; but Khrushchev too had been able to recommend a handful of his own most loyal supporters. There were others who owed nothing either to Malenkov or to Khrushchev. Between them, on the face of it, they made a queer, self-cancelling mixture, with Stalin demonstrably supreme, in a class entirely of his own. The old pattern of power was shattered: out of this melting-pot—there is no other name for it—a new pattern must inevitably emerge.

And soon it began to be clear that it would be a very new pattern indeed. We do not know now, we may never know, precisely what Stalin intended. All we know is that in breaking up the old pattern, in reducing the value of every single member of the supreme Party bodies, in bringing comparative outsiders so suddenly into the centre, Stalin was taking the first step towards the physical extermination of the majority of his oldest and most faithful supporters. Andreyev was completely dropped from the new Presidium. Beria was already weakened by the blood purges which had been organized to destroy his own apparatus in Georgia and elsewhere. On January 13, three months after the Party Congress, the public action started with the announcement to a fascinated world, to an appalled and terror-struck Russia, that the organs of state security had uncovered a plot organized by "a terrorist group of physicians," nine in all, seven of them Jews, who, working hand in hand with Zionist organizations and the American Secret Service, had successfully murdered Zhdanov and Shcherbakov (before his death during the war considered, with Zhdanov, as being a likely successor to Stalin) and tried to murder a number of Army leaders, including the distinguished Marshals Vassilevsky, Govorov, and Koniev. The doctors had all been leading specialists retained to care for the Party leadership. According to Khrushchev, three years later, one had been put in chains on Stalin's personal instructions, all had been beaten to make them confess. Two died under torture.[7]

Before this action there had been a Plenum of the Central Committee, of which the world knew nothing, at which Stalin had spoken and in vague terms threatened Molotov and Mikoyan. At the same time, also according to Khrushchev, he had "toyed with the idea" that his old drinking companion, one time commander-in-chief of the Red Army, Voroshilov, had been an English agent. "It's true—an English agent! A special tapping device was installed in his home to listen to what was said there."[8]

Again: "It is not excluded that had Stalin remained at the helm for several months more, Comrades Molotov and Mikoyan would probably not have delivered any speeches at this Congress."

"Stalin evidently had plans to finish off the old members of the Politburo." Beria and Kaganovich would certainly have gone too, perhaps others. Malenkov himself was clearly operating at this time hand in glove with Beria. But the only certain thing is that Stalin, whether because he had finally gone off his head, or because he justly feared a conspiracy against him among his oldest colleagues, was preparing, in an atmosphere of terror (the newspapers and radio were shrieking, "Vigilance! Beware spies!" at the top of their voices for weeks on end), to break the old pattern finally by judicial murder and to substitute a new subordinate hierarchy to carry out his will. Fearful things were going on behind the scenes, as the "trial" of the doctors was prepared by the extraction of confessions under torture and the arrest and liquidation of unknown thousands. On February 17 *Izvestia* recorded the sudden death of the chief of Kremlin Security, Major General Kosynkin. On March 3 it was announced that Stalin himself was critically ill. His death was announced at 6 a.m. on March 6.

Muscovites awoke to find the city completely sealed off by Beria's MVD troops with tanks and flame-throwers. The commander of Moscow Military District and the commandants of the Moscow city garrison and of the Kremlin guards were put under arrest. Early in the morning Stalin's heirs, crowded together in the Kremlin behind Beria's guards, issued their communiqué, which closed with the appeal that there should be "no panic and disarray." [9] By the time the day was over these men had announced the succession and shattered at a blow the hierarchy so carefully established by their late master only three months earlier. Five members of the Secretariat were sacked. The thirty-six-man Presidium was brought down to fourteen. Government ministries were reduced from fifty-two to twenty-five. A compact new body faced the future, with Malenkov as Prime Minister over four First Deputy Prime Ministers (Beria, Molotov, Bulganin, and Kaganovich). To please the Army, Marshal Zhukov was brought back from the limbo to which Stalin had consigned him (for being too popular) and installed as joint Deputy Minister of Defence, under Bulganin, with Marshal Vassilievsky. The new Secretariat consisted of Malenkov, Khrushchev, Suslov, Pospelov, Shatalin, and Ignatiev, in that order. Two of the men who had been exalted by Stalin, one of them a Khrushchev man, the other not, and now cast out by Malenkov, were Brezhnev and Kosygin, who were later to come back more strongly than before.

Taking all these circumstances together, it is not surprising that many Russians still believe that Stalin was murdered and that Malenkov and Beria, perhaps others, but not Khrushchev, for obvious reasons, had a hand in it. When tyrants die in Russia, especially on the eve of a new outbreak of atrocity, people's minds naturally spring to murder as the most likely explanation. Stalin was a murderer. Trotsky, a Russian, accused him of poisoning Lenin as the most natural thing in the world. Stalin's closest colleagues were soon to murder Beria when he had ceased to be useful to them. We do not know. If Stalin died a natural death, then Providence was very kind to certain of his successors.

[3.]

Khrushchev now, and for some time afterwards, played a waiting game. He took no public initiatives. He was well inside the inner circle as it presented itself to the waiting world. He was a member of the new Presidium, which, like the new Secretariat, had a definite order of seniority—Malenkov, Beria, Molotov, Voroshilov, Khrushchev, Bulganin, Kaganovich, Mikoyan, Saburov, Pervukhin. Beria had moved up to number two, still hand in glove with Malenkov (his troops had been essential for the execution of the coup—there is no other word for the destruction of Stalin's Presidium). Saburov and Pervukhin, technocrats first, were Malenkov's own protégés. All Khrushchev's protégés had gone but not all his friends. And he was still powerful in the reduced Secretariat. The Council of Ministers was packed with Malenkov men, and it was at once clear that Malenkov had decided to repose his main strength on the state government, which ran the production ministries, the Executive, consisting largely of the most able and often apolitical individuals, as opposed to the Party. It looked quite a good idea. Russia was going to move away from repression by the Party bureaucracy and into the technological age, in which administrative and executive brains would at last begin to count. Khrushchev had no foot in this camp, but as second Party secretary after Malenkov he shared control over an immense and still indispensable machine which, if he handled it well, he could transform.

He handled things very well indeed. In the days of confusion immediately after Stalin's death he did not put himself forward. He was honoured by being given charge of Stalin's funeral arrangements. But he kept in the background. He did not speak at the funeral. Malenkov, Beria, and Molotov spoke. The only one of these three to show any human warmth was Molotov, who, though he had been Stalin's butt, had also been, very largely, Stalin's creator and must in his queer way have loved the atrocious old man and regarded with misgiving and contempt the pushings and the public posturings of his new superiors.

The Malenkov regime started off with some spirit. Malenkov had succeeded to both Stalin's positions: the Premiership and the First Secretaryship of the Party. There was no pretence about a collective leadership. He set out at once to establish his position as the true heir, the supreme leader. But within ten days all that had changed. Malenkov did not operate in a vacuum. He depended, for the time being at least, very much on the old stagers who surrounded him. And these old stagers were very certain in their minds that there was to be no successor to Stalin, no supreme boss, no second Stalin with the power of life and death over each and every one of them. They would play their parts and accept the seniority of a much younger man, presentable and outstandingly able, provided he was content to appear as first among equals, as chairman, in effect, of a committee, a collective. Otherwise they would not cooperate. And so they acted, and although Khrushchev kept in the shadows he was central to their action. There was to be a meeting of the Supreme Soviet, the constitutional rubber-stamp, on March 14, at which the new order was to be proclaimed. But at the last minute the meeting was postponed. Instead, the Party Central Committee was convened to hold a plenary session, and at this session Malenkov rose to say that because of his responsibilities as Prime Minister he wished to be relieved of his post as First Secretary of the Communist Party. His resignation was accepted, but no successor was announced. The Secretariat now consisted of five members instead of six, but Khrushchev was listed first. With him was still Ignatiev, who, as Minister of State Security, had been so active in purging Beria's men. There was no need, as far as Khrushchev was concerned, for a formal title. He had the Secretariat in his pocket, therefore the Party, for what it was worth. He could pack the Party at will. And he was now the only man to have a seat on both the Presidium and the Secretariat. Malenkov, cut off from the Party apparatus, had to rely more than ever on his government machine—and on members of that machine introduced into the Presidium.

For a long time Khrushchev held back. He left the running to Malenkov, and it was Malenkov who appeared, whether as the friend and colleague of Mao Tse-tung, whether as the man who was quietly undermining Stalin's reputation, whether as the initiator of new approaches to the West or of a relaxation of the tyranny at home. For a long time Khrushchev did not have a word to say. He worked away behind the scenes, purging the Party of Malenkov supporters, rejuvenating it in his own way by quietly inserting his own men, his "Ukrainians" above all, into key positions all over the land—not without opposition, not without great circumspection.

This went on all through the summer of 1953, while controls were loosened, writers and intellectuals, long silent, began to raise their voices, and Stalin, though never criticized, was quietly relegated to the background. In July the appearance of a fraternally united collective was shattered by the sudden arrest of Beria and his murder, long before his execution was officially announced. We do not know whether Malenkov joined with the comrades in liquidating Beria, or whether Beria's removal was part of a growing movement against Malenkov. We do not even know the circumstances of his death. Khrushchev told so many stories, some of them grisly, all of them revealing a bland failure to understand that foreigners might see something odd in members of a cabinet getting together to seize one of their colleagues, however dangerous, however evil, however overbearing, and shoot him on the spot, without impeachment, without trial—so many stories, to so many different groups of foreign Communists, that they are not worth paying attention to. All that mattered was that Khrushchev and many others benefited from the murder of Beria, so richly deserved. Malenkov did not.

It was in August that Khrushchev struck his first really damaging blow, though still with public discretion. He felt strong enough to fire the Secretary of the Armenian Communist Party, Arutinov, the man who had dared make the first attack on his agricultural schemes. This could not have been done without the agreement of Mikoyan, who all through the Stalin terror had cherished his own native republic and seen that at least in Erevan the people did not starve. In September Khrushchev came out into the open. It was announced that he had assumed the formal title of First Secretary of the Party. And his first act was the seizure of Leningrad by the sacking of Malenkov's most favoured protégé, who himself had succeeded Zhdanov—Andrianov. But Malenkov was still strong enough for some time to make the government, as opposed to the Party, appear as the senior organ in the promulgation of all decrees.

It was a queer situation. All over Russia philosophers, scientists of every kind, artists of every kind, were rising, and being encouraged to rise, in revolt against the dead hand of Party obscurantists. All over the country all kinds of workers, from engineers to peasants, were being wooed with concessions. And all those who were fighting for more freedom saw Malenkov as their hope. The Party press, controlled now by Khrushchev, hit back. In those days of conflict with Malenkov, Khrushchev was unable to appear as a liberalizer. Malenkov was making the running here, and he could not be outbid. All Khrushchev could do was exalt the claims of a Party which was being purified and returned to Leninist ways. The purification meant the substitution of Khrushchev supporters for Malenkov supporters; the return to Leninist ways was intended as encouragement to all those revolted by the behaviour of the Party hitherto and all those who were inclined to see in Malenkov's concessions a too glib opportunism—and all those inside the Party who feared the Party's eclipse by Malenkov's state apparatus. Khrushchev had to go very carefully indeed. For the time being, in order to assert himself against Malenkov, he had to follow the unpopular course, the hard line at home and abroad. Especially at home.

In August, Malenkov had formally presented his new course of amelioration and reform. It was announced in a way unprecedented to the Supreme Soviet, without previous reference to the Central Committee of the Communist Party. It concentrated on the rapid development of "the light and food industries at the same rate as heavy industry," thus marking a dramatic and ardently desired break with the twenty-five-year-old concentration on heavy industry at all costs. Hand in hand with this went cuts in taxes and prices, designed to rally the masses of workers and peasants. This was Malenkov's supreme bid. Since it was a direct appeal, over the heads of the Party, to the people, it should have succeeded. It failed. Khrushchev was now strong enough to know that he had not only the backing of the Party as a whole, but also the backing of his colleagues in the Presidium and the Secretariat, the Army too; some saw Malenkov acting the demagogue in a bid for supreme power, which they were prepared to concede to nobody; others were more concerned with his deliberate attempt to undermine the authority of the Party, which included them; others genuinely believed that the Soviet Union could not afford more relaxation, could not afford to "raise sharply in two or three years the population's supply of foodstuffs and manufactured goods, meat and meat produce, fish and fish products, butter, sugar, eggs, confectionery, textiles, clothes, footwear, crockery, furniture and other cultural and household goods." [10] To this level had the pretender to leadership of 200 million people in the world's most advanced society been reduced in his appeal for confidence.

Khrushchev knew as well as anybody else that Malenkov was right in principle: if Russia was not to stagnate, Party and government *must,* in the quickest possible time, raise the abysmal standard of living and give the intelligent and enterprising their heads—always within limits. But this was to be done not by Malenkov but by Khrushchev himself. How to cut the ground from under the feet of the man who was making the running?

[4.]

He began with his first major speech in September 1953, and that speech was about agriculture. [11] Malenkov had said earlier that Soviet agriculture had turned the corner, was running on the right lines, and could supply what was needed. Khrushchev had another story, much nearer the truth. There was enough bread, he said, and there would be no shortage of bread grains. But there were intolerable shortages of everything else. For the first time the facts about agricultural production long known to Western experts, long concealed behind bogus statistics, were officially admitted to Russia and the world. As an example, not only were there 3.5 million fewer cattle than there had been on the eve of the war, and 8.9 million head fewer than there had been in 1928, twenty-five years earlier, on the eve of the collectivization, but there had also been a drop of 2.1 million head of all livestock during 1952; this, of course, was Stalin's last year, when Khrushchev had retired from the agricultural scene. All the same, although he gave a fairly hopeless picture, admitting failures which had never been admitted before, and although he put the catastrophic and scandalous state of Russian food production in perspective for the first time since it had collapsed in 1929, Khrushchev had only exhortations to offer. At no point in his speech did he so much as begin to hint at the true reasons for the continued failure: the system itself. And the impact of even what he did say was weakened by the wildly optimistic light in which he projected the future. The chief aim of this speech, seen in retrospect (this was not evident to outsiders at the time) was twofold: to suggest that Malenkov in his earlier assessments of the situation had displayed complacency amounting to frivolity, and to paint the past and the present in the gloomiest terms so that any further improvement would be attributed to him, Khrushchev, personally. At that moment of time the world had no idea that Khrushchev was preparing to identify himself with Soviet agriculture and to stake his reputation on a dramatic improvement. But he had a plan, and this plan was to bring him into the limelight and keep him there.

The plan had nothing to do with the quiet encouragement of the peasants to pull their weight by the judicious use of incentives, as proposed by Malenkov; still less had it anything to do with a radical reassessment of the system. The former was too slow, the latter too revolutionary. In effect, Khrushchev decided that for the time being the old-established collectives must be written off as a theatre of swift improvement. Instead there was to be a complete and dramatic switch. The whole weight of agri-

cultural investment, such as it was, was to be concentrated behind the opening up of an area, much of which had never been
cultivated before—the so-called Virgin Lands of Kazakhstan
and southwestern Siberia.

The scheme was launched, and by Khrushchev personally, in
February 1954, at the end of a special emergency conference of
agricultural experts in Moscow. The purpose of the conference
was to underline that Soviet food production was in even worse
case than Khrushchev had said five months earlier, and to show
that nobody could offer a convincing solution of the problem—
nobody except Khrushchev. Khrushchev's solution was simplic-
ity itself, and at the same time spectacular and gigantic and sudden in the beloved Russian tradition. Nothing had been done
for twenty-five years; now everything was to be done at once.
The stored fertility of vast areas of untilled steppe, immemorial
grazing grounds for nomad cattle, was to be tapped and exploited in a colossal operation which could not fail. During 1954
over 6 million acres of this land were to be ploughed up, sown
down to spring wheat, and harvested. By the end of 1955 this
total was to be brought up to 32 million acres. In this operation
120,000 tractors were to be engaged and 10,000 combine har-
vesters; 250,000 "volunteers," mainly from the Komsomol, were
to be transported to these vast empty spaces, where there were
no houses, no farm buildings, no public services, to build themselves first primitive huts, then new villages and towns as they
worked. The acreage involved is hard to visualize. Thirty-two
million acres was more than three times the acreage under cultivation in the whole of the Soviet Union on the eve of the collectivization. It was equal to the combined cultivated areas of Britain, France, and Spain.

I have described elsewhere the mood in which this immense
campaign was carried out, the muddles and the hardships, the
suffering, of the scores of thousands set down in the middle of
the empty steppe and told to get on with it. But in spite of all
this, the scheme initially succeeded. The prophecies that the
Virgin Lands would be turned into a dustbowl, that much of the
acreage was too arid or too contaminated with salt to grow
wheat, turned out to be true up to a point. But the first limited

harvest of 1954 was a success, which was what Khrushchev immediately needed.

He was very much alone in this venture. Malenkov would have nothing to do with it. Later Khrushchev was to say that Mikoyan and others had also opposed it. In allowing him to put it forward in his own name, the collective no doubt felt that if it turned out to be a fiasco it would be Khrushchev's personal failure and he would pay. But Khrushchev felt otherwise. He had produced the solution; it was a solution, thus, sponsored by the Communist Party and by the Young Communist League (the Komsomol), which, under Shelepin, was providing the volunteers and, in the process, trying to whip up the sort of mood among the young which had not been seen since the early days of the Five Year Plans and the building of Magnitogorsk and Komsomolsk. But he intended to take no blame. The conception was his; the drive was his and the Party's. Any failures that happened would be due not to him, not to the Party, but to the government, Malenkov's government.

And indeed he was soon attacking the governmental ministries for obstruction, lack of foresight, lack of imagination. The Ministry of Agriculture was to blame for everything under the sun; the industrial ministries were to blame for not providing tractors, ploughs, combines, spare parts; the Ministry of Housing was to blame for lack of houses and building materials; the Ministry of Transport was to blame for failure to move machinery in time; other departments were to blame for inadequate piped water and electricity. Never once did he attack the Prime Minister, the Chairman of the Council of Ministers, Comrade Malenkov, personally: he simply went on and on about the individual ministries, all of them responsible to Malenkov. And he made it appear that at every turn the Party, keen and self-sacrificing and dynamic, was being frustrated and obstructed by the state bureaucracy, the source of all evil.

This year, 1954, was Khrushchev's great year. Having got himself into the centre of the limelight with the Virgin Lands campaign, he never moved out of it. Soon he was laying down the law, as First Secretary, on every aspect of Soviet policy. By the summer of 1954 he had vociferously toured the length and breadth of the Soviet Union, a human dynamo, talking endlessly in marathon public speeches, projecting himself as the practical, downright man who knew how to get things done, establishing the image which was to sustain him for the rest of his reign. He had gone outside Russia too, attending the Czech and Polish Party Congresses.

He had his ablest supporters firmly established, sometimes as key individuals, sometimes—as in the Ukraine and Kazakhstan—in great depth, in all the key Party posts, and in some important republican government posts as well. Shelepin was running the Komsomol. Madame Furtseva, with whom he had the closest personal ties, ran Moscow (her husband was soon sent abroad as Ambassador to Belgrade). Kozlov ran Leningrad. Shepilov, whom he was soon to make Foreign Minister, edited *Pravda*. In July he achieved a major coup by getting his atrocious old ally, Serov, made head of the new Committee of State Security: Serov was nominally responsible to the Council of Ministers—i.e., to Malenkov—but he was Khrushchev's man. He was even able to save from destruction the sinister Ignatiev, who should have been shot, with others who were, for playing the leading part in faking the notorious "doctors' plot": Ignatiev had to leave the Secretariat of the Central Committee, but he was given a decent job in the provinces—by Khrushchev. In July, Khrushchev started interfering in foreign affairs; he was now undermining Molotov. Career Foreign Office diplomats were replaced in half a dozen Communist countries, including China, by Khrushchev's Party officials, who were thus controlled not by the Foreign Office at all, but by the foreign-affairs section of the Central Committee, responsible to Khrushchev.

[5.]

His endless travelling about the Soviet Union was paying off. It had taken him into regions he had never visited before and where his character was unknown. The world heard all about his public speeches, in which he addressed himself to the lower echelons in mass audiences, bullying, cajoling, exhorting, explaining with obsessive detail how collective farmers should go about their cultivations. This created the public image. But his talks behind the scenes were even more to the point. There he addressed in private the Party workers and with his extraordinary persuasiveness and authority convinced them that he was the man to win. He was fighting the chairborne ministerial bureaucracy; he was fighting for Party rights, for the very careers of those who listened to him.

Malenkov sat in Moscow, apparently powerless to compete on his own ground with this tornado of a rival, who, with no consistency of purpose, dashed about the country, selling panacea after panacea like a glorified cheapjack. Malenkov had sat too long in offices, operating the levers of power in the name of Stalin. He was used to manipulation and intrigue, knowing that, if only he pleased Stalin, he had only a handful of men to outmanœuvre; he had never in his life had to compete, as it were, in the marketplace for popularity. He relied on reason and intelligence, backed by absolute power. Now his power was far from absolute, and reason and intelligence, the appeal to the sophisticated, were not enough. He had attracted to him, among the technocrats and industrial managers, some of the keenest brains in the country, but these were not enough either. He had treated the Party apparatus, the middle and lower echelons of it, with the contempt it deserved, but he had not realized the power of the vested interests in these men who were still indispensable to the management of the country and who, manifestly inferior to the managers and the makers, were desperately afraid of the growing power of these and were ready to rally round Khrushchev as the man who would defend and exalt them. They could be coerced by only one force, an all-powerful political police, and with the breaking of the power of Beria's police and the rehabilitations, the amnesties, the dissolution of the labour-camp economy, this force no longer existed.

Malenkov appealed to the technocrats and the intelligentsia through reason and moderation, to the peasants by bribes and concessions. But the technocracy and the intelligentsia did not represent an organized force, and the peasants did not care, any more than the mass of the workers, who among the indistinguishable row of bosses was top and who was not. They took their concessions, their bribes, grumbled because they were not larger, and cried a plague upon all Communists. The only coherent force, apart from the Army (apolitical) was the Party apparatus. Khrushchev knew how to woo it. The senior Army officers, who for the most part, detested the civilian leaders, as all soldiers detest politicians everywhere, had no particular love for Khrushchev. But they disliked Malenkov with particular intensity for his very active part in the great Army purge of 1937. More immediately, they were apprehensive about the new emphasis on consumer goods and services. They wanted guns and tanks and rockets—like so many generals, more guns, more tanks, more rockets than any of them would ever have the skill to deploy.

In any case, Malenkov's promises of an easier life, more consumer goods, more amenities, were almost impossible to fulfil. In the first place the food was not there. Khrushchev's Virgin Lands scheme, represented as a means to produce more food quickly, therefore a step up in the standard of living, actually worked the other way. The factories which should have been turning over to consumer goods had to turn out agricultural machinery instead. It was an ingenious exercise in sabotage on the part of our hero. Sabotage in this context may seem a strong word: it is justified.

In December of 1954 Khrushchev went to China on a supremely important mission. He was determined to win Mao Tsetung to his side. In person, he handed over to China the Port Arthur and the Chinese Eastern Railway. In person he negotiated an important agreement whereby Russia was to supply China with imposing supplies of capital goods—a commitment which finally put an end to the new course. This was an extraordinary occasion. This great mission, which should have been conducted between prime ministers on an interstate basis, was conducted between Party secretaries on an inter-Party basis. Malenkov stayed behind. More remarkable, too, so did the Foreign Minister, Molotov. Khrushchev took with him Bulganin as a Deputy Prime Minister and Mikoyan as the expert on trade. The argument was won.

Malenkov had not given in without a struggle. Until August

1954, just a year after the formal inauguration of the new course, he had been able to exercise a certain control over Khrushchev. As early as March 1954 he had received a public snubbing, being forced to retract his statement that atomic war would mean the end of civilization and to reassert the traditional line that it would mean only the end of capitalism. But he was still strong enough in July to cause *Pravda* to delete certain reckless statements about Soviet atomic superiority from an outstandingly bellicose speech delivered by Khrushchev in Prague.[12] By the autumn, however, Khrushchev was ready for the kill. The turning point was in mid-August, when a great extension of the Virgin Lands campaign was announced, and announced in a manner that showed that the Party had won formal as well as actual command of the government apparatus. For the first time since Stalin's death the Central Committee came before the Council of Ministers in the promulgation of a joint decree.[13] Less than a fortnight later *Pravda* in a leading article exhorted the Party organizations to intensify their supervisory activity in all government departments.

When Khrushchev returned from Peking in October things moved very fast indeed. Saburov, once a Malenkov man, in his speech on the eve of the anniversary of the October Revolution announced that heavy industry was the very cornerstone of the Soviet economy. A few days later Khrushchev issued his first personal decree, signed by himself alone (it was about the need to find more subtle ways of conducting anti-religious propaganda!). On December 23 a very deadly blow was struck at Malenkov by the report in *Pravda* of the trial and execution of Abakumov, ex-Minister of State Security, Malenkov's close collaborator in the past, for his part in the "Leningrad Affair," the purge of Zhdanov's supporters, which had been organized by Malenkov. On January 24, 1955, Khrushchev signed his second personal decree, a very symbolic one, changing the date of the memorial day for Lenin. Here he was showing his power, but in a matter which was hard to criticize; the Lenin anniversary was henceforth to be celebrated on the anniversary of Lenin's birth, not, as hitherto, his death—a sunny thought. Exactly a fortnight later Shepilov, editor of *Pravda*, wrote over his own name a resounding article demanding priority for heavy industry, and on that day Mikoyan, one of the most ardent and radical advocates of Malenkov's new course (he had wanted to import food and consumer goods to raise the standard of living quickly, and to learn and profit by Western trading methods), lost his job as Minister for Internal Trade. On January 25 Khrushchev himself told the Central Committee that certain "vulgarizers of Marxism" had been committing the heresy of putting consumer goods before heavy industry. Using the sort of language that had been out of fashion, in public at least, since Stalin's death he stigmatized this heresy as a right-wing deviation and compared its exponents with Rykov and Bukharin.[14]

On February 8, Malenkov ceased to be Prime Minister.

The occasion was a meeting of the Supreme Soviet, but all the members of the Central Committee Presidium were on the platform in the great Kremlin hall. Malenkov, the man whom Stalin had groomed for so long, sat there too and listened impassively while, to the shocked surprise of the 1300 delegates, the Chairman of the Supreme Soviet of the Union read out Malenkov's request to be allowed to resign. He asked, of all things, to be replaced "by another Comrade with greater administrative experience." He went on: "I recognize clearly that my insufficient experience in local work has an unfavourable effect on the fulfilment of the complicated and responsible duties of the Chairman of the Council of Ministers, as well as the fact that I have not had the opportunity of being directly responsible for individual branches of the economy in another ministry or in any other economic body." [15] He went on to make his apology for agricultural shortcomings, for which he said he held himself responsible, and finished with a statement of his faith in the primacy of heavy industry.

What Malenkov in effect was saying was that he had played the role of *éminence grise* too long and was now paying for it. There was no argument about policy, only the statement that this genius of an administrator knew nothing about administration, and that this industrial overlord who had never had anything to do with agriculture had failed in his agricultural policies. His message was clearly taken, but it made no difference what the comrades thought. He had lost power, therefore virtue. The man with power, therefore virtue, was Comrade N. S. Khrushchev, who now took the stage. He was making a new Prime Minister on behalf of the Central Committee of the Party. He proposed Nikolai Bulganin for the job, praising his "great experience in the political, state, economic, and military fields." Bulganin had indeed been a good administrator; it was his solitary talent. The Central Committee was foisting a puppet Prime Minister on the Council of Ministers, which Malenkov had tried to make supreme. But Malenkov was still very much a figure to be reckoned with. Although he ceased to be Prime Minister, he was still a member of the Party Presidium, and it was not until the early summer of 1957 that he was finally crushed in the very moment when it looked as though he had triumphed over Khrushchev.

CHAPTER SIXTEEN

The Chieftain Finds His Voice

KHRUSHCHEV was sixty-one and bursting out all over with a vitality which seemed only to have gathered strength from a lifetime of strain and stress and peril and from the complex and taxing manœuvres through which, less than two years after Stalin's death, he had subdued his seniors as well as his only dangerous rival. He was not yet undisputed master of the Soviet Union (was he ever to be that?), but for a decade to come the Khrushchev story was to be the story of his country and also, to a very large degree, of the world.

This is not a history of the Soviet Union, or of the world. It is the story of one man's rise and fall. To recount all his activities as the spokesman and accepted leader of one of the two great powers would call for many volumes. Many volumes have indeed engaged themselves with aspects of this teeming subject, and I myself have written three of them.[1] In these pages I have tried to show the sort of man he was, his background, his changing environment, his path to the top. It remains to be shown how he ruled, how he himself was ruled by the combination of his own past and the forces engendered by a changing Russia and a changing world, and how he fell.

He was never to be the supreme autocrat, as Stalin was the supreme autocrat, though at times he came very near to it. This is not hindsight: during the whole of his period of ascendancy, in a continuous running commentary on his extraordinary and multifarious activity, it was my own persistent contention that the men who had raised him up could, and one day might, pull him down. In the end they did just this. They did more: by the timing of his fall and by their subsequent actions they demonstrated which aspects of the policies enunciated by Khrushchev had been in fact collectively agreed on, and which had been imposed on them by Khrushchev. The most important were then seen to have been agreed on; they were continued after Khrushchev's eclipse.

It is important to be clear on this immediately, and for two reasons, which interlock: it is the key to our understanding of Khrushchev's own rule, and it is the key to our understanding of the country over which he ruled, which is still with us today, and of the men who ruled with him, the survivors of whom destroyed him when he tried too hard to make himself an autocrat, and who continue to rule without him.

In February 1955 they agreed to the dethronement of Malenkov not because they thought Khrushchev would make a better tsar but partly for personal reasons and partly because they believed that the new course was heading for trouble. The irony of the situation was that the economists and the technocrats who had been nurtured by Malenkov temporarily gained from the fall of their champion. Saburov and Pervukhin were both promoted to be First Deputy Premiers under Bulganin, as was Mikoyan, a fervent advocate of the new course. Four other heads of production industries were also made deputy premiers, so that the government team, with Malenkov only one of eight deputy premiers, was extremely strong. Soon afterwards the Army too showed that it had a hand in Malenkov's fall. In March eleven new marshals were appointed, and of these the majority had worked with Khrushchev in the war. They stood, obviously, for the swift development of heavy industry, and very soon they showed that they were also interested in the rewriting of the history of the war in a way which would give the generals a proper share of the credit.

So although Bulganin, as Prime Minister, made public obeisance to the Party, which, he said, it was his sole and proper task to serve (using the identical formula which Molotov had used when Stalin made him Prime Minister in 1931), the new government and Party leadership were clearly intended to operate as a collective, concerned above all with putting heavy industry and agriculture on the right lines before trying to please the consumer. And very soon this was made specifically clear. Khrushchev might be First Secretary, and the First Secretary was clearly more important than the Prime Minister, but he was not to be as important as all that: there were to be no more decrees signed only by Khrushchev himself. "Lenin taught us," wrote *Pravda* on April 20, "the collective nature of work. He often reminded us that all members of the Politburo are equal [Malenkov was still a member of the Politburo, the Presidium] and that the secretary is chosen to execute the resolutions of the Central Committee of the Party." Khrushchev was thus constrained to publish in his own Party newspaper, edited by his own protégé, Shepilov, a solemn declaration of the limits of his own power. A few days later the Party theoretical journal, *Kommunist,* was even more explicit: "Lenin repeatedly stressed the importance of collective leadership in the Party and the country. To avoid any misunderstanding, Lenin said . . . that only resolutions agreed on by the Central Committee after they had been sanctioned by the Orgburo, the Politburo, or the Central Committee in plenary session should be implemented by the Secretary of the Central Committee of the Party. Otherwise the Central Committee cannot work efficiently." [2]

All during 1955 Party and government functioned outwardly as a tightly bound collective. It was for Khrushchev a year not of spectacular progress, but rather of consolidation and purposeful advance. He had put Malenkov down, but this deadly rival was still a powerful personality in his own right and still in a position to intrigue. Malenkov had not conceded defeat—far from it; and in May 1957, over two years after his resignation as Prime Minister, he came within a hair's-breadth of final victory. He did not conceal his long-range intentions. When he came to England in the early summer of 1956, technically as the head of a delegation of power-station engineers, actually to prepare the way for the imminent state visit of Bulganin and Khrushchev, he talked like any Western political leader in opposition. In a

short, quite private conversation, I asked him how he was enjoying his semi-retirement. He was not as retired as all that, he answered; there was plenty to be done. All the same, the change
made a welcome rest; he had more time for reading and getting
out into the open air (he was always, in spite of his poundage, a
passionate hunter in the Continental manner). Did he still
think his own views about the new course and heavy industry
had been right? Did he think some of his colleagues had been
wrong? He smiled—and unlike most Western politicians, this
man whose eyes could look like stones and who had behaved for
so long with such an extremity of nastiness, could still smile, on
occasion, with his eyes—and said, "I know that I was right and
that some of my colleagues were wrong. They will see this in due
course. But we have a collective government, and I am part of
that collective."

It is very necessary to remember the continued existence of
Malenkov as a very real threat when considering the actions of
Khrushchev between 1955 and 1957. Khrushchev had to go very
carefully indeed.

He did not take a very active part in the real domestic business of 1955. This was concerned with the overhaul of industry,
and it was presided over, not ineffectively, by Bulganin, working
with and through the strong team referred to above. Bulganin,
though weakened by drink and soft living, though never a
power politically, was by no means a negligible figure. He had
shown himself as a first-class industrialist in the days when these
were few and far between; he had, as Chairman of the State
Bank, shown financial acumen and had familiarized himself
with the ins and outs of the creaking economy; as Minister of
Defence he had got on well enough with the soldiers; he knew
how to talk to foreigners. At the Plenary Session of the Central
Committee in July 1955 he made a most important speech
which expounded the shortcomings of the industrial system, the
waste, the bottlenecks due to rigid and over-centralized planning, the way in which Soviet Industry as a whole was far behind
the West.[3] His speech was no less dramatic, and a good deal
more constructive, than Khrushchev's own speech about the

shortcomings of agriculture in September 1953. Bulganin worked very hard that year and achieved a good deal. Khrushchev let him get on with it; he had his eye on other things.

Khrushchev issued no more personal decrees, but he continued to hold the limelight. This was the year in which he finally made his name as the fountain of innumerable ideas. It was clear that he had decided that his best policy was to keep moving at all costs, ceaselessly making the headlines, nagging, exhorting, cajoling, and passing on to a new idea before the last one had time to get stale. Now he was going to save Russian agriculture by teaching the peasants to plant corn, corn everywhere, above all as a fodder crop, even where corn had never grown before and could not grow. The fodder was to increase the livestock population, and thus the meat supply: it was now that he earned the nickname, derisive rather than affectionate, of "Kukuruza"— this being the Russian word for corn. Later on he was to backpedal heavily on the corn crusade: even the newest hybrids would not flourish except in certain strictly defined areas. Certainly he forced corn on the very conservative peasantry in places where it should have been cultivated long before. No less certainly he caused tens of thousands of acres to be wasted. Balance of advantage, as was always the case with Khrushchev's bright ideas, was hard to strike. When it was not corn, it was concrete—reinforced concrete was the hope of the future; he would teach the Russians to construct their buildings out of prefabricated concrete units, which made for economy and durability and overcame the shortage of bricks in the vast areas where there was no timber. But he failed to make corresponding provision for the manufacture of cement. When it was not corn or concrete it was architecture: he launched with great panache a campaign against Stalin's overornamented, monumental architecture. There were to be no more of the wedding-cake piles which dotted the skyline of Moscow; apartment buildings were to be severe, economical, and functional. He made great fun of the lavish decoration of the Moscow underground, of the ponderous vulgarity of the rebuilt Krestyachik in Kiev—evidently quite forgetting that the Moscow underground had been his personal creation and that, as First Secretary of the Ukraine, he

had personally presided over the planning of the new Krestyachik.

While in public he sustained a nonstop performance on these
lines, which did nobody any harm but which did not do much
good either; privately he continued with his slow and skilful rebuilding of the Communist Party in his own image. But he was
also applying his mind for the first time to foreign affairs. Sooner
or later, if his progress was to continue, he would have to turn
himself into the spokesman of the Soviet Union *vis à vis* the
outer world; it had better be sooner than later. In the process he
would have to do to Molotov, still very much Russia's elder
statesman, what he had already done to Malenkov. Here he had
all the comrades on his side, including Malenkov himself, already committed to an anti-Molotov line. Just as Stalin had
made Molotov Foreign Minister in 1939 to bring home to the
world that he was about to abandon all ideas of collective security and make a deal with Hitler, so, if the Soviet Union was to
make a new start, Molotov would how have to go.

The pretext was the *rapprochement* with Marshal Tito. Although this did not turn out as Khrushchev had expected, the
fact that it took place at all was a defeat for Molotov, who still
believed that by weakening in the face of Yugoslavia the Soviet
Union would invite severe difficulties in her satellites, above all
in Poland. He was quite overborne. When, in May 1955, it was
decided to send a delegation to Yugoslavia, Molotov was already
fighting a rear-guard action. Some sort of *rapprochement* was
necessary, it was generally agreed, if only to put an end to a
situation (the defiance of the Soviet Union by a relatively tiny
power) which made Moscow look increasingly ridiculous. Molotov said, in effect, all right, but limit the occasion to a formal
meeting of heads of state. Khrushchev and others argued that
only by bringing the Yugoslav Communist Party back into the
fold, thus neutralizing it, could the danger of the example of the
Titoist heresy be overcome. The majority of the comrades
agreed. The delegation was to be led by Khrushchev, as First
Secretary of the Communist Party, not by Bulganin as Prime
Minister. Khrushchev's personal aim was to secure an international success for the Party he led and to make his first appear-

ance on the international scene as the spokesman of the Soviet Union. In the first essay he failed; in the latter, more important immediately to him, he succeeded.

[2.]

We have already glimpsed the man as he appeared in Belgrade, his first excursion into a land where he had to meet a foreign leader who was master in his own house. He made many mistakes, filed them in his mind for future reference, and did not repeat them. But, always accompanied by Bulganin and Mikoyan (who usually walked behind him), he was evidently and absolutely in command on all public appearances and in most private ones too. Whether he was rudely hectoring the astonished and embarrassed ambassador of a minor power in a private room at a vast public reception, whether he was holding forth about state relations (Bulganin's province) or industry and trade (Mikoyan's province), nobody contradicted him and, as I observed earlier in this narrative, he made felt, with no sign of conscious effort, the personal authority and power which dominated any assembly and helped to explain why a collection of the hardest and most ruthless opportunists in the world were accepting him as their figurehead, heir spokesman, their dynamo too. He was positive. He did not mind speaking out and making mistakes. It was highly necessary for the Soviet Union to speak with a positive voice; the colleagues, even the cleverest among them, were so conditioned by fear—fear of Stalin—that they seemed wholly incapable of speaking in public with positive commitment, even though, like Mikoyan or Molotov or Malenkov or Kaganovich, they might be downright and aggressive in their own closed sessions with the Central Committee and in their smaller cabinet.

Some of Khrushchev's mistakes were personal to him and spoke volumes about his authoritarian background *vis à vis* his subordinates, as when he ignored the existence of the workers on the bench at the turbine factory in Ljubljana: he had sprung from the workers and knew their weakness and how they had to be bullied and cowed; now he exploited that weakness, not troubling to conceal the fact that he regarded them as dirt—until he discovered that the Yugoslavs were members of a prouder, more upstanding people than his own.

But the greatest of all his mistakes was clearly a collective affair and, by itself, would have been enough to cause the failure of his own special mission—to bring Marshal Tito and the Yugoslav Communists into fraternal (i.e., servile) relations with the Soviet Party. At Belgrade airport he made what he took to be the most handsome apology for past Soviet policy towards Yugoslavia. It was intended as an earth-shaking gesture of a magnanimity beyond compare: Russia the Great was not accustomed to making apologies to minor powers—or, for that matter, major ones. It was an obviously prepared statement, agreed on by the Presidium in Moscow. Not only Khrushchev, but also his senior colleagues, took it unquestioningly for granted that Marshal Tito would be so overwhelmed by the magnitude of this gesture that he would be rushed off his feet into agreeing to anything Khrushchev asked of him. It did not work out like that. This is what Khrushchev said:

We sincerely regret what has occurred and are determinedly removing all those obstacles which have accumulated during this period. In this, we, for our part, must include the provocative role played in the relations between Yugoslavia and the USSR by the enemies of the people, Beria, Abakumov, and others, who have now been unmasked. We have carefully examined the material upon which those grave accusations and insults aimed then at the Yugoslav leaders were based. The facts have shown that this material was concocted by enemies of the people, despicable agents of imperialism who had joined the ranks of our Party by underhand means.

This kind of thing was good enough for Russians. In the eyes of the country which Stalin and his closest colleagues (Khrushchev himself, Bulganin and Mikoyan standing with him on the airport apron) had tried to batter into submission by all means short of military invasion, it was worse than no apology at all. As Tito raised his hand to stop the interpreter it must have seemed to him that this apology was not only adding insult to injury but was also sinister. There had been a good deal of evidence that the new leadership was trying to move away from Stalinist policies, but here they were in the very act of reversing one of his "mistakes" and quite unable to prevent themselves from reverting, as to the manner born, to Stalinist phraseology and lies. During all the conversations which followed, there was little warmth on both sides. State relations were resumed (Bulganin signed the agreement for the Soviet state), but inter-Party relations were not so much as mentioned in the communiqué. More than this, the communiqué contained a little phrase which was to prove epoch-making in the history of Moscow's relations with Communist Parties everywhere—which was, indeed, to herald the disintegration of the Communist monolith: "Differences in practical forms of socialism are exclusively the affair of individual countries." It was a trick sentence, as designed by Khrushchev. But it was the first trick in a long-drawn-out game which he was to lose in the end.

It was a trick phrase because, although it conceded "different paths to socialism," Khrushchev was already planning his next move. This was to be nothing less than the formal announcement that the Soviet Union had already achieved socialism and was now actively engaged in the "transition to Communism." This formulation was intended to put the Soviet Union into a different class from the aspiring satellites and Yugoslavia, and from China too: she was still the mentor and the guide, because a stage further on the journey to Utopia. This formulation, what is more, was taken by Khrushchev very seriously indeed: in years to come, the aspect of the Chinese challenge which enraged him above all others was Mao's claim that by his invention of the Commune system and his Great Leap Forward he had found a short cut to Communism which (by implication) the Russians had never had the wit to discover for themselves. More immediately, in putting forward this formulation, Khrushchev encompassed the humiliation of Molotov who, in one of his speeches (to the Supreme Soviet on February 8, 1955) had delivered himself of the harmless-seeming remark that in the Soviet Union "the foundations of the socialist society have already been built." He was not then challenged. Nobody publicly objected. But Khrushchev hugged it to himself. Seven months later the grand old man was forced to make a public apology in *Kommunist* and explain at length where he had been wrong.[4] This recantation, besides serving to discredit Molotov and to emphasize his isolation, also gave Khrushchev a dramatic way of posing as a Party ideologist—for the first but not at all for the last time. The Party, and Khrushchev, needed an opportunity to show that it was still an ideological force: Communist theory for some time past had been so swamped by economic and tactical expedients that it was beginning to look as though there was no reason for the Party's existence except as an apparatus of personal rule.

By that time (September 1955) Khrushchev had extended his power considerably. The Belgrade experience had taught him and his colleagues a good deal. They understood, as they had not understood before, that Moscow had a long and difficult row to hoe before it could gain the confidence not only of Yugoslavia but also of the remaining satellites. In this they were helped by Mikoyan, the Armenian, with his lively understanding of the feelings of subject peoples, who had so gloomily watched Khrushchev's efforts to make friends with Tito. At that Central Committee Plenum in July at which Bulganin exposed the failures of Soviet industry, Mikoyan insisted forcibly that if the Soviet Union was to get anywhere at all in its relations with the other Communist countries, except by force, it must make an end of the ruthless economic exploitation of the satellites, the attempted and foredoomed exploitation of China too, and start treating them as partners.[5]

At that meeting, too, in spite of Khrushchev's indiscretions in Belgrade, it was effectively decided that he had better be given as much rope, within reason, as he asked. This was nothing less than a recognition of his personal force and the need for personal force. At the end of the session he was able to strengthen his influence in the Presidium by importing into it one of his toughest and most vigorous aides, Kirichenko, who had served with him in the Ukraine and taken over the First Secretaryship of the Ukrainian Party after Stalin's death. To an enlarged Secretariat he brought three of his supporters, two from the provinces, Aristov, who had once run the great steel works at Magnitogorsk, and Belyaev, who had been in charge of the Virgin Lands campaign: with them came Shepilov, the young editor of *Pravda,* who was later to take over Molotov's job as Foreign Minister.

Also, behind the scenes there was very active preparation for the first Party Congress of the post-Stalin era, which was to be the famous Twentieth Party Congress of February 1956. The isolation and neutralization of Molotov were part of this exercise. So, in that same month of September, was the trial of a number of senior officials of the Georgian (Beria's own) security services. This was in effect a preview of the sort of charges Khrushchev was preparing to bring against Stalin in his secret speech. It involved the rehabilitation of a number of Stalin's most distinguished victims, notably Ordzhonikidze, the Georgian Party chieftain, one of Stalin's stoutest aides, who had been driven to suicide by his master. Nothing was said about this trial until November. Nothing was ever said about a speech which Khrushchev made in Sofia on his way back from Belgrade in June. Here, it was later discovered, only ten days after he had invited Tito to join him in blaming everything on Beria, he for the first time attacked Stalin openly (though in secret Party conclave), bringing out some of the charges which were to be elaborated in the secret speech.[6] This Sofia affair provides the direct answer to those who maintained that in some way Khrushchev was forced by his colleagues to make the secret speech: he was leading them and making it inevitable.

There were other preparations, more oblique, but in retrospect evident for what they were. Before he stood up at the Twentieth Party Congress, not only to denounce Stalin, but also to give Soviet policy towards the West a decisive new turn, Khrushchev needed to accomplish two more things: he needed to establish himself further as an international figure and also to secure for himself a first-hand impression of the leaders of the "imperialist camp," above all President Eisenhower of the United States.

The first was achieved by the very much publicized visit with Bulganin to India, Burma, and Afghanistan, during the course of which the Russian leaders allowed themselves to be garlanded and to be photographed in ways more reminiscent of vote-catching Western politicians than of Russian tyrants. They were indeed vote-catching. A new doctrine was being born, the doctrine of "peaceful competition." Khrushchev was reversing Stalin's policy, which was based on the assumption that all newly independent nations, freed from Western imperial rule but still preserving ties with their late masters, were in fact crypto-colonial lands, ruled by traitors (Gandhi, for instance, or Nehru) in the pay of the West. He was at the same time recognizing a fact of life—the existence of a vast new area of political neutralism—and preparing to bid against the West with material aid, not so much for its active support as to keep it neutral. But all the time he fulminated against the West, certainly trying to please the lately downtrodden and exploited, but more particularly with an eye to presenting himself as a true disciple of the Lenin who had been betrayed by Stalin in his later years.

The second aim he achieved by attending the first summit meeting at Geneva and there meeting the Western leaders, Eisenhower, Eden, Fauré. Molotov went too (he had not yet been publicly humiliated), and with him Bulganin and Marshal Zhukov, who was to talk with Eisenhower as an old comrade in arms. Here Khrushchev set out to create an impression of becoming modesty and constitutional correctness. Since nothing was to be decided at the summit meeting, he had nothing to lose and everything to gain by sitting quietly by while his Prime Minister did the talking. Indeed, he went out of his way to show that he was a man like other men. Not for him the noisy and flashy police guards with motorcycles and helicopters. He drifted about in a casual sort of way, kept his ears open, and for the first time in his life had a first-hand glimpse of what Western politicians were made of. He must have found it hard indeed to believe his eyes and ears.

CHAPTER SEVENTEEN

Old Dogmas, New Ideas

THE WORLD STATESMAN was now fledged and ready to take the stage. He was sixty-one, but except to a handful of specialists his name had been known for only three years outside Russia and Russian-occupied territory. Even to the specialists he had not appeared as a formidable pretender to the succession until late in 1954, so quietly had he been playing his hand. But now, by the end of 1955, he had established himself as the first among equals and also as a politician of a different breed from any known in Russia, tsarist or Bolshevik—indeed, as the first Western-style politician in Russian history. He was preparing for the great coup, which, if it succeeded, would at once establish him as the effective master of the Soviet Union, strong enough to break the survivors of the original Stalinists, who had been running the country in the days when he had been a modest district secretary, as well as the most able of his own contemporaries. It was an extraordinary transformation from the bullet-headed young tough of Yuzovka into the quiet, watchful, modest little figure at Geneva who could afford to sit by and allow Bulganin, Molotov, and Zhukov to argue with the President of the United States, knowing that if he chose he had only to raise a pudgy little hand to make them fall silent and listen to him.

What did he believe? Until now what he believed had not mattered one way or the other. He had been fully occupied with the day-to-day problems of helping Stalin "build socialism" and furthering his own career—interrupted but not set back while he fought the Germans on behalf of the people instead of fighting the people on behalf of Stalin. Since Stalin's death he had been even more feverishly occupied in helping his colleagues to hold the line, while at the same time manœuvring himself into the dominant position. He had not had much time for ideas. In any case, he was a man of action, not a thinker; even as a man of action he was a politician first, a balancer, a trimmer, an intriguer, a fixer, not in any way an intellectual or a theorist—an opportunist in the grand manner, operating within the rigid framework of a received ideology. But he was more than this: he was also a natural commander, as he had shown in Yuzovka, in Moscow, in Kiev; the characteristics of the ward politician had been developed out of all proportion by the circumstances of his career, the struggle for survival and advancement in the service of a brutal and pathologically suspicious tyrant.

He was still more, he was a dreamer—the quality we have noted in his eyes even in some of the earliest photographs and which began to manifest itself on a national scale with his grandiose plans for the redemption of agriculture. He dreamed of power: from the earliest beginnings in Yuzovka the vision of power had been his great driving force; there could have been none other to carry him through the fearful strains and the hazards, the brutalities, the humiliations too, of the steady climb to the summit. Nobody forced him to embark on this fearful undertaking, and it is to his credit that he never for a moment bemoaned his lonely fate in the manner so familiar among Western politicians, who, having schemed and plotted and manœuvred and toiled for high office, then, while clinging to it tooth and nail, demand our sympathy because life at the top is rough and hard and really rather trying. Khrushchev wanted power, and he visibly enjoyed his power: he did not grumble because the responsibilities of office kept him from hunting and fishing; he enjoyed the responsibilities of office and used his power to see that he got the best hunting and fishing whenever he felt like it. He was a happy potentate.

He also dreamed for Russia. He was very much a Russian with a profound instinctive patriotism which had its roots in the source of all Russian patriotism—Russian soil, the endless steppelands, the forests, the great, slow rivers, the marvellously fluid, unformed, embracing landscape, and the vast Russian skies; the sense of togetherness and community on a quasi-mystical plane with a suffering people, which could also co-exist, as it co-existed in the hearts of so many outstanding Russian patriots through the centuries, with the severities and brutalities of the most ruthless taskmasters when it came to sustaining the central autocracy—any autocracy, save only that it functioned. Thus a Suvorov, who loved his men and cherished them while he drove them, who despised the higher command and the whole system of government, would put down peasant rebellions, using his peasant troops, with savage rigour, although the rebels had risen in desperation against the ruling society he loathed and despised and against which he fought all his life.

[2.]

Khrushchev was not a Suvorov. But he had a feeling for the dumb masses of Russia, from which he had sprung and whom he exploited to the utmost in the interest of the central autocracy, first Stalin's, then his own. At work, as individuals on the bench, they did not exist; they were automatons, and faulty and suspect automatons at that. As a class, seen from his office in the Kremlin, they were dangerous, to be subdued. But when they were in manageable groups, visited off-duty, clustered round him in factories, on collective farms, in meeting-halls throughout the provinces, and drinking in his words, he drew strength from them and felt one with them. We are familiar with his manner of talk: he would tell them how to plant corn in squares instead of rows so that the stems would support each other and the pollen shaken loose from the branching inflorescence would fall more surely to be caught in the silky beards of the swelling cobs below; he would urge them to plant potatoes and then turn pigs out among them to fatten themselves and at the same time churn up and fertilize the soil; he would announce with the air of a man who had discovered the Second Law of Thermodynamics that the latest research had shown that two milkings a day were enough for any cow, and paint in glowing colours the increase in milk-yield gained from leaving the animals in peace to chew their cud—and the saving in man-power, or woman-power. The time-honoured custom, he said, was for "milk-maids" to milk their charges at least five times a day in the belief that the best milk came from the "last drop" of each milking. He enjoyed these homilies. He dotted them with ancient Russian proverbs and frequent invocations of the Almighty, whose existence at other times he scornfully denied. He was one with his peasants, he was Little Father too—and then he went back to Moscow and issued decrees designed to detach still further his beloved peasants from the land, their own little bits of land, their own little acres and their cows; to sack the peasant chairmen of thousands of collectives at a time and replace them with trusted Party workers from the towns, and then to sack these in their turn because they did not know how to make two blades of grass grow where none had grown before.

It was all, of course, for everybody's good. The Soviet Union, backward and oppressed, where millions lived on a bare subsistence level on potentially the richest land on earth, must be made to prosper in spite of the backwardness, the feckless millions who still clung to their dark superstitions and their drunken feast days. To this end they must be driven in the traditional Russian way—but with a difference. They had been driven, once upon a time, as serfs to enrich their masters. Now they were being driven to enrich themselves. The peasants had to provide the food to feed the factory workers, the miners, the foundrymen, and the administrators. The factory workers had to provide the material to build up a vast heavy industry which would look after arms to defy the outer world, and the highly articulated skeleton of a modern industrial economy which in due course would have machines to spare to multiply the amenities of the good life—when all would reap their reward.

This was the Stalin system. It was a shock system: to invite the cooperation of the people by letting them enjoy parts of the fruit of their toil as they produced it was too dangerous and too slow—and too irregular. The rewards must be deferred, and since people will not work for rewards indefinitely deferred, they must be coerced. This was the system Khrushchev had lived with all his life. Malenkov had tried to win popularity by abandoning it, altogether prematurely: it could not, must not, be abandoned while Russia was still lagging behind the West in productivity. Of course Stalin had driven too fast and too far. Of course in his last phase he had made further growth impossible by driving so hard and planning so rigidly, relying on forced labour as though the population of Russia was illimitable and all of it expendable, killing all initiative by terror. But the principle was correct; only the detailed application was wrong. The people were not to be trusted to know their own best interests; they must be chivvied, instructed, and coerced—sternly but no longer viciously.

About other nations he had thought very little. Less than any of Stalin's lieutenants had he been concerned with his country's relations with the outside world. During all the period of the rise of nazism and fascism in Western Europe he had been occupied with purely domestic tasks in Moscow. He knew at first hand about German efficiency and method, and feared them. For the rest, there is nothing to show that he had any ideas about the West more subtle and perceptive than the general view shared by the ordinary Party functionary.

In this there was grafted on to the ancient Russian suspicion of all foreigners, mixed with envy and contempt, the received conviction that the Western powers, England above all before the war, America after it, would go to any lengths in their inevitable and implacable hostility to the first "socialist" state. They had tried in vain to strangle it at birth; monopoly capitalism, expressing itself in imperialism and fascism of one kind and another, remained pledged to the destruction of the Soviet Union. Britain and France had tried to reach an accommodation with Nazi Germany at the expense of Russia, had been foiled, had in 1941 been only too pleased to see Russia and Germany tearing each other to pieces and, at the same time, to exploit the heroism of the Red Army in their own interests. At the end of the war, relatively unscathed and stronger than ever before, America had profited by the prostration of Europe to impose herself on the West European powers, substituting her own imperialist designs in Asia above all, and rearming West Germany to act as the powerful spearhead for a renewed drive against the Soviet Union.

This is what Stalin believed, and Khrushchev took his foreign-policy views from Stalin. When, after Stalin's death, his successors sought to modify Soviet foreign policy in the light of the nuclear facts of life, it is improbable in the extreme that Khrushchev had any new ideas to offer. In those early councils of 1953 and 1954, when Malenkov, abetted by Mikoyan, was attempting to ease the tension and achieve some sort of working relationship with the West, seeing clearly enough what Stalin in his last days was only beginning to see, his ideas must have seemed heretical to the man from the Ukraine, who had never had to give a thought to the complexities of coexistence in a catastrophic age. In this he was upheld by Molotov, the trusted expert on foreign policy, the aggressive and conservative stone-waller, as well as by many of his friends in the military hierarchy. But, as always, he learned quickly, and by the end of 1955 he was preparing to advance the Malenkov view as his own. Some years were to go by before, in the teeth of the Chinese, he formally produced as his own idea the view he had condemned Malenkov for holding—that nuclear war would mean the end of Communism as well as capitalism. But in February 1956, when he advanced the thesis that war was no longer "fatally inevitable," it was clear that a new understanding of the meaning of nuclear warfare was the reason for this reversal, not, as Khrushchev insisted at the time, a conviction of the overwhelming strength of the "socialist camp."

As far as the "socialist camp" itself was concerned—which then, of course, included China—here again there is no reason to suppose that in his early days as First Secretary Khrushchev thought of the European satellites as anything but obedient borderlands managed by indigenous Communist rulers loyal to Moscow and easily controllable in Moscow's interests. His visits to Prague and Warsaw in 1954 could only confirm him in this view: the Czech and Polish Communist leaders, Stalin's puppets, received him as their sovereign lord and provided him with the intoxicating experience of addressing in their proud and ancient capitals great meetings packed with local Communists who applauded him wildly and in a thousand ways showed that they looked to Moscow for leadership and guidance—which seemed to him entirely right and proper. Only later, in Belgrade, did it begin to dawn on him that a regime which called itself Communist might seriously question the Moscow leadership.

As for China, Khrushchev knew, as Stalin had known, that there could be no question of reducing Mao Tse-tung to the status of a puppet leader. Stalin, having done his best to prevent Mao from carrying out his revolution in 1948, was resigned to it when it came and made the best of it, using China's desperate need to impose terms which had to be accepted, deeply though they were resented, and profiting by the Chinese revolution to terrify America. Mao would accept from Stalin, the world's senior revolutionary, treatment which he would accept from neither Malenkov nor Khrushchev, both small and parvenu compared with him. Khrushchev was the first to profit by establishing a new and personal relationship on his visit to Peking in 1954; but he could see by then that if unity between Moscow and Peking was to be maintained a difficult and tricky passage lay ahead. The whole problem of world revolution was at issue here. The ultimate triumph of what Khrushchev thought of as Communism—i.e., the Soviet system—over what he thought of as capitalism—i.e., the hidden government of bankers and big industrialists—was taken for granted by him as a simple axiom of faith. But he, like Stalin, had no use for any revolution which could not be controlled by Moscow and exploited in the interests of the Soviet Union. The first challenge to the logic of this simple faith had been the Yugoslav defection. Would China pose a second, far more serious challenge? She would need extremely careful handling. But Marx was Marx, and Lenin was Lenin, and history was on their side. There might be storms, but in the end the "socialist camp" would hold together in face of the standing threat from America and America's European satellites: China would be retained, just as, quite soon, Yugoslavia would swallow her stiff-necked Balkan pride and return meekly to the fold.

The task, meanwhile, was to carry on: to hold the satellites together and raise their economic and military potential in the

Russian interest by intelligent handling; to sap the confidence and subvert the power of the West by playing on the differences between the Western Allies, by encouraging class warfare in the individual countries, by presenting the Soviet government as a steadfast force for peace in a world threatened by the irresponsible and malevolent "warmongering" of the Pentagon generals and Mr. John Foster Dulles, the American Secretary of State and apostle of "brinkmanship."

There was a further activity, which Khrushchev himself was the first to develop. Stalin had refused to have anything to do with the governments of ex-colonial countries, regarding them as "imperialist lackeys." Khrushchev and his advisers saw that this was a mistaken view. Nehru, for example, was certainly anti-Communist, but he was also manifestly anti-imperialist, except on his own account in such places as Kashmir. It was useless to expect India to carry out an immediate Communist revolution and throw out Nehru (anyway, who would control a revolution on those lines?), but it was criminal to throw her into the imperialist camp by refusing to treat with her. It was quite sufficient for the time being to make amicable noises and to grant with as much fuss as possible a modicum of material aid—aid without strings on long-term loans at a very low interest rate. Who would have dared to guess in 1953 that Moscow would soon be building dams for a country, Egypt, in which the Communist Party was illegal?

As for ideas of socialism, or Communism, in domestic politics, these were what the central government, the Presidium of the Central Committee of the Communist Party of the Soviet Union, said they were. And what they said they were was embodied in the system developed by Stalin. It stood for ultimate prosperity for all, abundance for all, to be achieved by the following-out of measures prescribed minutely from above. Only two items of Lenin's original concept of a Communist society survived. The first was that no individual, or quasi-autonomous group of individuals (such as a private or a joint stock company) was permitted to employ for its own financial gain any other individual. All were employed by the state, directly, as in industry, or indirectly, as in the collective farms; and the state drew the profits, to reward the overseers as it chose—or to sack them or destroy them as it chose. The second was that, through universal education, talent could rise freely to its own level, provided it behaved itself politically. One day, when abundance had been achieved, there would be enough for all, and then the slogan "From each according to his ability, to each according to his work" would be changed to the glorious declaration of full Communism: "From each according to his ability, to each according to his needs." But there was a long way to go, and it was still too early to bother one's head about what this really meant—if, indeed, it should prove to mean anything at all.

This, very roughly, was the position of Nikita Khrushchev as he prepared himself for the Twentieth Party Congress, to take place in February 1956. He had done all he could, and it was a great deal, to secure the renewed supremacy of the Party and to consolidate his own ascendancy in it. But he was still part of the collective. More than this, neither the Party itself nor he, nor anybody else, could begin to aspire to the absolute authority which Stalin had enjoyed. The Soviet Union had changed, and Stalin himself had changed it. This was a point which was never grasped by all those (there are still many) who believed in general that at any moment there could be a full-scale reversion to the Stalinist terror, and in particular that Khrushchev, once he had achieved supremacy (in June 1957), was an unquestioned and untouchable autocrat in the sense that Stalin was an autocrat from the moment of Kirov's murder in 1934 until his death in 1953.

[3.]

The Soviet system was Stalin's own creation. He had imposed it by the force of his personality on a land which, until 1928, had no system at all. Heavy industry was then under state control; trade and light industry, under the NEP, were run by private entrepreneurs; the peasants, still in an overwhelming majority, were masters of their own land and determined to stay that way. Stalin, assisted by his own growing band of supporters owing all they had to him, and using the old revolutionaries whom he later killed, operating through a monstrous and highly privileged political police force, built up the system where none had been before at a time when the relative simplicities of the demands of industry and agriculture required no more than cheap, or forced, labour provided by a backward and largely illiterate population which seemed then infinite and infinitely expendable. The men he raised up to run this brutal, wasteful system were his own creatures. He could make them and he could destroy them. They too were expendable.

It may be argued until Doomsday, and doubtless will be so argued, whether or not Stalin or anybody else could have transformed backward, agrarian, anarchic Russia into a modern industrial power more swiftly and effectively by other means. We do not know, because he did not try, and neither did anybody else. Could Peter the Great, or anybody else, have brought Russia into Europe in the seventeenth century by any other means than total brutality and slavedriving? We do not know: no other means were tried. Could the West, could America, in the twentieth century, have "contained" Communism by any other means than by lumping all "Communist" countries together and holding the line by force of arms at the cost of welding so many discordant elements into an apparently monolithic threat? We do not know: no other means were tried.

What Stalin did, he did. And in the process, however wastefully, he did in fact transform the face of Russia, creating not only a large force of skilled and semiskilled workers but also an entirely new class of managers, administrators, technologists, scientists, and engineers necessary for the detailed running of the increasingly complex economy—in a word, a bourgeois society with, latent within it, the demands and aspirations of all bourgeois societies everywhere, if, in this case, with a strong Russian accent. It is this, far more than the industrialization of the Soviet Union, which will be remembered as Stalin's great positive achievement. He brought education on the grand scale to this vast, backward, illiterate land. He introduced the idea and the possibility of self-improvement, and so brought self-respect to a people with a servile tradition. The tragedy was that he did not know what to do with this new society when he had made it: even as he created a literate people, he corrupted them with terror. To the end of his days Stalin treated this society, which he had himself conjured up, like dirt, unable to perceive that in so doing he was defeating his own purpose and depriving the state of the benefits which could accrue only from the full extension of its gifts and talents. But the literacy remains, a lasting monument, and, as terror wanes, corruption very slowly fades.

This was the situation which Stalin's heir inherited. Stalin with his police could maintain the pressure, even if it led to a slowing down of the economy. His surviving colleagues could not. Malenkov, and Khrushchev too, all the pretenders indeed, perfectly understood that unless one among them was given supreme authority, including absolute control of the police, there was no way of maintaining the Stalinist terror. But in surrendering all authority to one of their number they would be putting their own lives into hands which they could not control. Some of them had escaped with their own lives only by the providential timing of Stalin's death; never again were any of them prepared to see the powers wielded by Stalin transferred to any other individual.

There was no question at all of anything but a collective government, though Malenkov tried to seize, and for a few days held, more than his share of power. There was no question, therefore, of the resumption of arbitrary terror. And even if this had been on the board, they knew very well that it could not work. Soviet society had become too complex, too highly articulated, much too dependent upon the services of tens of thousands, hundreds of thousands, of highly gifted individuals. Terror might work when only a handful of men were effectively running the country in the crude early stages of a belated industrial revolution. That stage was now past, and terror could not work in an age when, if the economy was to progress, men of talent had to be recognized and given their heads. All this meant, inevitably, a relaxation of police rule. But the men who were forced to preside over this relaxation knew, none better, that when people are given a little they at once demand more, that revolutions are made not when tyranny is confident and absolute but when it begins to weaken. If they did not know this as a generalization about human behaviour, they knew it very well from their reading of Russian history. And they all had read Russian history.

This was their dilemma: how to liberate the productive forces from the Stalinist ice age without calling into being such a torrential thaw that they themselves would be swept away by it? They had been playing with this problem, without coming to grips with it, for nearly three years, blowing now hot, now cold, on the first painful, bewildered, ill-directed stirrings of the sleeping giant. Decisive action could not be delayed much longer. One great difficulty was the intricate network of vested interests represented by the members of the Party machine running their satrapies and sub-satrapies throughout the vast land, who did not believe, frequently did not want to believe, that the relaxation was serious. They constantly worked against the new mood being propagated from the centre. And, paradoxically, they were encouraged in this by the actions of Khrushchev himself, who, in his manœuvring against Malenkov and the government bureaucracy, had, with his stress on the primacy of heavy industry and the need for Party discipline and the more active interference of Party functionaries in the running of the economy, encouraged them to believe that they were very much the masters. They were all the stronger too, now that the political police had been called to heel and curbed. It was not only the people, above all the intelligentsia, who had to be told that indeed the Soviet Union was emerging from the Stalinist night; even more, the conservative but wholly indispensable Communist Party membership had to be made to understand that a wind of change was blowing and that they must bow to it or lose their jobs.

The argument in the Kremlin went on and on. We have seen that as early as June 1955 Khrushchev had committed himself in his speech to the Bulgarian Party leaders in Sofia, if nowhere else, to an exposure of at least a part of the iniquity of Stalinism. But as late as December 21 the collective had not finally made up its mind. Although all sorts of implicit criticisms of the Stalin system had been permitted and even encouraged; although many aspects of the consequences of that system, the hushing up of the truth, the active lies and the corruption, had been denounced by gifted writers who had not been shot (but some had been reprimanded and certain editors had been disgraced); although the Kremlin fortress, the very symbol of an occupying power in an alien land, had been thrown open to the public; although a thousand other things had happened and Stalin's name was under a cloud, no direct attack on him personally had been made. Beria was his scapegoat still. And on the anniversary of Stalin's birthday, December 21, 1955, he was given a special commemorative article in *Pravda,* with his familiar photograph on the front page.

But within weeks Khrushchev had got his way: at a meeting of leaders from all the Communist countries which took place on January 27 and 28, 1956, the assembled comrades were told a little of what was to come: Stalin, in certain of his aspects, was about to be repudiated. They had just a month to compose themselves and get their explanations ready (later the Chinese were to insist that they had not been warned, but this was not true). The hour had come, and it was Khrushchev's hour.

CHAPTER EIGHTEEN

The Secret Speech and the World Stage

THE TWENTIETH PARTY CONGRESS and Khrushchev's two speeches are part of history. For the Western world the most important matter was contained in those parts of Khrushchev's public speech—in the speeches of others too—which announced quite epoch-making modifications to the Leninist canon. These, formally embodied in Congress resolutions, inaugurated a new era in Soviet foreign policy. Peaceful coexistence, different paths to socialism, revolution without violence, and the abandonment of the doctrine of the inevitability of war: the Soviet Union had formally renounced her role as the spearhead of violent revolution and the single-minded destroyer of the bourgeois world. The importance of these modifications—which amounted to a rewriting of Leninism—was not grasped in the West at the time because of the not unnatural tendency to regard all Soviet statements of policy as exercises in deception. The vital difference between propaganda—for example, Stalin's peace propaganda—designed to deceive, in line with Lenin's formula, and doctrine solemnly laid down as part of received truth was not easily distinguishable. This aspect of the Congress, which was a collective act, was also obscured by the excitement aroused by the criticism of Stalin started by Mikoyan and Suslov, moderate enough in tone but radical in content, and then by the violence of Khrushchev's denunciation in secret session.

Because of certain peculiarities of timing, because, too, Khrushchev was not forward among those who criticized Stalin publicly, a legend grew up that it was only at the very last minute decided that the speech should be delivered and either that the role of Stalin's prosecutor was wished on a reluctant Khrushchev by his colleagues or else that, on impulse, he suddenly decided to steal the limelight for himself. Both explanations are improbable, if not impossible.

In the first place, the speech was over 20,000 words long—a fifth of the length of this book—and was put together in a most careful and calculated way. Out of the huge mass of material available to Khrushchev, a very great deal was left out, and what was chosen was very carefully selected to display Stalin, from 1934 onwards, as an enemy not of the Soviet people but of the Communist Party, and Stalin's own anti-Trotsky, anti-Bukharin Party at that. This was a difficult undertaking because there was no clear-cut division in time: the judicial murders of different sorts of Party members overlapped. Stalin was denounced for the torture and murder of many of those who had themselves murdered for him and who had triumphed with him at the Congress of the Victors in 1934. But he was emphatically not denounced for his action against the Trotskyites and the Bukharinites, the old left and right oppositions, even though the most distinguished of those were not finally tried and shot until deep into the period of the "personality cult." Nothing was to be said against the excesses of the collectivization or of the great terror in so far as it affected ordinary, non-Party citizens. A little had to be said about the great Army purge of 1937 because the marshals were demanding a formal restoration of the Army's good name (in fact Khrushchev did not satisfy them; later he had to go a good deal farther in the way of rehabilitating the murdered generals). In short, the speech was a smokescreen as well as an exposure. It could not conceivably have been prepared at the last minute; months of thought and discussion had gone into it.

Nor could the speech have been wished on Khrushchev by his colleagues. If it was to be made at all, it had to be made by the First Secretary of the Party. As we know, Khrushchev was already holding forth against Stalin's crimes in Sofia in June 1955. It was he who was making the pace. The emphasis on the personality cult may well have been insisted on by others seeking to find ways and means of convicting Khrushchev out of his own mouth, should he ever look likely to develop a personality cult of his own. If this was so, Khrushchev himself and his allies got their own back. Some of the cleverest passages in the speech were aimed at the discrediting of Malenkov, Kaganovich, Molotov, and Voroshilov—Malenkov above all—by associating them in various ways, obliquely but unambiguously, with certain of Stalin's "mistakes" and excesses. It is possible that Khrushchev inserted certain of these short passages at the last minute, or impromptu, as he read. But whether he did this or not, there was no subsequent retraction. And this meant that support was strong enough, even in February 1956, to enable him to associate Malenkov, for example, with Stalin's refusal to listen to the man at the front, Khrushchev, at the time of the Kharkov encirclement and to hold up the "Leningrad affair" (which everybody knew was Malenkov's vicious purge of Zhdanov's men) as an example of Stalin's behaviour at his worst. Similarly, in his equivocal remarks about the murder of Kirov he was going out of his way to suggest the complicity of Molotov and Kaganovich.

The immediate outcome of the Congress as a whole and the secret speech in particular was all in Khrushchev's favour. With his formal and public announcement of the coexistence, no-more-war, revolution-without-violence theses, as with his endorsement, through Mikoyan, of a more flexible attitude to economic problems and his overdue recognition of the very evident fact that the capitalist walls of Jericho would not fall at the flourish of a trumpet, he had stolen Malenkov's thunder and established himself as the man who was committed to easing the fearful international pressures which had the effect of cutting the Soviet Union off from the outside world, burdening her with excessive arms expenditure, and inhibiting her development as a modern power among other modern powers. With his denunciation of the Stalin terror, selective as it was, he was telling the Soviet people that they might start living like human beings instead of sustaining a sort of underground existence in a land occupied and controlled by a hostile power; at the same time he was serving notice on the dyed-in-the-wool Stalinists that they must reckon seriously with the wind of change and adapt themselves to it or perish. But by his strong emphasis on Leninist revivalism and the power of the Party he was making it quite clear that the march to better times would be conducted under strict Party leadership. Even as he was drastically modifying the most sacrosanct of Lenin's remaining precepts (Stalin had long ago done away with the rest) he needed Lenin, he and his supporters all needed Lenin as never before. Stalin had been his own authority. What authority had Khrushchev? He could only hope to legitimize himself by presenting himself as the proper heir of Lenin and the defender of the true faith. This was a complicating factor and was to remain so. It was to be the direct cause of many of the waverings and contradictions of the next decade. The farther Khrushchev moved away from Leninism, and it was to be very far indeed, the more he needed to invoke Lenin in support of his "revisionist" or, not to put too fine a point on it, anti-Leninist policies. The Chinese later were to make the most of this.

Meanwhile, in February 1956, Khrushchev had said the right things: all that was now needed was to produce policies to match his words. This was harder.

[2.]

The Soviet Union was in turmoil; so, soon, were the European satellites; so, a little later, were the Communist Parties of the world. The secret speech, as such, was never published. But enough had been said by Mikoyan, Suslov, and Malenkov too in their public speeches to throw the Communist world into a tumult of half-incredulous excitement. And soon, long before the American State Department issued to the world the version of the speech we all know (a version never contradicted and, in any case, confirmed piecemeal in months and years to come), it was all over the Soviet Union.[1] What happened was that at tens of thousands of Party meetings, all down the scale, the speech was read out and then discussed. I have never met a rank-and-file Party member who had ever had the speech in his hands and been able to read and ponder it for himself. But within a matter of weeks all had had it read to them, and, as can be imagined, none retained more than a general idea of its contents, luridly lit up by bits of detail, differing from individual to individual. The shock was immense.

As the monuments came tumbling down, as streets and factories and cities were renamed—in the end not even Stalingrad, the hero city, now Volgograd, was excepted—people tried to take stock and failed. The experience was traumatic, especially among the young, who had not suffered at first hand from Stalin (though most of their parents had) and had been brought up to think of him as their idol, the fixed point round which the universe revolved.

I remember asking a correct, well-groomed, and very young Soviet diplomat to tell me what it meant to him personally. He had just poured me out a drink at one of those immense formal parties. He stared at me, and his eyes were suddenly stricken. "How can you ask me that!" he exclaimed. "How can you possibly ask me that?" Tears stood in his eyes, he swung away violently to hide them, tried to put his glass down on the table behind him but smashed it against another, and fled from the room.

The questioning was intense. It ranged from the violent rebellion of the students at Tiflis University, revolting against the destruction of the greatest of all their countrymen, to the insistent, nagging doubts of millions. "Very well, Stalin did terrible things; we knew that, though we did not understand how terrible. But what about these others, what about Khrushchev? They told us to worship him. They shared in his tyranny and profited by it. How can they hope to be respected now, when they turn against their dead leader when he cannot answer? At least he was great and strong and not afraid of anyone. Harsh and cruel he may have been, but harshness was what Russia needed, and how difficult to draw the line between cruelty and necessary hardness. How he would make this lot run like rabbits, if he could suddenly appear among them!" Others, more thoughtful, asked what was wrong with a system which could allow such a tyranny to establish itself. Khrushchev had not said a word in criticism of the system. But none of these criticisms

were ever publicly voiced until much later. It was left to Togliatti, the Italian Communist leader, to suggest that the Russian
comrades should surely, in the light of Khrushchev's revelations,
be asking themselves some heart-searching questions about the
very nature of the Soviet system and, in all humility, seeking
ways and means of changing it.[2]

In the Soviet Union, Khrushchev got his way: among his colleagues because he was clearly the only man with the boldness
and resource not only to cast down the Stalin idol but also to
ride the storm created by this act;[3] among the Party as a whole
because he put the Party unequivocally first; in the country because he was clearly the new master. But even at the summit of
his power he was never respected as Stalin had been respected.
The only man who inherited a shadow of this respect was Molotov, who kept clear of the pack and who retained a certain dignity through all the humiliations which were soon to be heaped
upon him.

[3.]

The composition of the new Party machine showed clearly
enough where Khrushchev's strength lay and also where he
sought support. The voting membership of the old Presidium
remained unchanged, indicating that Khrushchev's ascendancy
was the outcome of a fairly delicate balance of forces; but promotions of a number of his strongest supporters to candidate
membership and to the enlarged Secretariat showed that he was
losing no time in consolidating that ascendancy. He now had, on
one or the other body or both, a number of figures who owed
their advancement to him and to nobody else—most notably
Aristov, Brezhnev, Madame Furtseva, and Shepilov, among
others. Most significant of all was the elevation of Marshal Zhukov to be a candidate member of the Presidium. This was a clear
indication that Khrushchev had swung the Army behind him in
return for its first share in high policy-making. The composition
of the new and enlarged Central Committee made this quite
plain. Zhukov as Minister of Defence, two other generals as

Deputy Ministers of Defence, Sokolovsky as Chief of the General Staff and two generals occupying key commands, made a formidable showing among the ranks of the senior *apparatchiki*.

Immediately after the Twentieth Party Congress, Khrushchev made an innovation of some importance. He established for the first time a special bureau of the All Union Central Committee for the Russian Union Republic. He himself was chief of this bureau, which was staffed for all practical purposes with his own creatures. This gave him a double hold over the vast Russian Republic, which stretched all the way from the Ukraine and Byelorussia to the Pacific Coast, from the Central Asian Republics and Caucasia to the Baltic and the Arctic Ocean. But the main purpose of the bureau was to create a series of new jobs to reward men whose support Khrushchev needed. He was to need all the underpinning he could devise and all the support he could muster before a year had gone by.

[4.]

When the history of twentieth-century Russia comes to be written, if people are still interested in history a hundred years from now, I think it will be seen that it was in February 1956 that Khrushchev achieved the summit of his career. The Soviet Union lay at his feet: there was nothing he might not do, and this was never again to be true. We have followed the growth and development for sixty-two years of an individual making his way by devious means, with the aid of good qualities and bad, to the loftiest and most exposed position in the land. He was now in the position to rule.

But he could not rule. Stalin had been stronger than Russia and had moulded Soviet society in his own image. The image was now broken, and by Khrushchev; but Russia was stronger than Khrushchev, who could survive at the top only by submitting innumerable hostages to fortune and by trying to ride the whirlwind which he himself had unloosed. For eight years and more he was to succeed in this, but then it became too much for him and he fell. After the Twentieth Party Congress he was no longer in any way a free agent; for the rest of his career he was feverishly reacting to events which he could not control. Russia was taking charge.

This may seem a paradoxical view, even a perverse one. The natural view, I suppose, is that, after the Twentieth Party Congress, Khrushchev still had a long way to go before he had achieved supremacy, that the moment of total victory was when, in the autumn of 1957, he broke Marshal Zhukov and brought to heel the Army, which had helped him destroy his old comrades and rivals, the "anti-Party" group, earlier that year—Molotov, Malenkov, Kaganovich and others; that the moment of supreme triumph was in the autumn of 1959 when, as the acknowledged master of the Soviet Union, he achieved his apotheosis by visiting as an equal the President of the United States. Then he returned to Moscow to say in effect: I, Khrushchev, as the strongest man in the Old World, have come to an understanding with the head of the New World: between us, General Eisenhower having demonstrated his good will and his genuine desire for peace, we can police the world and ensure prosperity and peace for all mankind. "Our country and the United States," he had said at Dnepropetrovsk in July 1958, "are the two most mighty powers in the world. If other countries fight among themselves they can be separated; but if war breaks out between America and our country, no one will be able to stop it. It will be a catastrophe on a colossal scale." [4] This was the promise. The meeting at Camp David was the seal.

But already when Khrushchev destroyed his old comrades, the "anti-Party" group, he depended utterly for his victory not only on Marshal Zhukov, whom he was soon able to put down, but also on a host of individuals in the great Party machine (far more than Stalin had ever depended on), many of whom had views of their own, some of whom were, seven and a half years later, to take over the government and the Party from him, nearly all of whom were to survive his fall. And already in 1959 he was under the heaviest pressure from a third power of immense potential and disconcerting proximity, the China of Mao Tse-tung. The greatest pressure of all, however, came from the people of the Soviet Union, some highly articulate, the mass not articulate at all but hostile all the same.

He was doomed to go on learning. And if we compare what he wanted and hoped to do in 1956 with what he in fact did do between 1956 and 1964 we shall see how much he had to learn and how every lesson learned entailed some sort of retreat interrupted by ugly counterattacks and covered by noisy alarms—but always retreat.

[5.]

What he set himself to do, for all practical purposes, was this: at home to preserve the Stalinist system purged of its grosser excesses, to ease the central tyranny just enough to win the cooperation of the people on lines laid down from above; abroad to achieve a political *détente* with the West which would ensure the avoidance of a major nuclear war, while at the same time leaving him free to exploit revolutionary movements directed against Western interests, to undermine by all possible means Western positions and Western unity, to woo the neutralists and wean them away from the West, to threaten with nuclear arms which he did not intend to use; within the Communist world to regenerate the socialist camp by easing police pressure and Soviet demands, while ensuring that the consequent increase in economic efficiency should be harnessed to Soviet interests. What he set out to achieve, in a word, was Stalinism without tears. And just as much later, at the height of the quarrel with China, he was to defend his tenderness towards Nehru's India by declaring with all his old brutality, "Certainly we are supporting Nehru; but we support him as the rope supports a man to be hung!" [5]—so he might have said, "Certainly we are allowing more freedom; but the freedom we allow is the freedom of the regiment."

He did not see the insuperable contradictions latent in all his policies. It is to be questioned whether he ever saw them. His mind was agile to a degree, strong, and even supple; but it was not lucid and it was not subtle. Like the minds of so many able politicians, it was not creative and it was the reverse of contemplative. It was essentially a mind swift in reaction to exterior pressures and stimuli, and when the pressures and stimuli were contradictory, as frequently they were, his reactions were contradictory too. This need not surprise us. The philosopher politician is a rare phenomenon; and when a national hero does emerge of this kind, who creates his own framework of reference in the interests of a coherent and organic body of thought and action, the philosophic level is usually pretty inferior, producing a Bonaparte, a Bismarck, a Hitler, or a Stalin.

It was Khrushchev's overwhelming vitality and drive which, coupled with his quickness and ingenuity, produced the impression that he was really going somewhere, and thus obscured the truth; namely, that his mind was a politician's mind, the sort of mind found in all men who rise to power by persuasion and intrigue and who repose their power on the consent of the persuaded. Khrushchev did not restore Stalinism without tears, driving the Soviet Union on to an ever-rising level of prosperity, shattering the unity and strength in the West, and presiding from Moscow over a regenerated socialist camp and an increasingly active and successful world revolutionary movement. Far from it: he did away with most of the tears, but the system he established also did away with the strongest elements of Stalinism, while retaining some of the weakest; after a quick rise in productivity and prosperity when the sluice-gates were first opened, continued interference from the centre—unsystematic, often contradictory—put a stop to increased food production and seriously slowed down industrial production; he left the West at least as strong as he found it; the socialist camp was not regenerated at all, but fragmented; the world revolutionary movement was thrown overboard; the neutralists were forced into disillusionment; and if vast areas of the world one day come to look to China for salvation, this will be only because the leaders of the free world are as hopelessly bound by their own preconceptions as Khrushchev was by his.

With all this, our hero will go down to history as Khrushchev the peacemaker.

[6.]

This was not an easy title to win, and probably not the one he most coveted. Even of that he was not sure until October 1962, when he took his rockets out of Cuba.

The first lesson came quite soon after the Twentieth Party Congress, when, with Bulganin, Khrushchev visited London. It was his first excursion into an enemy headquarters (Geneva was neutral ground), and he was very much on the defensive, as well he might have been: the peasant boy from Kalinovka, still not formally confirmed as the head of a great power whose strength he himself hardly appreciated and whose backwardness and muddle he himself had lately been exposing for all to see, was meeting face to face, on his own ground, the Prime Minister of a people notorious for their old-world perfidious diplomatic skills and implacable hostility to Communism. The Prime Minister was Mr. Eden. At that time, as part of the general practice of subversion, Russia was being unusually active in stirring up trouble in the Middle East. As far as Khrushchev was concerned, the Middle East was Tom Tiddler's ground, a promising theatre for essays in "competitive coexistence." He discovered with a sense of shock that to London the Middle East was not Tom Tiddler's ground at all: it was oil, and the oil from the Middle East was vital to the life of Britain, so vital that if the Soviet Union started serious trouble it would lead to war. Khrushchev, of course, knew all about Middle Eastern oil and Britain's interest in it, but he had seen it as just one of those interests of the capitalist brigands which he could quite happily and safely work to undermine—as he was working to undermine, without creating any particularly sharp reaction, what was left of the British position in India. He absorbed the shock: Russia's freedom of action was not quite so complete as he had been led to believe. It was a pity.

On the same visit he had another shock. This was at a dinner given in his honour by the Labour Party at the House of Commons. Mr. Gaitskell produced a list of two hundred Social Democrats held in prison in the various European satellites and asked him for his personal intervention in their interest. Very much on the defensive indeed, he took this as a calculated insult. There were no Social Democrats in Russia, he said (in fact they were all dead), and what went on in other countries was no concern of his. He refused to have anything to do with the list. It had been well enough for him, at that same meeting, to hold forth to Labour leaders about the iniquities of British policy before the Second World War, policy which Labour had often opposed; but the slightest question of his own good faith could only be a calculated insult. The man whom nobody he had had to deal with in forty years had ever dared answer back was finding it difficult to accommodate himself to a world in which Gaitskells and George Browns could openly attack him.

This particular attack must also have seemed part of a plot. He knew, as the West at that moment did not, that under the impact of de-Stalinization the satellites were beginning to boil over. Instead of being grateful for the new mood in Moscow and rallying round the Kremlin with a will, base elements were preparing to exploit this new mood in the interests of nothing less than counterrevolution. There is not the least doubt that Khrushchev did believe in a plot. He had, when all was said, the authority of Mr. Dulles. When the factory workers in Poznań started rioting on June 28, the Poles themselves for a moment spoke of imperialist provocation, but almost immediately changed their minds when they realized that the country was on the edge of going up in flames. Moscow, however, would have nothing of the revised Polish view that police tyranny and atrocious working and living conditions lay behind the rioting. A month later Bulganin himself went to Poland to stiffen the government's resistance, insisting with total conviction that the Poznań riots had been "provoked by enemy agents" and speaking of the "lunatic plans of international revolutionary agents." [6]

Even if Bulganin, or Khrushchev, did not believe this to be the whole truth, it was the thing to say; the Polish Party leaders were expected to say it. They were expected to fall into line with the Stalinist tradition, the Khrushchev tradition. But the tradition was broken. The Polish leaders, whose total subservience had been taken perfectly for granted by Khrushchev, went out of their way to dwell on the social causes of the result; they drew the conclusion that the only way to put an end to an inflammable situation was by further "democratization," not by a stepping up of repression. When the Soviet press demanded severe punishment for the rioters[7] the Polish leadership paid no attention, released many of those who had been arrested, and gave lenient sentences to the rest, with not a word about imperialists agents or enemies of the people.

Democratization was not a word that had occurred in Khrushchev's speech. He was alarmed. He was also very much on the defensive, this time against some of his own colleagues. Wild things had been said at home under the impact of the assault on Stalin, but these had been checked by one or two leading articles in *Pravda* laying down with some precision just what it was safe to criticize Stalin for.[8] The Russians knew how to take a hint. Wilder things had been said in Hungary, but then the Hungarians were notoriously wild, and they had a new leader, Gerö, who was no less loyal or obedient to the Kremlin than Rakosi, his predecessor, who had been sacrificed as an earnest of better things to come. Wild things had been said and done at Poznan; these were a matter for the Polish Party and police. But the wildest, most outrageous, most dangerous of all the things said and done during those turbulent months was the quiet, unemphatic refusal of the Polish Party leaders to do what Moscow told them.

It was in September that Khrushchev decided to appeal to Tito to redress the balance. He was in imminent danger of being overthrown by the Stalinist faction in the Kremlin, headed by Molotov and Kaganovich, who, if the East European empire continued exploding, would soon win the support of many more. For the first (but not the last) time a Russian Communist leader was appealing to a foreign statesman to come to his aid in a fight with his own colleagues. It was an extraordinary situation. Tito had become an example and a symbol to all those satellite leaders who, no longer wholly subservient to Moscow, wished to ingratiate themselves with their own peoples while achieving a measure of independence for themselves. Khrushchev sought to exploit his extraordinary authority by getting him to convey to the satellite Parties that if they went too far with their own de-Stalinization he, Khrushchev, their true friend and protector, would be overthrown by reactionary elements—such as Molotov—who would soon put an end to more liberal policies.

Tito, for his part, already had dreams of appearing as the accepted leader of a new sort of European Communist movement, independent of Moscow, and cooperation with Khrushchev seemed to be his best hope. The situation at times verged on the farcical—as when Khrushchev insisted on summoning the wretched new Hungarian First Secretary, Gerö, to meet Tito in Yalta and thus make himself acceptable to the Hungarian dissidents. But how deadly serious it was for Khrushchev was shown at this same Yalta meeting when Tito himself and a high-ranking Yugoslav delegation were received not only by Voroshilov, as titular President of the USSR, and Bulganin, as Prime Minister, but also by a group of Khrushchev's closest personal supporters —Kirichenko, Madame Furtseva, Brezhnev, General Serov of the police, a highly political general, and an admiral. This reception committee amounted to a demonstration. Molotov, Malenkov, Kaganovich kept away; even Mikoyan was not there.

It was all in vain. Inside Russia the qualified rehabilitation of Stalin, which Khrushchev himself had initiated, proceeded fast. Already in September, Kaganovich, long out of the picture, had been given an important ministerial post. In Poland and Hungary events were moving the other way. Gomulka, imprisoned by Stalin and lucky to be alive, was now put forward in Poland as the man who was going to take over the leadership and do away with the Polish Stalinists forever. This was going too far. It had to be stopped. On October 19, the eve of the critical meeting of the Polish Central Committee at which Gomulka was to be elected First Secretary, Moscow acted. Without warning, the Poles in Warsaw found themselves confronted by an unprecedented and terrifying threat: Khrushchev and Mikoyan, flanked by Molotov and Kaganovich breathing fury, arrived by air to say that this nonsense must stop. Khrushchev did most of the talking, ranting and threatening outrageously.[9] But it was a different Khrushchev, now tacitly acknowledging that he was one with the Stalinist faction he had fought so hard for so long.

The threats were backed by force. Warships of the Soviet fleet stood off Gdynia; tanks of the Soviet Army moved to encircle Warsaw. But Gomulka and his supporters stood firm. Rather than surrender to Soviet demands they would appeal to the people of Poland to fight. The Russians recognized defeat when they saw it and went home. But for days it was touch and go. The Soviet troops still stood in readiness and Warsaw felt itself a beleaguered city. It was during these days that Gomulka, dedicated Communist as he was, managed to rally behind him all patriotic Poles, including the spiritual leaders (themselves lately let out of prison) of a nation that was still bitterly anti-Communist and almost wholly Roman Catholic.

Worse was to come. On October 24 Hungary went up in flames. Still shocked by their experience in Warsaw, the Moscow comrades wavered. Until their confrontation with the Poles, the Stalinists could fairly say to Khrushchev, "We told you so, this is where your policies have led us!" After the Polish act of defiance Khrushchev, though very much on the defensive, could retort, "I told you so! A show of force by us will only lead to counterforce."

Now Hungary . . . It was a difficult situation. How to give way before the Poles in order to maintain a certain basic unity and yet not give way before the Hungarians? For eleven days the argument in Moscow went on. In Budapest the rebels seemed to be having things all their own way. Imre Nagy had become Prime Minister on October 24, on October 30 single-party rule was formally abolished, and it was announced that the Russians had been asked to take their troops out of Budapest and had agreed to do so. It was clear, it is still clear, that the collective in Moscow had decided to recognize the government of Imre Nagy. The turn-round occurred on October 29. There was a curious crossing of the wires. Fresh troops were marched into Hungary on that date, even while a Soviet declaration of coexistence was being drafted, to be published three days later, on the very day that poor Nagy proclaimed Hungary's neutrality and asked the great powers to guarantee it.[10] On November 3 Soviet troops were in position round Budapest and the frontier was closed. Next day, while Hungarian leaders still negotiating with the Russians were treacherously seized and sequestrated, Soviet troops attacked. The Soviet press had already declared the line which was to be maintained for a long time to come: the Hungarian rising had nothing to do with popular discontent; it had been staged by counterrevolutionary forces directed by fascist elements in West Germany and Austria. Nagy himself was an active accomplice of these elements—or, alternatively, his government had collapsed. No matter, the rising was put down in blood with total and concentrated savagery.[11]

We do not know the precise role played by Khrushchev throughout this affair, which will forever be associated with his name. We do know that while Soviet troops were still poised to strike at Warsaw, and while Moscow was still trying to decide what to do in Budapest, there was a very peculiar intervention: Chou En-lai, the Chinese Prime Minister, interrupted a journey to Burma to fly first to Moscow, then to Warsaw, where he greatly reassured the Poles. He could not have done this without a direct invitation from Moscow, and the invitation could only have come from Khrushchev. Khrushchev had lately shown a certain recklessness in appealing to Marshal Tito for help; he now appealed to Chou En-lai and thus had the distinction of being the first man in history to invite China into Europe.

There was an interesting postscript to this affair. Some years later, at the Moscow Conference of all the Communist Parties in November 1960 (and, later still, more publicly), the Chinese, savagely working for Khrushchev's overthrow, were to claim that the Russians had been cast into total confusion in the autumn of 1956, and that they, the Chinese, had themselves persuaded Moscow on one hand to refrain from using force in Poland, on the other to employ it decisively in Hungary[12]—their argument being that military intervention in Poland would have meant war between two Communist governments, whereas in Hungary military intervention was necessary to destroy a counterrevolutionary government. (Also Poland was hemmed in between Russia, East Germany, and Czechoslovakia and could not hope, as Hungary could hope, to link up with the West, or Tito's Yugoslavia.)

This may or may not be true. It sounds probable. Certainly some Poles believed they owed their salvation to the Chinese. Certainly Gomulka believed he had established a special relationship with Mao Tse-tung, seen by him as a moderating influence, and was to be bitterly affronted when, just a year later, at the Moscow Conference of November 1957, he was coldly told by his hero to toe the new, hard Soviet line.[13] Certainly Khrushchev stood in need of help and high protection: already in 1954 he had established his own special relationship with Mao. October 1956 was a dangerous month for him, and it is deducible from all sorts of internal evidence that he then owed his survival as First Secretary to the man who was so soon to be his bitterest foe. From the point of view of China in 1956 it would have been disastrous for the Communist world to fall into still greater confusion through the public dethronement of the man who had just dethroned Stalin.

It came very close to it. From October 1956 until February 1957 the world was to hear little of Khrushchev, who spoke out only to condemn Soviet students who had been demonstrating against the Budapest massacre and to make a number of statements designed not merely to check criticism of Stalin but, further, to reverse his own line. Thus on New Year's Eve, at a Kremlin reception, he declared, "When it is a question of fighting against imperialism we can state with conviction that we are all Stalinists. We can take pride that we have taken part in the fight for the advance of our great cause against our enemies. From that point of view I am proud that we are Stalinists." [14] And again, a fortnight later: ". . . in our opinion Stalinism, like Stalin himself, is inseparable from Communism. . . . God grant, as the saying goes, that every Communist may fight as Stalin fought." [15]

Molotov, meanwhile, very quietly had been appointed to be Minister of State Control. Furthermore, a plenary session of the Central Committee just before Christmas was a most remarkable occasion. Neither Khrushchev, the First Secretary, nor any of his closest supporters spoke at all. The higher Party apparatus as laboriously built up by Khrushchev might not have existed. And the chief decision of this Central Committee, meeting without its proper leadership, was to set up what could only be called an anti-government, a body of economic and technological leaders who might have been chosen by Malenkov, presided over by Malenkov's Pervukhin.

CHAPTER NINETEEN

Victory: The Dictator by Consent

IT WAS a shattering reversal of fortune. Within ten months of the triumphant Twentieth Party Congress, Khrushchev had raised against himself and his new Party machine a most powerful coalition of the old Stalinists, symbolized by Molotov and Kaganovich, and Malenkov with his economists and technocrats. They did not at once attempt to purge the Party; leaving it intact for the time being to act as a stabilizing force in the satellites, at home they simply bypassed it, reducing it to ignominy. In so far as it existed as an ideological force, Mikhail Suslov acted as its spokesman. But the real government of the Soviet Union was already in the hands of the men who were soon to be denounced as the "anti-Party" group. In so far as the Party now quite legitimately consisted of Khrushchev and his personal supporters, this is precisely what they were. During November and December 1956 and January 1957 they were victorious. In February, Khrushchev started to fight back. In June he triumphed and his enemies were scattered and crushed.

The battleground was the whole of the Soviet Union; the campaign reproduced in essentials, but on a bigger scale and with an urgency born of desperation, the features of the campaign which had ended in Malenkov's resignation of the Premiership in 1955. Then Khrushchev had been fighting Malenkov's governmental machine, committed to the new course, and had won the support, or at least the benevolent neutrality, of the old Stalinists. Now the new men and the old were united for

the sole purpose of putting Khrushchev down, for the time being shelving the differences between them. But the new and unlikely coalition repeated the mistake made by Malenkov three
years earlier: they relied on the power of the central government organs to impose their will on the country as a whole, neg-
lecting the country. Once again they were to pay for the total
inability, shared by all those who had helped Stalin run Russia
from the centre, to understand the mood outside Moscow. Once
again the man who so many years ago had put on his sheepskin
and moved about the Donbas in a sledge was able to mobilize
the provinces against the centre.

He did not, of course, appeal to the people over the heads of
his colleagues in the Presidium. The people did not enter into
this struggle at all, although it was fought out over the whole of
Russia. He appealed, as always, to the vested interests in the
Party apparatus, tens of thousands of individuals in enviable
jobs who saw their positions threatened by the new government
bureaucracy embodied in Pervukhin's State Economic Commission. This was comparatively easy. He did more. He broadened
his appeal to attract all those provincial ministerial officials and
industrial leaders who had suffered so long from the dead hand
of Stalinism and from the clumsiness, the red tape, the arbitrari-
ness, and the sheer inefficiency of rigid control by monstrously
swollen central ministries.

He was not content to appeal: he thought up a scheme which
was designed to achieve the impossible, to win the support of
both the provincial Party officials *and* the provincial state
officials, to say nothing of the factory directors. And this scheme
he presented at a new plenary session of the Central Committee
in Moscow, which met on February 13. There must be an end,
he said, of these giant ministries which were trying to run from
their offices in Moscow the entire productive forces and the entire administration of an immense country which sprawled over
one-sixth of the land-surface of the globe; 200,000 enterprises,
100,000 administrative organizations scattered throughout this
vast territory from Brest-Litovsk to Vladivostok, from Murmansk and Kamchatka to Baku and the borders of Afghanistan,
all with widely differing problems, had to look to Moscow for

the detailed direction of their operations. It was an impossible situation. What he proposed was to divide up the USSR into a number of administrative regions, each run by an economic body which would control and coordinate its whole productive life, industry and agriculture too: *Sovnarkhozy,* People's Economic Councils, which would smash through the network of centralized red tape, bring an air of reality to planning, and fully engage the talents of all gifted men on the spot, at present frustrated at every turn by the Moscow bureaucracy.[1]

This scheme was presented to the world, which had not yet understood how close to destruction the great Khrushchev stood, as a coolly calculated economic reform with decentralization in the interests of efficiency as its aim. Reform it certainly was, but the new proposals raised more questions than they answered. What was really being brought forward was yet another instalment in the drama of Khrushchev's survival. By stumping the country, by sending out the message via his own Party network, he had, while his colleagues glumly schemed against him in Moscow, offered to key men of all kinds throughout the provinces the promise of undreamed-of advancement, increased scope and promotion for tens of thousands. And it was with the knowledge of their support that he faced his enemies at the Central Committee meeting—to such effect that, instead of rejecting out of hand the plan which, if carried out, would wreck their careful schemings, the Central Committee voted that the Party Presidium and the Council of Ministers should draw up a detailed series of proposals. The Party, Khrushchev's Party, was back in strength. Shepilov, who had been dropped from the Secretariat in December, was restored to office, and Frol Kozlov, Khrushchev's Leningrad right hand, was brought to Moscow to strengthen the Secretariat.

Khrushchev had made a remarkable comeback, but he had not won the campaign. His Central Committee speech was not published until six weeks after it had been delivered, and even then it was offered only as a guide to "a general popular debate," not as a laying down of the law. The debate went on from March 3 to May 4, and during the whole of April the Soviet Press had little space for anything else. According to Khrushchev himself, who continued to stump the country instead of staying in Moscow to keep an eye on those who were working against him, no less than half a million meetings were held throughout the land.[2] But on no solitary occasion did the opposition, which now included Bulganin and Mikoyan as well as the Stalinists and Malenkov, make a public reference to the reforms, either for them or against them.

During the debate all sorts of pressures came to light. In appealing to the provincial figures, Khrushchev inevitably affronted the very powerful republican party secretaries, all his own creation. At the same time, in the excitement over new "spoils," the leading figures in every district demanded their own economic council—and, indeed, in the end Khrushchev had to break up the country into more and smaller fractions than he had originally proposed. At the same time, also to win support where it was vitally needed, he had to exempt certain ministries from the general process of destruction. He had a new ally, however, and derived much strength from it—none other than the Army under Zhukov as Minister of Defence. What personal reasons decided Zhukov to back Khrushchev, what promises he was given about the curbing of Party interference in Army affairs, we do not know. But the breaking down of the vast unwieldy economy into quasi-self-sufficient areas was, on the face of it, an idea that would have appealed strongly to the marshals with their territorial and frontier commands. It meant that these commands would themselves gain in self-sufficiency, comprehending within their areas complete cross-sections of industry, presided over by local officials who could be directly influenced by the local Army commanders.

In May the reform became law. Pervukhin gave up his post as economic overlord. The new state committee for long-term planning, the only statewide economic organization left, was set up under an obscure but reliable back-room member of Khrushchev's Party machine. The opposition to Khrushchev had its back to the wall.

[2.]

But it was still, as far as Moscow went, very powerful, and it was desperate. Khrushchev and his Secretariat were once more in full control of the Party, and the Party had snatched economic power from the men who had thought most about it. But the men who had been displeased by the break-up of the central ministries made a formidable array of malcontents, and although the candidate, or non-voting, members of the Presidium were Khrushchev's creatures, the senior members of that Presidium remained. Khrushchev left them behind in Moscow and took Bulganin on a trip to Finland. During their absence—during the absence also of Kirichenko, Khrushchev's only entirely dependable supporter among the voting members of the Presidium—Malenkov and Molotov convened a meeting of the Presidium for June 18. On June 14 practically the whole Presidium turned out to meet Khrushchev and Bulganin on their return from Finland, and one of the most fascinating documents of the time is the photograph which appeared on the front page of *Pravda,* showing Malenkov, Molotov, Kaganovich, Mikoyan, Suslov, and all clustering round the returned heroes, beaming joy and good will, half smothered with flowers.[3] All was made up. The comrades, recently at daggers drawn, were all boys together. The collective was restored. Dear Nikita Khrushchev, beaming too, was even more equal than the rest. It was an act to end all acts, even in Russia. It was inconceivable that these cloudlessly happy warriors could be plotting against their leader, so lately restored to his proper authority.

Only four days later, at the Presidium meeting, Khrushchev, who had undoubtedly believed that it was only a matter of quite a short time before he could finally rid himself of his old comrades, found himself isolated. He was attacked with savagery, not only for playing ducks and drakes with the economy but also for trying to jettison the principle of collective leadership. "Talk less, and give the people more to eat!" said Molotov. Other stories of this kind were later put about by Khrushchev's supporters, who had an interest in confusing the issue. There were to be plenty of stories like this circulating round Moscow

during the months to come, but all we know with any degree of
certainty comes from Khrushchev's own admission that he was
voted out of the First Secretaryship by a strong majority of the
Presidium, that he then confounded the victors by refusing to
resign until this verdict had been confirmed by the Central
Committee in full session. "But we are seven and you are four,"
exclaimed Bulganin; to which Khrushchev retorted, "Certainly
in arithmetic two and two make four. But politics are not arithmetic. They are something different." [4]

He got his plenary session. It was the first appeal to any sort of
inner-Party democracy since Stalin, aided by Molotov and Kaganovich, at long range by Khrushchev too, had formally abolished it in 1926. While the comrades of the Presidium waited for
their decision to be endorsed (Molotov was to be First Secretary,
Malenkov Prime Minister, Khrushchev Minister of Agriculture!) the Khrushchev faction staged a spectacular operation.
With the help of Marshal Zhukov and the Army's transport
planes, Khrushchev's supporters were rushed into Moscow from
the remotest provinces, while those who were already there
staged a filibuster until the majority for Khrushchev was assured; Madame Furtseva is said to have held forth for six hours.

On June 22 the Central Committee met—in all, 309 individuals, 215 of whom applied to speak. First they listened to the
high-level attacks on Khrushchev; then they started replying.
Molotov, Malenkov, Kaganovich reiterated their charges. They
particularly attacked Khrushchev's "milk-and-butter Communism"; he had lately taken to boasting rather wildly about
"catching up and surpassing" America in food production
within a very few years. They in their turn were accused of sabo-
taging the decisions of the Twentieth Party Congress.

And then, according to Polish reports, Zhukov went a stage
further: he directly attacked Molotov, Kaganovich, and Malenkov for their behaviour during the great purge years and said
that if they did not look out he would prove his point by pub-
lishing relevant documents of the period. This seems highly
likely. Zhukov and all the Army marshals had been working
very hard to secure the complete rehabilitation of the purged
Army officers, and it is a fact that three weeks later, speaking to

the workers at a Leningrad factory (one of hundreds of speeches being made up and down the land to brand the "anti-Party group"), he declared that Molotov and Kaganovich had been reluctant "to surrender the privileges they had enjoyed thirty years ago," that they "had opposed the unmasking and calling to account of those individuals who bore the main responsibility for the violations of legality which used to occur." And the reason for this, he said, was that they themselves "feared to accept responsibility . . . for their illegal actions before the Party and the people." He then went on to give details which were only hinted at by *Pravda* when it reported his speech next day.[5]

Be that as it may, the Khrushchev faction triumphed. For a time it must have appeared touch and go, because during the course of the plenary session Khrushchev's own most bright-eyed protégé, Shepilov, made an irreparable miscalculation and spoke against his master and protector. He, together with Khrushchev's opponents in the Presidium, and all those who spoke against him in the Central Committee, were doomed. Of the eleven full members of the Presidium, Kirichenko, Mikoyan, and, belatedly, Suslov supported Khrushchev. Of the seven attackers, Molotov, Kaganovich, Malenkov, Saburov fell immediately; Pervukhin was reduced; Bulganin was spared for the time being for tactical reasons; Voroshilov was practically senile and did not count; he was also a distinguished figurehead and a link with the revolutionary past, worth preserving.[6]

The new Presidium, now fifteen full members instead of eleven, bristled with Khrushchev's men. Furtseva, the first woman to achieve this honour (it did not last long), was elevated to full membership; so was Marshal Zhukov. Aristov, Belyaev, Ignatov, and two old warhorses, Shvernik and Kuusinen, were brought in too to supplement Khrushchev himself, Kirichenko, Mikoyan, Suslov, and Voroshilov. There were nine candidate members instead of five, rich in Khrushchev appointees, and including Kosygin, who had been a full member during Stalin's last four years and then dropped from the Party machine to busy himself with economics. This flood of promotions gave an insight into the way Khrushchev had had to buy support. It is a point to bear in mind. The Council of Ministers was also given a major shake-up, still with Bulganin as nominal Prime Minister.

The rout was complete. The old collective was destroyed, its leading members broken and humiliated—Malenkov sent to his power station in Siberia, Molotov to Outer Mongolia. Any further opposition to Khrushchev would have to come from among the people he himself had raised up, or whose support (as in the case of Zhukov) he had bought. The only two immediately effective figures left from the pre-Khrushchev era were Mikoyan, "the great survivor," and Suslov, not a personality to capture anyone's imagination but rather a tough operator with a very long head, a natural *éminence grise*.

The coup did not cause a great upset throughout the country. Nobody cared much about Malenkov and Kaganovich; Shepilov (rather unfairly) was regarded as a young man in a hurry who deserved his fate. But Khrushchev made a serious mistake in his treatment of Molotov. Nobody loved Molotov, but almost everybody respected him; he was elderly and far from well, and for him to be sent off like a parcel to wear out his weak heart on the remote Mongolian heights was too much. Khrushchev had to pay attention to this feeling in due course. "Vyacheslav Mikhailovich finds the mountains unhealthy?" he is said to have remarked one day. "We can't have that. We had better send him to The Hague. It's low enough there even for him!" [7] But he did not go to The Hague; he was diverted to Vienna, there to preside over the Soviet delegation to the Atomic Energy Commission, there to spend restful years attending occasional parties and taking gentle walks in the parks.

[3.]

But if there was no strong feeling about the coup, there was still a good deal to be done in bringing the country under control, particularly the intellectuals, and most particularly the young. The Russians were not struck dumb, as the West was struck dumb, by the spectacle of a Soviet leader deposing his colleagues without actually shooting them. They took this for granted. Indeed, they took a great deal for granted. And one of Khrushchev's first acts as supreme master was to indicate very firmly that a line was to be drawn and that he would draw it.

He staged an imposing offensive against the writers, who had been getting out of hand. But in his eyes (and, indeed, in fact) this was in no way a literary action: it was a high political action, for the writers represented nothing less than the spearhead of a political movement directed against the Party Establishment. The symbolic sacrifice was Vladimir Dudintsev, whose novel, *Not by Bread Alone,* published in instalments in *Novy Mir* in the late summer and early autumn of 1956, had attacked the corruption and the greed of the Party bureaucracy and had become the focus of innumerable feverish, entirely spontaneous student meetings in Moscow and elsewhere. "Tell me your attitude to this book, and I will tell you what you are!" one Moscow student declaimed. And another: "Our literature has been the literature of a great lie! At last it is becoming the literature of great truths." During that winter all sorts of writers, mostly young, had been raising their voices in what amounted now no longer to criticism of individual wrongs, which was permitted, but in implicit criticism of the system which encouraged such wrongs. This had to be stopped. The writers and the artists had to be put back where they belonged, firmly under Party control. They were to be allowed to criticize, but only what the Party thought fit that they should criticize. Khrushchev himself intervened, the first of a long series of interventions which was to show the immense, perhaps the superstitious, value of this peasant, who had never been to school, who had afterwards taught himself to read fairly widely, but who in his heart despised the intellectuals (whose weapons he nevertheless feared), set upon harnessing the intellectual life of the country to the cause.

After the writers had stubbornly and demonstratively refused to be overawed by the routine Party spokesmen, backed by the hated Party hacks among their own colleagues, who had been fulminating against them during the early part of 1957, in May the Central Committee itself had convened a special conference of writers, et cetera, with a grand reception in the Kremlin. At the conference Khrushchev himself laid down the law in a series of speeches which, when they were at last published in August, came to serve as the official line for years to come: the official line, of course, was freedom within strict limits.[8] But at a celebrated garden party at his own villa on the outskirts of Moscow, which was never officially reported, he showed the iron hand. He violently attacked so-called Communists among the writers who showed themselves worse citizens than many who were not Party members. He attacked by name the poetess Margaret Aliger, who fainted away under the shock. And he threatened. The Hungarian uprising, he said, would never have occurred if the Budapest government had had the courage to shoot a few of the rebellious writers in good time. Should a similar situation begin to emerge in the Soviet Union, he said, he would show that he was made of sterner stuff. He would know what to do: "My hand would not tremble." [9] He was equating the unrest among the writers of the Soviet Union with the bold and reckless clamour of the Petöffi Circle in Budapest, which had in fact triggered the Hungarian revolt. His words shocked his audience in that cheerful villa garden.

The shock was deeper than Khrushchev himself realized, although he had certainly intended to shock; it was the first time since Stalin's death that shooting and terror had been threatened. It was the first time, moreover, that any of the younger writers and all but a handful of the surviving old had been exposed directly to the atmosphere of careless violence which for decades had been the natural air breathed by the Kremlin leadership. Khrushchev almost certainly had no intention of shooting anybody. What appalled his audience, except the most hardboiled among them, was the cheerful way he talked about shooting, after all he had said to discredit the Stalin terror. They had come to believe that the shootings, the sentences in labour camps to living deaths, inflicted on so many of their vanished colleagues, had been the outcome of deliberate and solemn policy decisions arrived at by a harsh tyrant with proper, if frightful, gravity: so will men always seek dignity and significance in their own sufferings. Now they were face to face with a chunky little man in a panama hat, carelessly talking about shooting a few of them to encourage the others and clearly lacking the faintest appreciation of the real meaning of his own words. For the first time they understood that they did not count at all and that, although, for very good reasons of state, their new master was not a killer and would almost certainly be very sparing of executions as long as he was in charge, casual violence was, and would be, very much a part of his nature.

Milovan Djilas records his sense of outrage when, one evening in Moscow, Zhdanov told, "as if it were the latest joke," what had happened to the Leningrad satirist Zoschenko, after he, Zhdanov, had attacked him viciously as a supreme example of the negative, "cosmopolitan" peddler of Western decadence. "They simply confiscated Zoschenko's ration coupons [which in those days meant starvation] and did not give them back until after Moscow's magnanimous intervention." [10] The spirit of brutal, cheerful cynicism behind Zhdanov's "joke" was what the Soviet intelligentsia saw for themselves that they had to reckon with after Khrushchev's garden party.

It was largely because Khrushchev revealed this mood too candidly (Stalin had always been careful to conceal it behind the appearance of an aloof and taciturn regality) that he never won the respect in Russia that the West thought was his due. It came out in many ways repeatedly: the ward politician who went hand in hand with the statesman in him came out, inside Russia, in a thousand ways, and frequently also marred his performance as a statesman. The violence came out more rarely. It came out with the wanton execution of Imre Nagy in 1957. It came out at another meeting with the writers (who went on fighting back) in 1963 when the young poet Yevtushenko was defending abstract artists at a meeting of intellectuals. "I am certain," Yevtushenko said, "that some of the formalistic tendencies in their work will be straightened out in time." To which Khrushchev retorted, "The hunchbacked are straightened out by the grave!"

But he had learned a good deal between 1957 and 1963, and he allowed Yevtushenko to answer him with a straight rebuke: "Nikita Sergeievich, we have come a long way from the time when hunchbacks were only straightened out by the grave. Really, there are other ways!" [11]

Remembering the climate in which he had lived for the

whole of his adult life, we should not underestimate the effort it must have cost Khrushchev to restrain himself, as he succeeded in doing for a great deal of the time, from lapsing into violent solutions when confronted not only by intractable problems but also with active dissent among his colleagues. The violence was never far below the surface. The man who could stand in a rage before a meeting of Communist leaders and tell Peng Chen, the Mayor of Peking, that his venerated master, Mao Tse-tung, was nothing but another Stalin, "oblivious of any other interests than his own, spinning theories detached from the realities of the modern world" [12] must very often have regretted the passing of the days when anger could find immediate expression in personal violence.

People have speculated, I myself have speculated in the past, about whether Khrushchev's tirades really reflected lost temper or whether they were coolly calculated acts—as, for example, his extraordinary performance in the Palais Chaillot after the fiasco of the Paris summit conference in 1960. Of course he knew precisely what he was saying in Paris when he banged the table and ranted like a man possessed about the perfidy of General Eisenhower; but he was also allowing himself to be carried away, and to one who was there it was clear that behind this act, and others like it, there was a very real welling up of rage, the rage of frustration above all. This man who stood at the head of one of the two great powers, who had intrigued and manœuvred and slogged and murdered his way to the pinnacle of power, who was conditioned by thirty-five years of Stalinism to sweeping away all opposition, found it at times unbearable to discover himself in situations in which he could do nothing—nothing to the master of Communist China who defied him, nothing to a President of the United States who broke all the rules of international double-crossing by assuming personal responsibility for the activities of his absurd secret service in the matter of the U-2, nothing, short of shooting or imprisonment, to artists who painted nonsense pictures or poets who said the Jews had had a bad deal.

"I have not met people like you for thirty or forty years!" he burst out at the notorious dinner given by the Labour Party in 1956. This was one of the most revealing of all his remarks. He was, of course, partly thinking in terms of "ideology": there had been no Gaitskells, no Bevans, no George Browns in Russia for all that time; Khrushchev had helped to kill off their Russian equivalents—and in half a dozen European countries too. But, more personally, he meant that in all that time he had not met a group of men (outside his closest colleagues) who had the effrontery to answer back, even to heckle him. And faced by this situation he did not know what to do.

[4.]

There was another side. He could no longer shoot as a matter of course. This, as we have seen, was largely because he knew very well that the spirit of the times, the stage of development which the Soviet Union had now reached, ruled out arbitrary violence in the Stalin manner, ruled out, also, labour-camp solutions. More than this, however, it is perfectly clear that he himself dreamed of a Soviet Union—and worked hard for it—which should be rich and prosperous, sufficient unto itself and an example to the world. He did not want to shoot; his destiny forbade it. Lenin had been the great Founder; Stalin had been the great Consolidator and Defender; Khrushchev was to be the great Liberator and Provider, and woe betide anyone who tried to stop him! He, none better, was aware of the immense changes that had been wrought in the Soviet Union since Stalin's death, and he was bitterly aggrieved when the Soviet people did not thank him, or at once demanded more, or when foreigners quite failed to understand the nature of the changes. Thus, on his return to Moscow after his London visit in 1956, still harping on that Labour Party dinner which had produced so traumatic an effect, he said:

If these Labour Party leaders had had friendly intentions towards the Soviet Union, they would have found other questions to ask. After all, they know perfectly well that we are doing all we can to correct the mistakes made in a number of cases in the past, and that innocent people who were convicted are now being rehabilitated, and that not only in the USSR, but also in the people's democracies, legal proceedings of doubtful validity are now being re-examined.[13]

He was speaking here with perfect sincerity. He had gone to London as the chief spokesman of a great power which was engaged most actively in putting its house in order and making Russia a country fit for Russians to live in. He and his colleagues, but most particularly he, had acted with extreme boldness at the Twentieth Party Congress only three months earlier, and at considerable personal risk, to prepare the ground for this transformation. He expected to be taken at his own face value. In a speech at Birmingham he had spoken with modesty and dignity, setting what he thought should be the tone of the visit:

We have come to your country with the very best intentions. We are very pleased with the hospitality shown us by the government of Great Britain and the British people. Anyone can tell by looking at people's eyes and the expression on their faces that the common people of Britain are happy about our visit. I do not want to exaggerate the significance of myself and N. A. Bulganin as persons. But we represent a great and interesting country—the Soviet Union. You can like us or not like us, but the Soviet Union will not cease to exist.

And from this great height the representative of 200 million people, already disposing of the hydrogen bomb, very soon to send the first man into space, feverishly coping with the problems of de-Stalinization in the Soviet Union and in the satellites (which were soon almost to overwhelm him and sweep him away), was dragged down by a handful of so-called socialist politicians to discuss the fate of 200 wretched little oppositionists who, if they still survived in prison (in Rumania, in Hungary, in Bulgaria) could consider themselves lucky to be alive. This is not a criticism, far from it, of the British Labour leaders: Khrushchev had still a great deal to learn if he aspired to lead the Soviet Union to the sunny uplands, and this little matter of 200 imprisoned Social Democrats, all men of distinguished character and high position, imprisoned by Stalin, was one of the lessons in the course. It would have been a hard lesson for any politically minded Russian backed and enclosed by the tradition of authoritarian rule. "After the liquidation of the classes," Khrushchev once said to a group of French socialists questioning the premises of single-party rule, "we have a monolithic society. Why, therefore, found another party? That would be like letting someone put a flea in your shirt." For Khrushchev personally, with his particular background, it was impossibly hard, and he never quite learned it. But he went on trying to the end.

He was not merely angered by political opposition, at home or abroad; he was angered by anything and everything that stood in the way of his personal vision of a decently ordered society, firmly guided and controlled from above, but engaging the active and devoted cooperation of the people at large. His anger would come out in all sorts of ways. He was angry with bad workmanship. "The joints between the pipes," he said of a new show hotel in Sverdlovsk, "had been very badly made. And I, as a former fitter, was extremely indignant; even before the Revolution pipe-joints in the mines were cleaner and better finished than in this hotel at Sverdlovsk!" (But this was a long way from the man who had been once used to charging bad workmen with deliberate sabotage.) He was angry with the writers and the painters who abused their splendid new freedom to work for the cause by undermining the cause, or by frivolling away their time on daubs that might have been made by donkeys' tails. He was angry with parents of the younger generation who encouraged their children to look for white-collar jobs instead of going to factories and construction sites to lend a hand and learn about life. "It is no secret, after all, that some parents reason thus: 'But my daughter has completed the ten-year course—she cannot possibly milk cows!' She can drink milk, but she considers it beneath her dignity to milk cows!" He rejoiced when things went right. "There were some persons, even scientists, in the USSR who tried to prove that the Dutch have some breed of cows, better cows than our Moscow ones, and that our Moscow cows will never be able to compete with them. However, our Soviet cows have derided these scientists and have supported the Central Committee!"

And again, about a good crop of corn: "Here is the complete

ready-made meal! Here is beefsteak! Here is bacon! What will these plants look like in a month and a half's time, at harvest time? Then the cobs will be half a metre long! Now you will understand why I go on so about corn!"

And again: "We are getting richer, and when a person has more to eat he gets more democratic!"

[5.]

But he was an uneasy democrat. He also had plenty of bad advisers. It is clear, if it was not clear before, that the majority of his senior colleagues had set their minds against any return to terror; these must often have restrained his own harsh impatience. He had at his side the remarkable figure of his wife, full of restraint and dignity and sense, who must time and time again have borne the brunt of violent explosions and calmed him down, diverted his wrath, and headed him away from ill-considered actions; but she could not be with him all the time, and she could not stop him in full flight once he had started speaking. He had a son, twenty-one in 1956, a young engineering student who appeared to be the model of the more studious, politically disengaged new generation of students, and who could tell him what his contemporaries were thinking. He had a daughter, Rada, who was livelier, and through her he must have had a window into the mood of the rapidly growing and important class formed by the children of the elite with their total disenchantment with Party ways and Party maxims, their passion for foreign travel and foreign clothes and foreign ways.

But there is no reason to suppose that Khrushchev understood his children any more perceptively than the run of busy, impatient Western fathers faced with the incomprehensible ways of children who rejected everything they stood for; certainly he did not change his notions to fit theirs. Moreover, Rada Khrushcheva was married to a young man called Adzhubei, very much the sort of young man to marry the master's daughter, talented, energetic, born to run with the hare and hunt with the hounds, a most dubious mixture of the so-called "jet set" at its most lurid and the ambitious, intriguing politician: a protector of the very young and talented when it suited him, but also fathomlessly cynical. There must have been times when the young writers, the young painters, economists, and thinkers would have been happier if Khrushchev had not had in his house a son-in-law who liked abstract painting and understood the problems of contemporary youth; they would have known better where they stood.

Khrushchev also had to rely very much for too long on some of the most depraved political climbers, as well as on some of the most vicious place-men. Whereas his senior colleagues—those, like Mikoyan, who were there before him, those who had come up with him or under his mantle—were wise in the ways of tyranny and firmly set against any return of terror, any accretion of arbitrary power on the part of any individual, there were others. These were the ones who had learned their political manners under Stalin, who had climbed to the middle echelons by the very means Khrushchev had used (but they lacked Khrushchev's largeness and humanity), who had survived by sycophancy or back-stabbing or both, but who, when Stalin died, had by no means completed their climb and were not going to be put off by a little thing like the death of a tyrant and his subsequent disgrace. Khrushchev himself very much depended on a large number of these men for his final victory over the anti-Party group. Some of them disappeared into limbo when their usefulness expired; but there are to this day many of their kind still occupying vital positions in the Party apparatus throughout the Soviet Union.

They were at their strongest in the two or three years after the defeat of the anti-Party group. And at the Twenty-first Party Congress in February 1959 the most prominent among them made a vigorous attempt to have the case against the fallen leaders reopened. Spiridonov, the Leningrad chieftain, Ignatov, one of Khrushchev's appointees to the Presidium and the Secretariat, and Shelepin, the recently promoted chief of state security (later to be active in securing Khrushchev's downfall) were particularly violent. In their speeches they hinted that what they were really working for was the trial and execution of the late Khrushchev opposition. But Shelepin's speech, in a passage in which he accused the anti-Party group of behaving like "Trotskyists and rightists" was censored by *Pravda;* and the general tone of Khrushchev's most powerful colleagues was to condemn the fallen in passing, as a blight which had now been removed.[14]

More dire still than the influence of these vicious Young Turks who had been raised up by Khrushchev, who himself still depended on them, was the figure of Ilychev as head of Agitprop and Khrushchev's cultural adviser—a narrow, crass, ill-tempered sectarian, who believed not only in strict Party control of the arts and the humanities (Khrushchev believed in that) but also that the only way to secure this was to place and retain in positions of authority prime specimens from among the old-guard Stalinist Party hacks. What seems to have happened, in effect, was that Khrushchev did not swallow Ilychev hook, line, and sinker, but gave him his head when another touch of the whip seemed to be called for. Khrushchev himself knew very well that there could be no flourishing intellectual life in the Soviet Union, and no real change in the manners of the middle-rank Party leaders, unless on the one hand men with ideas were encouraged and, on the other, the Party hacks were shown again and again that the wind of change was real and not a sham. But he depended on the Party hacks, and at the same time he was still deeply suspicious of intellectuals and determined not to let them take him for a ride.

Thus, at the height of the Pasternak scandal, after the Komsomol leader, Semichastny, had attacked this great and noble writer with the language of the gutter, Khrushchev let it be understood, without saying so explicitly, that he was angry with the way the whole affair of *Dr. Zhivago* had been handled and had sharply blamed his subordinates for meddling in things they did not understand. But Semichastny survived and was later promoted to be chief of state security. And when Pasternak's enemies got together after the poet's death to destroy his mistress, Khrushchev allowed it to happen; and it was his son-in-law, Adzhubei, who came to England triumphantly bearing ridiculous documents which he said were proof of Madame Ivinskaya's guilt as an embezzler. So arrogant was he that he was deeply affronted when these documents, which might have come out of a child's home forgery kit, were regarded in London with raised eyebrows.

It is impossible to separate Khrushchev himself from this sort of thing. He could speak, as we know, with wisdom, moderation, and even vision in his public utterances; on occasion he could make Western statesmen look tawdry, narrow, and tenth-rate. He could preside over a meeting of farmers, or builders or writers or Communist functionaries like an amiable and infinitely tolerant Father-God, interjecting occasional comments, salty or benign. He could talk to individuals, often of low rank, in a human and personal way so rare in a professional politician as to be almost unique, reminiscing about the past, regretting that he had been too busy to read more, regretting that his position in wartime had cut him off from all those who had to live under fire. He could be simple and spontaneous and in love with Russia—and still laugh at himself:

On New Year's Eve I was coming back to Moscow from just outside. I spent the whole of December 31, from early morning, in the woods. It was a poetic day, a most beautiful Russian winter's day, and it could only have been a Russian winter's day, because not everywhere are there such winters as we have in Russia. Of course, this is not something national but a phenomenon of the climate and of nature—I would not like you to misunderstand me. That day the forest was especially beautiful. Its beauty was in the trees covered by powdery hoarfrost. I remember, when I was young, reading a story in *Ogonyek,* I forget who the author of that story was. It contained such phrases as "dear silvery shadows." The story was probably well written, but perhaps at that time I was less fastidious about writing. Never mind, I liked the story, and today I can still recall the impression it made on me. I liked especially the description of trees in their winter garb. The winter forest on New Year's Eve was so beautiful that it impressed me strongly. Perhaps the shadows were not silvery, but words cannot express the deep impression the forest made on me.[15]

And so on. All this, and much more besides, was a prelude to an attack on abstract art.

And now the modernists, the abstractionists, want to paint these
fir trees upside down and claim it as the new and progressive in art!

He was not always so gentle, and in private he showed himself
at home with the language of the Semichastnys and the Spiri-
donovs. Thus, on the occasion of his notorious visit to the abstract painting exhibition at the *Manezh* in Moscow:

Dmitri Stepanovich Polyanski [then Prime Minister of the RFSSR,
now one of the three or four outstanding figures of the Kosygin
government], told me a couple of days ago that when his daughter
got married she was given a picture of what was supposed to be a
lemon. It consisted of some messy yellow lines which looked, if you
will excuse me, as though some child had done his business on the
canvas when his mother was away and then spread it around with
his hands.[16]

And to the young painter Zheltovsky:

You're a nice-looking lad, but how could you paint something like
this? We should take down your pants and set you down in a clump of
nettles until you understand your mistakes. You should be ashamed.
Are you a pederast or a normal man? Do you want to go abroad? Go
on, then; we'll take you free as far as the border. Live out there in
the "free world." Study in the school of capitalism, and then you'll
know what's what. But we aren't going to spend a kopek on this
dog-shit. We have the right to send you to cut down trees until
you've paid back the money the state has spent on you. The people
and government have taken a lot of trouble with you, and you pay
them back with this shit. They say you like to associate with foreigners. A lot of them are our enemies, don't forget! [17]

The picture begins to emerge. It presents itself as an image
not unlike the images of innumerable pillars of the Establishment in the Western world, with particular reference to self-
made ones, oscillating uncertainly between sentimental and aggressive impulses, wishing they understood more but still frightened of what they do not understand, not wanting to be behind the times but detesting the times all the same, longing
to be loved but tempted by impatience into violence, enrap-
tured by a sunset but half ashamed of their softness. All this with
a difference. Western pillars of the Establishment do not give

tongue to every contradictory idea that comes into their heads; they do not rise to the top by actually shooting, or conniving at the shooting, of their rivals; and they do not enjoy the power of life and death over young painters, or anybody else, who defy them by wearing funny clothes and painting fir trees upside down. But, all in all, it says a good deal for Khrushchev that he did not shoot.

CHAPTER TWENTY

A Visionary Imprisoned by His Past

W E LEFT the main line of Khrushchev's career at the moment of his triumph over the anti-Party group, but as far as his domestic situation is concerned there is little more to relate. In October 1957 he felt strong enough to break Marshal Zhukov, without whom he could not have weathered the June crisis, willingly assisted by certain generals who either were jealous of Zhukov or genuinely disagreed with his policies or had put their money on Khrushchev.[1] It is generally supposed—Khrushchev himself let it be supposed—that Zhukov went because he was actively building up his own personality cult (he had posed on a white stallion for a life-size portrait!) and was defying Party control of the Army. No doubt he was doing both these things, but it is likely that there was also a more specialized reason. Zhukov was removed only a few days before the successful launching of Russia's, and the world's, first spacecraft, which was to bring about a radical change in Soviet strategic thinking. Khrushchev personally was soon to emerge as the champion of rocket defence of massive deterrents, as opposed to those conventional arms and armies which were Zhukov's dream-toys.

In August 1958 the time had come to get rid of Bulganin. This was quite easy, since Bulganin had voted against Khrushchev in 1957 and had only been kept on as Prime Minister for reasons of expediency and decorum until such time as Khrushchev judged the moment ripe to take the Premiership himself and make himself formally the head of state.

It should not be thought, however, that all was plain sailing from the breaking of Zhukov and the calling of the Army to heel in October 1957 until the end, almost exactly seven years later. On the contrary, there was a running series of clashes in the higher reaches of the Party, and the composition of the Presidium and the Secretariat changed a good deal in those seven years. Khrushchev had reached his apogee and could climb no higher, but this was not true of the men who had supported him, either out of conviction or in return for promotion or both. The sort of struggle which had engaged Khrushchev personally throughout his own career continued among his subordinates. Some fell by the wayside, some more or less held their own, some prospered. They clashed about domestic policy, about foreign policy, and about their own self-advancement. The Presidium which finally voted Khrushchev out of office in October 1964 was by no means the same Presidium with which he faced the Communist Parties of the world at the great Moscow Conference in November 1957, but it would be tedious and out of place to follow all the changes step by step: they tell us nothing about the master's methods which we do not already know.

[2.]

The Moscow Conference was Khrushchev's first great occasion as the supreme victor, and it was a triumphant occasion, Mao Tse-tung attended the conference in person and, shoulder to shoulder with Khrushchev, laid down the law to the rest of the Communist world. The Chinese were deeply gratified because for the first time they were accepted by the Russians as equals: they were invited to assist in the drafting of the famous Moscow Declaration, intended as a reassertion of centralized Party discipline and of Communist militancy after the shattering consequences of the de-Stalinization. Khrushchev was only too pleased to demonstrate to the outer world and to the unruly in the "socialist camp," to Marshal Tito too, who was presuming too much in his eyes, that Russia and China were one. But even as they celebrated their unbreakable unity and threatened the heretics in Poland, Yugoslavia, Italy, and elsewhere, Khrushchev himself must have been aware of trouble soon to come.

In the first place, he himself was simply manœuvring for temporary advantage and was concerned with tracing a hard line not from conviction but only for reasons of expediency; whereas Mao, he knew, reacting from his "hundred flowers" mood,[2] was arguing from conviction. In the second place, more importantly, there was already in existence a profound misunderstanding. Khrushchev was naturally pleased, to put it mildly, with the sputnik's performance a month earlier. But he was less emotional about it than either the Americans, who were cast into the depths of despair and self-questioning, or the Chinese, who were beside themselves with joy. The Soviet Union, they said in effect, long master of the hydrogen bomb, now led America in intercontinental missiles. The socialist camp, headed by the Soviet Union, would now proceed in every way to demonstrate its militray superiority over the imperialists. The East Wind, in Mao's words, was prevailing over the West Wind. It was in his speech to this conference that Mao also lightly observed that nuclear war would mean the end of capitalism but not of Communism: if 300 million Chinese were killed, there would still be 300 million left alive.[3]

Khrushchev clearly listened to this sort of arithmetic with a sinking heart. He understood what nuclear warfare meant. He also knew that there were not 600 million Russians, but only 220 million. He had a more sophisticated appreciation, furthermore, of the capacities of the American deterrent and the long way the Soviet Union had to go between the appearance of a sputnik swallow and a thermonuclear summer. He was building up the Soviet Union, not inviting its destruction. His ballistic missiles were instruments of state power to be deployed with discretion in the interests of defence and power balance, not to be used as the spearhead of the revolutionary struggle for the benefit of remote countries of which he knew nothing and for which he cared less. Furthermore, he had not the least intention of placing either the atom bomb or his rockets at the disposal of the socialist camp, or of telling China how to make them: they formed part of the paraphernalia of his, of the Soviet Union's,

power relations with the United States, and that was the end of
it.

He was right to be gloomy. Within a month the Chinese,
home from Moscow, were writing:

The absolute superiority of the Soviet Union in intercontinental
ballistic missiles has placed the striking capabilities of the United
States in an inferior position. . . . The Soviet intercontinental ballistic missiles can not only reach any military base in Central Europe,
Asia, or Africa, but also force the United States, for the first time
in history, into a position from which it can neither escape nor
strike back.[4]

Within six months of that the Middle East crisis had blown
up. Anglo-American troops had made their landings in Lebanon and Jordan, and the Chinese were demanding, and seeming
to expect, an apocalyptic reaction from the Russians:

. . . if the U.S.–British aggressors refuse to withdraw from Lebanon
and Jordan, and insist on extending their aggression, then the only
course left to the people of the world is to hit the aggressors on the
head! . . . The imperialists have always bullied the weak and been
afraid of the strong. The only language they understand is that of
force.[5]

Khrushchev thought otherwise. Although Bulganin was still
nominally Prime Minister, he addressed himself personally to
President Eisenhower as one head of state to another with an
appeal for an immediate summit meeting "before the guns begin to fire." He wrote: "We address you not from a position of
intimidation but from a position of reason. We believe at this
momentous hour that it would be more reasonable not to bring
the heated atmosphere to boiling point; it is sufficiently inflammable as it is." [6]

A little later, when the immediate panic had subsided and it
was clear that the Anglo-American troops were not going to
move on into Iraq, he withdrew his acceptance of Eisenhower's
counter-offer of a summit within the framework of the Security
Council—whether to appease the Chinese or for other reasons
we do not know. But the stage was set for the grand movement
which was to transform the peasant from Kalinovka, the district

Party official, the city boss, Stalin's lieutenant, the victor in deadly conflict with the toughest and most uninhibited set of politicians in the world, into a major statesman, into the great peacemaker who brought the Soviet Union to the threshold of a new age into which he himself could not enter.

The irony was that, for all his wisdom and vision, the one instinctive and deep, the other far but vague, he was moving where he did not want to go. He moved backwards into the future, trying to stand at bay, but always giving ground to the forces he himself, to his own greater glory, had unloosed. Or, because he was all those things, a peasant, a ward politician, a power-seeker on a grand and ruthless scale, as well as a dreamer and, towards the end, a statesman, he was incapable of an all-embracing and coherent design. He wanted to bring prosperity and glory to Russia, but his temperament was too opportunistic and his received ideas were too limiting to allow him to see the prerequisites for this. Instead of sitting down with his advisers and saying, in effect, The times have changed since Lenin gave us our direction, what must we do to escape from our own past? Let us experiment, carefully, systematically, and always on a small scale, with radical ways and means of revising the whole system which is so rusty in the joints: the industrial system with its rigid and over-centralized planning; the collective farm system which deprives the peasants of a personal interest in the land; the social system subordinated, in effect, to the interests of Party careerists and place-men—instead of doing this (which is now what his successors are in fact trying to do), he constantly sought dramatic and personal solutions which were going to change the face of the Soviet Union overnight without, wonder of wonders, disturbing the existing, the Stalinist, framework, solutions which were almost always ill-considered and frequently irrelevant. Just as he believed until after the Cuba crisis in 1962 that he could have things both ways in his relations with the West, achieving peaceable state relations with governments which he strove restlessly to embarrass and undermine, so at home he believed until the very end that he could have things both ways by inventing magical panaceas to be applied within the basic framework.

Thus, once it had been agro-towns, then the cultivation of corn, then the Virgin Lands, then putting townsmen in charge of the farms; now it was abolishing the Machine Tractor Stations, suddenly investing millions in artificial fertilizers, encouraging the theories of Professor Liberman[7]—and then drawing back when he looked at the details. It was sending half a million people to develop Siberia. It was catching up with America in the production of meat, butter, milk, and eggs in five years by trying one expedient after another to discipline or bribe the peasants into growing more fodder crops to feed and fatten more beasts. But nothing was basically changed: the great ideas man was now in a position to put his ideas at once into practice; but the ideas were apt to contradict each other, and they were often dropped for new ones before they had been properly tried.

With the ideas went people, who were dropped and promoted, often for no visible cause, but clearly because they opposed or supported the master's ideas. For there was indeed frequent opposition, some of it from Khrushchev's closest supporters, as when Madame Furtseva, Khrushchev's most faithful protégé (until she plummeted from the heights in the winter of 1961, to be restored later on a lower level as Minister of Culture), reproached him angrily for denuding Moscow, her Moscow now, of skilled builders to send them on a wild-goose chase into deep Siberia (they soon drifted back).[8] Nothing was coordinated, nothing harmonized.

But the same applied to the opposition: some opposed Khrushchev on one count, others on another, others on another still. After Cuba, at the end of 1962, there was a great coming together of all who differed from him about anything, and for a few months his position was more shaky than it had been at any time since the early summer of 1957. But he survived, and 1963 was the year of the great disciplinary action against the writers and artists referred to earlier—against the independent-minded elite, in effect; all those, whether engineers, soldiers, lawyers, scientists, technicians, to say nothing of students, whose way of thinking was made articulate by the writers. This was the last occasion on which Khrushchev sought strength from the Stalinists. This attempt, too, petered out. And in the autumn of the following year he went.

He went not because he was reactionary and not because he was liberal, but because he was erratic, unpredictable, unmanageable, now increasingly dictatorial; because, after a solid decade of incessant uproar about agriculture, food production was once more static and showed no signs of rising; because, after all his economic plunging, industrial growth was slowing down most dangerously, consumer goods were still in short supply, and the quality of what was being turned out was often atrocious;[9] because the country was confused and bewildered, not stimulated any more, by his restless dynamism; because in pushing the very necessary quarrel with China to extreme lengths, and concentrating now not on ideological differences, not any longer on China's reckless belligerence, but on the great power aspects of the dispute, he was shattering to small pieces what was left of Communist unity; because in pursuing his understanding with America he was giving too many hostages to fortune; because, in the end, he was showing signs of megalomania—as, for example, his essay in personal and private diplomacy through his son-in-law Adzhubei, aimed at coming to an understanding with West Germany.

All this was true. Khrushchev was not a tidy and efficient administrator—we have seen enough of his career to understand why this was so—and the Soviet Union desperately needed tidy, efficient, and systematically experimental administration above all else. He was not a coherent policy-maker: as we observed earlier, his great strength was his swift and bold reaction to events; he was not a moulder of events. And the Soviet Union needed badly a coherent line of policy, many-headed, domestic and external. He was impatient in action: patience he had to a very marked degree, but it was the patience of the man who is prepared to watch and wait until he is in a position to act; once the opportunity for action had come he was impulsive. He was authoritarian and intolerant of opposition and also vengeful: hence the bitterness of his quarrel with Mao Tse-tung and his

determination to push to the uttermost extreme his vendetta
against the man who dared try to supplant him as the father-
figure of the Communist movement, who said that through his
communes he had found a short cut to full Communism, who
worked determinedly and deviously for the ruin of the Soviet
rapprochement with America, who pursued policies which could
all too easily lead to nuclear war and the destruction of all that
the Russians had built up (and then complained because Khrushchev would not give him an atom bomb), who accused the
Soviet Union of betraying the Revolution by working to make
herself prosperous and strong—who, on top of all this, hinted
that the day might come when China would demand the return
of large areas of Siberia, including Vladivostok, which had been
ceded to a strong Russia by a weak China under a series of "un-
equal" treaties with the tsars.[10]

It was not until after the Cuban crisis that Khrushchev finally
made up his mind that there was one object to which all else
must be sacrificed, and that this was peace, first for the preservation of the Soviet Union, then for the preservation of the world;
peace to be achieved by an understanding with the United
States which would also strengthen the Soviet Union in face of
China. He had, indeed, desired this above everything else for
some years, but he had been unable to bring himself to face the
full implications. When he put those rockets into Cuba it was
the last kick against his destiny. Until then he had convinced
himself that he could still reach an understanding with America
without losing his freedom of action.

It had been a long and thorny progress. He had abandoned
Stalin's collision course with the West, once and for all, at the
Twentieth Party Congress in 1956, had been affronted because
the West did not understand what he was doing, and felt injured
because it objected to the rules of his new game: physical coexistence, ideological war *à outrance*. In 1958, at the time of the
Middle Eastern crisis, he had made his first appeal to the West,
but he was unable to perceive that so long as he proposed to use
ugly weapons, such as Berlin or megaton bombs, to intimidate
the West whenever, for whatever reason, it seemed expedient,

there was not much hope of an ardent response to his appeals. In 1959 he defied Mao Tse-tung and consummated what to his mind was without a doubt the climax of his career, the invitation to him, Nikita Sergeievich Khrushchev, the peasant leader of backward Russia, to visit the President of the United States as an equal—from log cabin to White House in its twentieth-century variation. But even then, because of his determination to have things both ways, he was unable to gain the full benefit of this apotheosis—for the very good reason that nobody then, or for some time afterwards, knew what it had cost him: the deliberate break with Communist China, which for long remained a most carefully guarded secret.

He held to his course, none the less, and made all preparations for a triumphant summit meeting to take place in Paris in June of the following year. He held on although he was under the greatest pressure from China, and also from those of his colleagues in Moscow whose appreciation of the Sino-Soviet situation differed from his own, until the spectacular incident of the shooting down of the U-2 spy plane in May 1960. The U-2 was there because, in spite of the spirit of Camp David, in spite of Khrushchev's warm and flattering references to Eisenhower's peace-loving and statesmanlike qualities, he was still unable to bring himself to abandon his freedom of action as the leader, challenged now (but few people knew this) by Mao Tse-tung, of a worldwide revolutionary movement—even though the responsibilities involved in leadership of any revolutionary movement had for some time been nothing but a hindrance to the peaceful development of the Soviet Union.

It is impossible to tell Khrushchev's real attitude to the U-2 incident. The signs are that he was at first prepared to take it in his stride, exploiting it for propaganda purposes to the top of his bent (the way in which he at first concealed the fact that the Russians had captured the pilot alive, thus leading the Americans to make ridiculous statements which were at once proved false, was a choice example of his cheerful cynicism). The tone changed only when President Eisenhower broke all the rules of diplomatic protocol by assuming personal responsibility for the flight. This clearly bewildered and angered Khrushchev, making him look a fool for having so loudly insisted on his "trust" in Eisenhower.

On the other hand, there was reason to suppose, even before the U-2 incident, that Khrushchev's attitude to the Paris meeting had changed for domestic reasons. What had gone on between Mao and Khrushchev at the Peking meeting late in 1959 was known only to the two principals and their inner cabinets. The fact that Khrushchev had refused to give the Chinese samples of atomic bombs and know-how in the summer of 1959 was not published to the world until very much later.[11] The withdrawal of Soviet technicians from China in the winter of 1959 was also only partly understood by the outer world, which, in any case, had no knowledge of the scale of this operation, its catastrophic effect on the Chinese economy, and the bitterness and rancour which it aroused. But in April 1960, with the publication in Peking of the celebrated articles for Lenin's anniversary,[12] Khrushchev had to reckon with the fact that the Chinese were beginning to hit back—though in a way still calculated to conceal the issues from the outside world—and that very soon Communist leaders all over the world would be asking for an explanation. Was this a good time to pursue, regardless of the rumblings from his great Chinese neighbour and the alarm in the "socialist camp," his policy of conciliation with the United States? It seems likely that the U-2 incident was perfectly timed to give him a breathing space, to supply a pretext for cooling off towards America, to allow him to appear no less anti-imperialist than the Chinese—and then to turn round and settle with the Chinese and all the doubters on his own side.

At any rate, this is what he did. In Paris, in June, he broke up the summit conference with the maximum of publicity and *brouhaha* and treated the world, on television, to the spectacle of a man beside himself with fury and outraged indignation. As had already been suggested, he was acting, and he knew what he was saying, but the genuine anger was there. All his pent-up frustrations came welling out in a carefully contrived show of violence: he was angry with President Eisenhower, by all means; but he was angry with Mao Tse-tung; with all those on his side who were not wholehearted in their support; with Comrade Ulbricht, who was going on about a German peace treaty; with life itself, which was perversely preventing him from having all things his own way.

It all came out in this display, which made responsible on-lookers think he had gone off his head. And then he went to Berlin to tell Ulbricht he would have to wait for his treaty, and then to Bucharest, to the Rumanian Party Congress, to insult the Chinese delegates, to attack Mao Tse-tung in the sort of terms he had once used in attacking Trotsky, and, before the astonished gaze of Communist leaders from East Europe and elsewhere, to reveal that for some months past relations between China and the Soviet Union had been working up to the point of cold war.[13]

[3.]

From 1960 until the end, the course of Khrushchev's career was dominated by the Chinese quarrel. This was made public to the Communist Parties of all the world at the secret Moscow Conference of November 1960, at which Khrushchev repeated his Bucharest performance, this time in face of much tougher opposition in the person of Teng Hsiao-ping, who stood up in the Kremlin hall in the heart of Moscow to accuse Khrushchev of betraying the Revolution and to declare in so many words that China proposed to take the leadership from Russia.[14]

The differences were papered over in the formal Declaration at the end of the conference, which is all the outside world knew about it. But the leaders of 81 Communist Parties had seen for themselves that it was war to the knife between Khrushchev and Mao, between the two great Communist allies; and although many of them deeply resented the way in which Khrushchev, aided above all by Suslov, had railroaded them into declaring their support (in the grand Stalin manner, not even permitting the various delegations to consult together in their hotels), they were so shocked by the shrillness and bitterness of the Chinese counterattack that all came to Russia's support, save for two or three equivocators in Southeast Asia and the British Dominions and Albania, that tiny country cut off from the European Communist bloc by Yugoslavia, whose dictator, Enver Hoxha, glorified Stalin and declared in round terms that Khrushchev was a traitor.

From 1960 onwards it was quite impossible to understand Khrushchev's foreign policy, and a good deal of his domestic policy too, except in the light of his life-and-death struggle with China, but it was not until the winter of 1962–1963 that the deadly reality of the conflict was at last revealed by both sides to the world.[15] One day it will be an interesting and instructive exercise for somebody to make a detailed study of Soviet foreign policy between 1958 and 1963 in the light of what everyone now knows about the Sino-Soviet quarrel—a period which included the meeting between Khrushchev and President Kennedy in Vienna in the summer of 1961 and the Cuban crisis in October 1962.

[4.]

During all these years Khrushchev had China on his back, but it was not until after Cuba that he felt able to abandon all pretence, and it was not until the signing of the nuclear test-ban treaty in August 1963 that he publicly acted in defiance of Peking. Even at the Twenty-second Party Congress in October 1961 he refused to attack China by name, using Albania as a cover-name for the great Asian power, just as the Chinese used Yugoslavia as a cover-name for the Soviet Union. He then had his chance to take the measure of the new American President at the Vienna meeting which cast President Kennedy into gloom.

From Khrushchev's point of view this meeting was in no way a climacteric; it was no more than a useful exploration. An aged and amiable national figure whom nobody would accuse of either dynamism or power mania had been succeeded by an extremely young and brash-looking professional politician with no experience at all of large affairs of state. The scion of a parent who was a caricature of American reaction, backed by his father's millions and an immensely powerful political machine, Kennedy had only just managed to defeat Nixon, who, on his earlier visit to Moscow, had failed to impress Khrushchev (and not only Khrushchev) as a proper Presidential candidate. With this narrow victory, the new young President looked likely to be the prisoner of Congress, and yet the most striking thing about him to the outsider in those early days was his patent ambition and his self-assurance. Our hero, who was himself not noticeably diffident and uncertain, may well have echoed Lord Melbourne's observation about Macaulay: "I wish I was as cocksure about anything as Macaulay is about everything!" He needed to see this young man with the toothpaste-advertisement smile and a very youthful head of hair. He needed to decide whether he really was a President or only a personable figure manipulated by unseen hands—and, if so, whose hands.

In Vienna he did not set himself out to be unpleasant to Kennedy; far from it. He made what he took to be a number of friendly overtures. He said, for example, that he had nothing against Eisenhower: he was quite sure that Eisenhower had not in fact known about the U-2 flight, but had only assumed responsibility "in a spirit of chivalry." He assured the young man that the invitation to the President of the United States to visit Moscow was still open. He contrived a small, token agreement on Laos. To demonstrate his good intentions and hs power over the Stalinists, he pointed out that he, Khrushchev, after all, had pushed through the Austrian peace treaty, overruling Molotov to this end. But he was adamant about Berlin and he contemptuously scouted the idea, pressed by the President, that the Soviet Union should sit back and contract out of ideological warfare, refusing to lend encouragement and aid to revolutionary movements in other parts of the world.[16] There could be no immunization against the spread of ideas, he insisted. He was also negative on the question of a nuclear test ban; he still had tests to make.

Khrushchev was quite unconscious of the deeply depressing effect this encounter had on the young President. He was simply being himself, and by now people in responsible positions should know what that meant. They should also know how to take hints. There was nothing in his attitude and his behaviour to upset the President's seasoned diplomatic advisers, some of whom had been through it all before and knew what to expect.

When Kennedy asked what they made of it, one of them replied that it was "par for the course." [17] But the young President was new to this dreary game, which Khrushchev had grown old in and which he rather enjoyed. He was, in fact, a young man in a hurry; when the meetings were over he exclaimed that if Khrushchev really meant what he said about Berlin there would be war.

That the President was a young man in a hurry Khrushchev himself could see. This sort of hurry was alien to his temperament. It could also be dangerous. He knew, none better, that the Soviet Union, with China on her flank, must indeed come to some sort of understanding with America. But this had to be achieved gradually and in proper form. There was no immediate threat from China—or, rather, the immediate threat was not to the Soviet Union as a state but to the Soviet Union as the head of an ideological empire. A too swift accommodation with Washington could only assist China in this matter. America had to be taught that the Soviet Union was still very much a power—and who, in any case, was America? Was it Kennedy? Then who was Kennedy? At the end of the Vienna meeting Khrushchev had satisfied himself that Kennedy was a person, and a strong character into the bargain. But what did he really believe? This was by no means clear. Might there not also be an element of brittleness in his evident strength? This would have to be tested. And so it was tested, first in the Berlin crisis which culminated in the horror of the Wall, then in the Cuban affair.

[5.]

The Cuban affair, we have already observed, was Khrushchev's last great fling. It was also, for him, the beginning of the end.

The breach with China was, in October 1962, still not officially public. Khrushchev himself was committed to it, and all Communists everywhere knew he was pushing it very hard: the Communist movement was disintegrating under the impact of this gigantic conflict, and, as the Communist movement disintegrated, the base of Russian authority over a large area of Eastern Europe and over the Communist Parties everywhere, legal or illegal fifth columns in effect, was rapidly dwindling. Khrushchev's one great asset, which he exploited unremittingly, was universal fear of nuclear war. The Chinese talked with insane recklessness about "paper tigers," about the hollowness of the American threat, about the cravenness of all those comrades who showed themselves afraid of the hydrogen bomb. It was only their talk that was reckless; they were in fact behaving with extreme circumspection. But it was easy for Khrushchev to present them as belligerent warmongers who, given half a chance, and through their policies of encouraging active revolutionary and liberation struggles, could push mankind into nuclear catastrophe. Communists all over the world were no more anxious to be incinerated than their capitalist co-nationals.

The great asset of the Chinese, on the other hand, was twofold: they led the field in protesting against the authoritarian ways of the Soviet Communist Party, which many of the comrades resented, and they pointed out unceasingly and with truth that Khrushchev had shelved the world revolution in the interests of the power and prosperity of the Soviet Union, and was seeking a *détente* with the loathsome American imperialists to this end.

At the time of Cuba, Khrushchev was under immense pressure to reassert the power and glory of the Soviet Union both as a state and as the unique headquarters of the world revolutionary movement. He had very little to show for his strenuous and unsettling years at the summit. The economy was in bad shape: industrial growth was slowing down and consumer goods were still in short supply and abysmally poor in quality. Agriculture had relapsed into its previous state of chronic malaise: there had been colossal mistakes in the Virgin Lands and elsewhere. Khrushchev's constant boastings had become a joke, and his restless plunging and endless expedients were producing a widespread mood of frustration and unsettlement. Corruption, speculation, the short-circuiting of central planning by illegal means on an immense scale still continued.[18] The young, in millions, cared nothing about the government and less than nothing about the Party. The conventional forces had been run down in favour of rocket weapons, causing dangerous discontent in the Army. The satellites were restless. The Communist movement was falling to pieces. The quarrel with China was being deliberately exacerbated to the point of no return. The understanding with America, headed now by a tough and pigheaded young President, whom nobody understood, but who was certainly too young and inexperienced to be allowed to hold up the Soviet Union to ransom, was as far away as ever.

The Cuban revolution and America's attitude to it indicated that in no part of the world where the United States could assert herself was there the least chance of a revolution, Communist-inspired or otherwise, being recognized by the United States, which meant that the Soviet Union would have to renounce all pretensions to revolutionary leadership, or else, sooner or later, meet America head on and teach her a lesson. Kennedy's fumbling of the Bay of Pigs affair and his acceptance of the Berlin wall suggested that he might be the President most amenable to such a lesson: in spite of his self-assurance there was an indecisive look about him; also, he was not putting up much of a fight for his ideas in Congress.

Cuba was the opportunity. It was greatly stimulating, it was even a little intoxicating, to see a Communist regime amazingly established within a stone's throw of the American mainland. But there, unbelievably, it was, and most demonstrably under Russian protection. But it could not last long. Sooner or later there would be a massive American invasion, and then what? If the Soviet Union than did nothing, the damage to her prestige would be irreparable; yet what could she do without bringing herself into full-scale conflict with America? How could she defend Cuba effectively without attacking the mainland in a full-scale atomic assault? And that, of course, would also end in the destruction of the Soviet Union.

There was just one move open, and Khrushchev took it—whether out of conviction or under great pressure, we do not know: establish rocket bases in Cuba in the utmost secrecy, and Cuba would be safe forever. The rockets did not have to be used —heaven forbid! But once their presence in combat readiness was revealed, no matter how America might rave, she could not invade without inviting the full-scale nuclear war which he,

Khrushchev, knew that no government in its senses could conceivably invite over the possession of an island, no matter how near, no matter how hostile.

Khrushchev's military advisers probably saw no further than this. He himself almost certainly saw a good deal further. Once the inevitable uproar had subsided, the whole balance of East-West strategy would have changed. The young President would have learned his lesson. The Soviet Union would emerge with such authority that she could afford to turn her back on China, and could then, at leisure, start to deal with the United States on the basis of a *fait accompli,* pending the time when China would have made her own atom bomb.

The plan broke down. Although the installation of the rockets in Cuba was carried out more swiftly than anybody in the West could have imagined, the installations were in fact discovered before they were complete and operational. America was faced not with a *fait accompli* but with a major and revolutionary strategic deployment which had not been completed. For Khrushchev it was a perfect reversal: just as with his *fait accompli* he had proposed to force upon Kennedy a retreat which could be avoided only by risking, if not launching, a nuclear war, so now Kennedy could do the same to him, and he could no more afford to appear as the aggressor than Kennedy, nor could he threaten the destruction of civilization with his long-range intercontinental missiles rather than call off what, to put it mildly, was the deliberate continuation of a highly provocative action under the eyes of all the world.

It was a neat equation, and the American President solved it. It was a question of nerve, and the American President, horribly isolated, proved that his nerve was good. Kennedy's solution depended on the assumption that Khrushchev was not prepared to launch a nuclear war over Cuba, just as Khrushchev's initial action had depended on the assumption that Kennedy would not be prepared to launch a nuclear war to reverse a *fait accompli* in Cuba. Kennedy's assumption was correct. Khrushchev's assumption was probably correct; but we cannot know this.

There was no hysteria about his subsequent action. We have it on the authority of Kennedy's biographer and personal aide

that the famous letter which marked the collapse of the Soviet attempt to humiliate the United States in its own hemisphere was
not hysterical but perfectly reasonable.[19] He was still under
pressure. The second letter, which tried to qualify the surrender
by insisting that America should abandon some of her bases in
exchange for his taking the rockets out of Cuba, showed that
some of his colleagues, military or civilian or both, thought his
retreat too absolute and were determined to make him salvage
something from the debacle. It is doubtful if Khrushchev himself was interested in half a loaf. The Soviet Union had lived
with the American bases in Turkey for a very long time and
could go on living with them. He had gambled for very high
stakes and lost; side bets were unimportant. The only thing to
do was to present himself as the man who, by bold and decisive
action, had made it impossible for America to invade Cuba, and
then, his purpose accomplished, to engage in a high and mighty
and statesmanlike gesture of conciliation calculated to secure
the peace of the world.

He was also looking ahead. He knew very well that the Chinese would soon be gleefully exploiting his retreat, as indeed
they did. He knew very well that he had jeopardized his main-
line policy of *détente* with America, and that, after using Gromyko and others to deny the very existence of "offensive"
weapons in Cuba, he would have his work cut out to persuade
President Kennedy to believe his word about anything ever
again. The retreat must be complete: there must be no bargaining about anything outside Cuba. And so it was.

The days of having things both ways were over. *Détente* with
America must now be put above all other things, cost what it
might. This first meant publicly clarifying Moscow's position *vis
à vis* Peking. And so, in the winter of 1962–1963, came the first
direct and undisguised Soviet attacks on China.[20] The Chinese,
who had been calling the Cuban retreat another Munich, replied with even more vehemence, reposing their whole case on
Khrushchev's betrayal of the Communist cause. Communists
who had supported Russia against China were beginning to
wonder; they would have to go on wondering. All during the
first half of 1963 Khrushchev and Mao manœuvred to put each

other in the wrong, Mao with overwhelming attack, Khrushchev coldly, but almost absently. His eye was on America. The Chinese were to be kept in play. Let them overstep themselves by all means, but he was not going to incur the odium of precipitating the final breach—not yet. When at length a very high-powered delegation arrived in Moscow to have things out—after each side had done its level best to provoke the other into calling off the meeting—Khrushchev absented himself and left them to batter their heads against Mikhail Suslov, who had stage-managed the great conference of the 81 Parties in November 1960.[21] More than this, he returned to Moscow, while the Chinese were still there, to meet the American President's envoy, Averill Harriman. He was easy and relaxed. He was having his way. He was in the process of wiping out the nasty taste of Cuba by making a large public gesture and establishing, while he publicly snubbed the Chinese, a "special relationship" with America. He told Mr. Harriman a good deal about the Russian quarrel with China. And on August 4 he signed the celebrated test-ban treaty, which reduced the Chinese, by now back in Peking, to apoplexy and caused them at last publicly to declare that as far back as 1959 the Russians had refused to help them with the atom bomb, which had amounted to the unilateral breach of a treaty of mutual technical assistance signed in 1957.[22]

Khrushchev was once more the world statesman, moving back to the spirit of Camp David—and beyond. His great aim now was to liquidate all possible obstacles to a further improvement of relations with America. As far as he was concerned, the quarrel with China had moved right out of the sphere of ideology: China, growing strong, working towards her own nuclear weapons, was a potential threat to the Soviet Union as a power. All the emphasis now was on frontier incidents, both real and imagined.[23] The day might come, and soon, when he, Khrushchev, might need a frontier incident as an excuse to react violently to destroy Chinese nuclear installations while there was still time. This, of course, was never said. It has never, to my knowledge, been suggested. But it must have been present in the mind of the man whose career we have traced and who had the boldness and logic to stake so much on the Cuba gamble. Six or seven hundred million Chinese, headed by a bitterly hostile demi-god, and pressing against the vast, empty hinterlands of the Soviet Far East (some of which, as they pointed out, had been stolen from them by a Russian tsar),[24] could, suitably armed, be a terrifying threat.

In 1964 China exploded her first atom bomb. For the rest of that year Khrushchev's immediate preoccupation was to arrange a great international conference of Communist Parties designed to secure the submission of China or her formal expulsion from the world Communist movement. He was losing support against China all the time, so the matter was urgent. He met stubborn resistance, for a variety of reasons, from Communist Parties hitherto loyal—from the Poles inside the Communist bloc, from the Italians outside, from many others. Communist Rumania was leading the field in exploiting this largely hidden conflict in her own interests by having the effrontery to play off Moscow against Peking; the monolithic satellite *bloc* was falling to pieces, and Khrushchev was making things worse by trying to bully into submission peoples who knew that they no longer needed to submit. There was one thing only that held the European satellites together: it was no longer fear of Moscow; it was fear of Germany.

The situation was complicated beyond measure for Khrushchev by the impending American elections. The assassination of President Kennedy in November 1963 had been a shattering blow. He had known where he was with Kennedy. It had been he, not Kennedy, who had been taught a lesson by Cuba. But there had been no reversal of Kennedy's policies by Johnson, so all was still well. Now it might be Goldwater, in which case his dream seemed likely to be doomed. It was almost certainly because of this that he fixed the date of the preliminary conference which we was to prepare for the great all Party conference for December 15, 1964: the American elections were to take place in November. It was almost certainly because of this that, in good time for the American elections, he decided, without consulting his colleagues of the Presidium (so they afterwards said), to send his son-in-law, Adzhubei, to Bonn.

There was only one possible interpretation of this: he was

preparing the great coup which would convince American opinion of his good intentions and cut the ground from under Sena-
tor Goldwater's feet. He was moving to an accommodation with
West Germany. He was getting ready to sell Comrade Ulbricht
down the river. He was finally admitting the logic of all his policies, and he knew how to cut his losses. He had taken this decision on himself. He was the master of the Soviet Union, who had
weathered so many crises, and he was going to behave like the
master. He had a vision, and he was going to act on his vision.

His colleagues dissented. There were various sporadic actions
designed to sabotage his great design. Then, while he was far
away on the Black Sea, they met and made their decision. All
those who had ever opposed the old master on anything drew
together to bring him down. They did not, most of them, oppose the main line of his policy (their subsequent actions
proved this), but they were against his suddenness and his pre-
cipitance; they were against the hostages he was preparing to
give to fortune; they were against the muddle he was making of
the economy, the endless "hare-brained" schemes, which led nowhere, which had no systematic direction; above all they were
against his final assumption of absolute authority. They summoned him back to Moscow on urgent business. They had the
police in their pockets through Shelepin, who was duly rewarded, and they had the Army behind them. One after another
they stood up—some of them owing all they were to him—and
separately arraigned him: for economic failure, for agricultural
failure, for administrative failure; for his uncoordinated plunges
and sudden switches of domestic policy; for his opportunism and
lack of consistency; for his endless boasting. They attacked him
for the unrest in the satellites; for pushing the Chinese quarrel
to such bitter extremes and so making even an appearance of
amity impossible, thus fatally dividing the Communist world.
They attacked him for being ready to sacrifice too much too
quickly for the sake of an understanding, necessary as it was,
with America. They attacked him for his overtures to Bonn.
Above all they attacked him for alienating so many good soldiers, so many able officials, and for promoting sycophants and
yes-men to high office. They attacked him for encouraging a per-

sonality cult of his own, in breach of solemn promise, for encouraging the glorification of his person and for trying to govern and make policy with too little reference to his colleagues and through his own personal network of favourites. They said he was too old. They said the government of the Soviet Union and the leadership of the Communist Party were too serious to be left to the uncontrolled, uncontrollable impulses of a man who was showing himself ever more incapable of playing his part in a team. They demanded his resignation.

He defended himself and hit back. He had brought the Soviet Union through the great change; he had acted decisively and boldly when others had been afraid to act; he had secured the peace and laid the foundations for prosperity. And in fact he had done all this. He may well have asked who else could have done as well. But, in doing it, he had served his purpose. He had rushed the Soviet Union to the brink of a new era, which would have little to do with the assumptions of forty-seven years. The comrades knew this. They also knew that our hero, more than many of them a prisoner of his past—and what a past!—could never be the proper guide as they moved into the promised land. They needed time to think.

CHRONOLOGY

(ENTRIES IN ITALICS REFER TO GENERAL RUSSIAN
HISTORY; ROMAN ENTRIES REFER TO KHRUSHCHEV'S LIFE)

1894	Khrushchev born at Kalinovka in Kursk Province *Accession of Tsar Nicholas II*
1903	*Lenin splits Russian Social Democratic Labour Party into Bolshevik and Menshevik wings at Second Congress in London*
1904–5	*Russo-Japanese War*
1905	*The 1905 Revolution; Moscow Rising*
1906	*First Duma, or Parliament*
1909	Khrushchev moves to Yuzovka (later Stalino, now Donetsk)
1909–18	Works in factories and at the pithead
1914	*Outbreak of First World War*
1917	April (old style, March): *Revolution; abdication of Tsar; formation of Provisional Government* November (old style, October): *"October Revolution"; Lenin overthrows Provisional Government* December: *Establishment of the CHEKA*
1918	Khrushchev becomes a Bolshevik and joins Red Army
1918–20	*Civil war and Allied intervention*
1920	Khrushchev back to Yuzovka as assistant manager of a mine
1921	*Introduction of New Economic Policy (NEP)*
1921–22	*Famine* Death of Khrushchev's first wife
1921 or 22	Khrushchev to Yuzovka Mining Technical School
1923	Becomes a *Politrook* at Yuzovka Technical School
1924	January: *Death of Lenin*

(1924)   May: *Eclipse of Trotsky*

1925   Khrushchev appointed Party Secretary of Petrovsko-Mariinsky District in Stalino Region

Attends Ninth All Ukrainian Party Congress with Kaganovich in chair

Attends Fourteenth All Union Party Congress
Defeat of Zinoviev and Kamenev

1926   First recorded public speech at Ukrainian Party Conference in Kharkov

1927   Promotion to Stalino Region Party apparatus

1928   Promotion to Kiev Party apparatus
Exile of Trotsky
First Five-Year Plan; start of collectivization

1929   Transfer to Moscow as student in Stalin Industrial Academy
Deportation of Trotsky

1930–31   *Famine*

1931   Promoted Party Secretary of Baumann and Red Presnaya Districts, Moscow

1932–34   Second Secretary, Moscow City Party Committee; rises to First Secretary, Moscow City Committee, and Second Secretary, Moscow Region
Murder of Kirov

1935   First Secretary, Moscow City and Region; Candidate Member of Politburo of Central Committee of All Union Central Committee

1935–38   *Years of the Great Purge and the Treason Trials; destruction of the old Bolsheviks and most of the Red Army higher command*

1938   Promoted to be First Secretary, Ukrainian Central Committee

1939   March: Full member of the All Union Politburo
September: As First Secretary for the Ukraine and civilian member of the Kiev Military Council, moved into occupied Poland

1940   Supervised sovietization of eastern Poland

1941–45   Saw service as Politburo representative on various fronts; lieutenant-general

1944   Appointed to be Chairman of the Council of Ministers

(Prime Minister) of the Ukraine, while retaining First Secretaryship of Ukrainian Central Committee

1945   To Warsaw as chairman of the commission of experts which planned the city's reconstruction

1946   *Famine in the Ukraine*

1947   Temporary eclipse and demotion

1948   Restored to full powers in the Ukraine

1949   Called to Moscow as Secretary of the Party Central Committee and First Secretary of Moscow Region Party Committee

1950   Overlord for Agriculture

1952   October: As Politburo member and Party Secretary, delivered report on "Amendments to the Statutes of the All Union Communist Party" to Nineteenth Party Congress; Malenkov delivered the report on the state of the Party on behalf of Stalin

1953   January: *"Doctors' Plot"*
March: *Death of Stalin.* Malenkov Prime Minister and First Secretary, Khrushchev ranked after Malenkov, Molotov, Beria, and Kaganovich
September: First Secretary of All Union Communist Party

1954   Khrushchev to Peking with Bulganin, etc.
Virgin Lands Campaign

1955   February: *Malenkov replaced by Bulganin as Prime Minister*
Visits to Yugoslavia, Geneva, India, etc.

1956   February: Twentieth Party Congress and secret speech
Visit to London
Defiance in Poland
October: *Hungarian Revolt*

1957   May: Recovers threatened position. Decentralization of Industry
June: Smashes opposition of Anti-Party Group (Malenkov, Molotov, Kaganovich, Shepilov, and others)
October: *First man in space: Major Yuri Gargarin*
October: Dismissal of Marshal Zhukov
November: Moscow Meeting of world Communist Parties, attended by Mao Tse-tung

(1957)	March: Khrushchev takes over Premiership from Bulganin
1958	Summer: *Middle East Crisis; concealed disagreement with China* Autumn: *Berlin Crisis*
1959	February: *Macmillan to Moscow* November: First visit to the United States; Camp David
1959–60	Winter: *Quarrel with China develops behind scenes;* Khrushchev refuses to give China atomic know-how
1960	May: Shooting down of the U-2 June: Abortive Paris summit meeting Khrushchev's Party Congress in Bucharest November: Chinese quarrel publicized to 81 Communist Parties at Moscow meeting, but still concealed from the world
1961	Summer: Vienna meeting with President Kennedy Autumn: Twenty-second Party Congress; first public attack on Chinese policies (China disguised as Albania)
1962	October: Cuban crisis
1962–63	Winter: Chinese quarrel finally brought into the open
1963	Disciplinary action against writers, etc. August: Nuclear test-ban treaty. Professor Liberman's debut. Disastrous harvest November: *Assassination of President Kennedy*
1964	Preparations, in teeth of world Communist Party resistance, for a conference of all the Parties (preliminary conference December 15) for a showdown with China September: Adzhubei to Bonn October: Resigns all offices; succeeded by Brehznev (First Secretary) and Kosygin (Prime Minister)

NOTES

CHAPTER ONE

1. Boris Pasternak, *Dr. Zhivago*, translated by Max Hayward and Manya Harari. London, 1958, p. 16. (New York: Pantheon, 1958.)
2. Madame Olga Ivinskaya and her daughter Irina. For the story of her arrest, trial, and sentencing, see *The Observer* (London) for October 1, 1961.

CHAPTER TWO

1. Khrushchev talking to a group of foreign visitors, quoted by Harold H. Martin in *The Saturday Evening Post*, November 7, 1964, and *The Sunday Times Magazine* (London), December 13, 1964.
2. Both Khrushchev's own remarks about his past and the statements in official handouts vary and contradict each other so much that one has to read between the lines. As Khrushchev approached his zenith the official biographies added more and more details calculated to glorify his revolutionary beginnings and also, more particularly, his activities in the Red Army during the civil war. Since his fall these claims have been forgotten.
3. *Polytyka* (Warsaw) No. 28, July 11, 1959. Quoted by Lazar Pistrak in *The Grand Tactician: Khrushchev's Rise to Power*. London, 1961, p. 10. (New York: Praeger, 1961.)

CHAPTER THREE

1. See Note 2 to Chapter 2.
2. Decree of September 26, 1918.
3. Harold H. Martin, op. cit.
4. More confusion. Details of the death of Khrushchev's first wife are supplied largely by his second wife, but there are conflicting accounts.
5. It has been said that Khrushchev and his children lived with his parents in Yuzovka before his second marriage. For a most vivid eyewitness description of the workers' quarter in Yuzovka on the eve of the 1914 war, see the second volume of Konstantin Paustovsky's autobiography, *Slow Approach of Thunder*, London, 1965.

CHAPTER FOUR

1. Merle Fainsod, *Smolensk under Soviet Rule*, Cambridge, Mass.: Harvard, 1958. This extremely well-edited compilation gives a more vivid and factual insight into Soviet living conditions in the 1930s than all other books put together.

2. Ibid., p. 49.
3. Ibid.
4. *Partinoye Stroitelstvo*, No. 2, 1930. This was not Malenkov's solitary literary effort. He wrote a good deal.
5. Pistrak, op. cit., p. 21.

CHAPTER FIVE

1. *Pravda*, October 7, 1926.
2. Pistrak, op cit., p. 29. Here I must emphasize my debt to Mr. Pistrak. Although I do not agree with some of his views, the range and depth of his researches into Khrushchev's early career, and particularly his reading of the Ukrainian press, etc., make his book, *The Grand Tactician*, indispensable for all who follow in his footsteps. I have drawn on him freely. Besides supplying a number of quotations otherwise inaccessible, he showed me where to look in the course of my own researches into the years of obscurity.

3. Quoted by Pistrak, op. cit., p. 31. from *Visti VTsVK* (Kiev), October 22, 1926.

CHAPTER SIX

1. *15 Syezd VKP (6) Stenografichesky Otchet.* Moscow, 1927, p. 1318.
2. Pasternak, op. cit., p. 178.
3. Winston S. Churchill, *The Hinge of Fate*, Boston: Houghton Mifflin, 1951.
4. J. V. Stalin, *Problems of Communism.* English ed., Moscow, 1947, p. 480. It is interesting to record that the comparable figures for 1851, before the emancipation of the serfs and with a much smaller population, were: cattle, 20,962,000; sheep, 37,527,000; pigs, 8,886,000; horses (in 1882), 21,203,900.
5. Milovan Djilas, *Conversations with Stalin.* London, 1962, p. 98. (New York: Harcourt, Brace and World, 1962.)
6. This story does not appear in the standard version of the secret speech to the Twentieth Party Congress of the Soviet Communist Party; but it was in wide circulation in the Soviet Union before the speech was published in the West, and was certainly told by Khrushchev.

7. The secret speech of February 24, 1956. This speech, in the version issued by the U. S. State Department, has never been challenged and is tacitly accepted by Soviet officials when Stalin is under discussion. The version referred to throughout this book was printed by Bertram D. Wolfe, together with an exhaustive commentary and analysis, under the title *Khrushchev and Stalin's Ghost*, New York: Praeger, 1957.

8. For a brilliant account of this period, as for Stalin's life and work in general, see I. Deutscher, *Stalin*, London and New York: Oxford, 1949.

9. *Pravda*, May 26, 1930. Resolution of Moscow Party *aktiv*.
10. *Pravda*, June 3, 1930.
11. For the story of Nadezhda Allilu-

lyevna see especially Deutscher, op. cit.; Pistrak, op. cit.; V. Kravchenko, *I Chose Freedom,* New York; Scribner, 1946; and A. Barmine, *One Who Survived,* New York: Putnam, 1945. Barmine says that he received the true story of her suicide from her brother, who was his friend.

12. See in particular his remarks about Ilya Ehrenburg and his exchanges with Yevgeny Yevtushenko at "cultural" meetings on December 17, 1962, and March 8, 1963. These are reported *in extenso* in *Encounter Pamphlet* No. 9, London, 1963; and Priscilla Johnson's *Khrushchev and the Arts,* Cambridge, Mass.: Harvard, 1965.

CHAPTER SEVEN

1. J. V. Stalin, op. cit., p. 502.
2. Ibid., p. 356.
3. Lenin's testament, which may be read in Wolfe, op. cit., was quoted in the secret speech and published for the first time in the Soviet Union in *Kommunist,* No. 9, 1956. In it Lenin, on his deathbed, alarmed at Stalin's growing power, characterized the Secretary General in terms which have since been echoed widely, and urged the comrades to remove him from office. It was generally believed that this testament had been discussed at a plenary session of the Central Committee in May 1924, when it was decided, in spite of protests from Lenin's wife, Krupskaya, to suppress it and not make it known to the delegates to the Thirteenth Party Congress, then imminent. Khrushchev, however, in his secret speech, said it had in fact been made known to that congress (which he did not attend). Pistrak, op. cit., says it was actually distributed to delegates in the Congress Bulletin of the Fifteenth Party Congress in December 1927, which Khrushchev attended as a delegate from Stalino Region.

4. John Scott, *Behind the Urals,* New York: Houghton Mifflin, 1942.
5. *Pravda,* July 16, 1931.
6. See also Pistrak, op. cit., pp. 76-78.
7. Victor Serge, *Portrait de Staline,* Paris, 1940.

CHAPTER EIGHT

1. *Istoria metro Moskvy; Raskazy stroitelei metro,* Moscow, 1935. This volume apparently appeared in two versions, one longer than the other. The long version was in my possession, and I made notes from it, but the volume has been lost. Pistrak quotes very extensively from both versions, and I have followed him. All the quotations in this chapter, except where otherwise indicated, are from one or the other of these versions.
2. *Pravda,* September 6, 1933.
3. *Pravda,* February 7, 1935.
4. *Piat let metro.* Moscow, 1940, p. 34.

5. *Moskovsky Komsomol na metro.* Moscow, 1934, p. 29.
6. El Campesino (Valentín Gonzalez), *Listen, Comrades: Life and Death in the Soviet Union.* London, 1952, pp. 72-73. (New York: Putnam, 1952.)
7. Ibid., p. 74.
8. Ibid.
9. Z. Troitskaya. *The L. M. Kaganovich Metropolitan Railway of Moscow's Metro,* English edition, Moscow, 1955.
10. See especially *Pravda,* November 10, 1955.

CHAPTER NINE

1. The literature on this period and on the terrible years which began with Kirov's assassination is immense. But Khrushchev's secret speech (in Wolfe, op. cit.) should be supplemented by a general account of the mood of the times, the best of which is in Deutscher, op. cit., and Kravchenko, op. cit. dividual defectors, e.g., Barmine, op. cit., and Kravchenko, op. cit. Trotsky in his own works and the two émigré Russian periodicals, *Sotsialistichesky Vestnik* and *Bulletin Oppozitsy*, kept up a running commentary on the development and multiplication of Stalin's crimes.
2. *Sotsialistichesky Vestnik*, especially December 22, 1936, and January 17, 1937.
3. Deutscher, op. cit., p. 356.

4. Secret speech, pp. 128, 130.
5. December 1957.
6. Secret speech, p. 156.
7. Ibid.
8. Ibid., p. 214.
9. *Pravda*, August 23, 1936.
10. *Pravda*, January 31, 1937.
11. Pistrak, op. cit., has many further instances.
12. Secret speech, p. 106.
13. Secret speech, p. 110.
14. Secret speech, p. 114.
15. *Pravda*, November 23, 1936.
16. *Pravda*, January 31, 1937.
17. *Pravda*, March 17, 1937.
18. *Pravda*, June 6, 1937. It will be seen that the national daily newspaper of the Soviet Communist Party made good reading in these years. It is now much duller.

CHAPTER TEN

1. A. Weissberg, *Accused*, New York: Simon & Schuster, 1951.
2. *Visti VTsVK*, June 21, 1938 (quoted by Pistrak, op. cit., p. 145).
3. *Visti TSsVK*, May 23, 1938 (quoted by Pistrak, op. cit., p. 147). Pistrak is indispensable for his detailed study of Khrushchev in the Ukraine.
4. *Bilshovik Ukrainy*, No. 7, 1938, p. 25.
5. *Visti VTsVK*, June 24, 1938 (quoted by Pistrak, op. cit., p. 148).
6. For the most comprehensive account of the forced-labour system see D. J. Dallin, *Forced Labour in Soviet Russia*, New Haven: Yale, 1947. Out of a multitude of examples of personal narratives by survivors, I would instance two classics: *Eleven Years in Soviet Prison Camps* by Elinor Lipper, Chicago: Regnery, 1951, and *World Apart* by Gustav Herling, New York:

Roy, 1951. But many others, not so beautifully written, provide shattering insights into conditions over the years, one of the latest being *A Hidden World* by Raphael Rupert, New York: World, 1963.
7. Djilas, op. cit., p. 14, said that in 1944 he appeared to be drunk all the time. He was certainly rather gloomily drunk on the only occasion I saw him.
8. Secret speech, p. 124.
9. W. Baczkowski, *Towards an Understanding of Russia*. Jerusalem, 1947, p. 33; quoting from A. Dotsenko, *The Winter March*, Warsaw, 1935.
10. Resolution adopted by the Seventh Conference of the Bolshevik Party, April 1917. Stalin, of course, supported this resolution.
11. *Bilshovik Ukrainy*, No. 6, 1938, p. 13.

CHAPTER ELEVEN

1. *Pravda,* June 29, 1939. But, in the light of hindsight, Molotov's speech to the Supreme Soviet of May 31, 1937, showed which way the wind was blowing. The full English text of both these contributions is in *Soviet Documents on Foreign Policy,* Vol. III, selected and edited by Jane Degras, London, 1953.

2. *Krasnaya Zvezda,* September 23, 1939.

3. The classic account of the Polish deportations is *The Dark Side of the Moon* (Anonymous) with a Preface by T. S. Eliot, New York: Scrib-

ner, 1947. The most adequate account of the Katyn Wood affair is Joseph Mackiewicz, *The Katyn Wood Murders,* London, 1951. See also Lieutenant General W. Anders, *An Army in Exile,* New York: Macmillan, 1949.

4. Details in the Soviet press of the period are curiously confirmed by a Gestapo report, of all things, quoted in Konrad Kellen, *Khrushchev: A Political Portrait.* London, 1961, pp. 66-67. (New York: Praeger, 1961.)

CHAPTER TWELVE

1. Grigoire Gafencu, *Prelude to the Russian Campaign.* London, 1945, p. 212.

2. But he liked to talk about the war and his part in it, and his regret that he had not been able to share the hardships of the fighting men, in informal conversation: it was clearly a deep and decisive experience for him.

3. This story has never been told and probably never can be told. But Khrushchev saw, unfolding under his eyes, the transformation of a people alienated from their government and hostile even to their own Army into a passionately fighting nation, wholly scornful of the Party, but carrying it on their backs and in the end making a symbolic leader out of Stalin, because they had to have a figurehead and he had a certain grandeur.

4. Secret speech, pp. 192 and 240.

5. Oleg Penkovskiy, *The Penkovskiy Papers.* London, 1965, p. 45. (New York: Doubleday, 1965.)

6. The so-called Commissar Order. For the story of German crimes in Rus-

sia (and elsewhere) see particularly Gerald Reitlinger, *The Final Solution,* London, 1953, and my own *Gestapo: Instrument of Tyranny,* New York: Viking, 1956.

7. This was a rare occasion. One of the saddest things about the Russian war was the stubborn refusal of the authorities (Stalin) to allow either members of military missions, of which I was one, or Western journalists anywhere near the front, with the result that the outside world knew all too little of the real and tremendous story.

8. As the Politburo's representative he was a member of the Military Council of the Stalingrad Front. In *The Battle for Stalingrad,* by Marshal V. I. Chuikov (New York: Holt, 1964), who commanded the 62nd Army at Stalingrad, we have glimpses of him encouraging the troops, giving them pep talks, and acting as an intermediary between the defenders of the city and the higher command. The Military Council maintained its headquarters under heavy bombardment in

the middle of the battle zone on the right bank of the river. Chuikov does not indicate whether Khrushchev lived in this headquarters or not; but it seems improbable that

he spent some months in a dugout virtually surrounded by the German 6th Army without our being told about it later.

9. Secret speech, p. 180.

CHAPTER THIRTEEN

1. I am here describing what I myself saw.
2. Stalin introducing the first postwar Five Year Plan, February 1946.
3. Secret speech, p. 190.
4. *Trial of the Major War Criminals,*

Vol. IV, Nuremberg, 1948, p. 31.
5. Ibid. (American Prosecution Speech). See also Reitlinger, op. cit., and Crankshaw, *Gestapo,* cited above.
6. Priscilla Johnson, op. cit., p. 12.
7. Quoted by Pistrak, op. cit., p. 165.

CHAPTER FOURTEEN

1. Djilas, op. cit., p. 135.
2. Ibid., pp. 136-38.
3. Secret speech, p. 204.
4. Marshall MacDuffie, *The Red Car-*

pet. London, 1955, p. 200. (New York: Norton, 1955.)
5. Ibid., p. 199.

CHAPTER FIFTEEN

1. Waste of manpower still remains a major feature of post-Khrushchev agriculture.
2. For a glimpse into rural conditions as they are to this day, see the short novel about a collective farm, *The Dodgers* by Fyodor Abramov, London, 1963 (published in New York by Grove Press as *The New Life* and by Praeger as *One Day in the New Life*). This story was first published in the Soviet Union under Khrushchev in the Leningrad journal *Neva*.
3. *Moskovskaya Pravda,* June 28, 1950.
4. *Izvestia,* February 13, 1951.
5. March 4, 1951.
6. *Pravda,* October 6, 1952.
7. Secret speech, pp. 202, 204.
8. Ibid., pp. 242, 244.
9. *Pravda,* March 7, 1953.
10. *Pravda,* August 9, 1953.
11. *Pravda,* September 15, 1953.
12. E.g., "We know that bourgeois poli-

ticians are idle gossips. They gamble on people with weak nerves. They think they can intimidate us. But we cannot be frightened because if they know what a bomb is, so do we." Thus in 1954 Khrushchev was taking precisely the same line about the bomb for which he was later to pillory the Chinese with their "paper tiger" slogan.
13. *Pravda,* August 17, 1954.
14. He did not mention Malenkov by name at least in the published version of his speech. But the sense was clear.
15. But immediately after this meeting, according to S. Bialer, a member of the Propaganda Department of the Central Committee of the Polish Communist Party, who fled to the West early in 1956, Malenkov was openly accused of responsibility for the Leningrad affair in a secret circular sent out to Party officials.

CHAPTER SIXTEEN

1. *Russia Without Stalin,* New York: Viking, 1956; *Khrushchev's Russia,* London, 1959; *Moscow v. Peking: The New Cold War,* rev. ed., London, 1965. The best political account of the Khrushchev era to 1962 is *The Kremlin Since Stalin* by Wolfgang Leonhard, New York: Praeger, 1962.

2. *Kommunist,* No. 6, 1955.
3. *Pravda,* May 20, 1955.
4. *Kommunist,* No. 14, 1955.
5. S. Bialer in *Hinter dem Eisernen Vorhang,* No. 10, 1956.
6. Richard Lowenthal in *The New Leader,* February 9, 1959.

CHAPTER EIGHTEEN

1. Information derived from many personal conversations in Moscow and elsewhere.

2. Palmiro Togliatti in an interview, *Unita,* June 17, 1956. It was Togliatti who, from the grave, helped to bring about Khrushchev's downfall. He went to the Black Sea, a dying man, to meet Khrushchev and make a formal protest against his pushing the quarrel with China to extreme lengths and also against his high-handed attitude towards the fraternal Parties everywhere (see Chapter Twenty). Togliatti died before he could deliver his memorandum. But the Italian Communist press, in the teeth of objections from Leonid Brezhnev, then President of the Soviet Union, now Khrushchev's successor as First Secretary, published the text. This took place at the beginning of September 1964, and the Togliatti memorandum was clearly used by Khrushchev's opponents as a sharp weapon in their armoury.

3. For an elaboration of this argument, and for a more detailed assessment of Khrushchev's achievements, see Crankshaw, *Khrushchev's Russia,* cited above. Malenkov may very well have calculated in the first instance (and with some reason) that Khrushchev would be unable to ride the storm, which would leave the way clear for his return to power.

4. July 28, 1959. He had said the same thing earlier in the summer to a visiting group of American Senators.

5. *The Observer,* November 11, 1962.
6. July 21, 1956.
7. September 22, 1956.
8. See especially *Pravda* of July 6 and 24, 1956.
9. Information derived from personal conversations with Polish Communists in Warsaw at the height of the crisis.
10. For the attitude of the Soviet press towards the Hungarian crisis as it developed, see Leonhard, op. cit.
11. *Pravda,* November 4, 1956. See also ibid., November 3, 1956, the first occasion on which the Russians published for home consumption an all-out denunciation of the "counter-revolution." It was our old friend General Serov who carried out the arrests.
12. Crankshaw, *Moscow v. Peking: The New Cold War,* cited above, p. 170.
13. Information from personal conversations with East European Communists.
14. Quoted in Leonhard, op. cit., p. 232.
15. At a reception at the Chinese Embassy, Moscow, *Pravda,* January 19, 1957.

CHAPTER NINETEEN

1. *Pravda*, March 30, 1957. Khrushchev had actually delivered this speech six weeks before it was published.

2. Leonhard, op. cit., p. 237.

3. *Pravda*, June 15, 1957.

4. The proceedings of these crucial meetings are still obscure. Moscow was full of "true stories." Khrushchev himself let fall remarks from time to time in later years, none of them conclusive. An indication of the vituperative atmosphere may also be found in speeches made by delegates to the Twenty-first Party Congress in January 1959.

5. *Pravda*, July 16, 1957.

6. Khrushchev had already, in his secret speech, made it clear that he had a stranglehold on Voroshilov. Secret speech, p. 226.

7. This is an example of the stories which used to go round Moscow, apparently with Khrushchev's deliberate encouragement. They emanated as a rule from very high Communist circles. Another example was the story, purposefully spread (whether true or not), that Khrushchev had sharply blamed his underlings for the Pasternak affair, asking them whether any of them had in fact read *Dr. Zhivago* and, on receiving the answer "No," retorting that he himself had now read it and that it should never have been banned: "You should have printed a very small edition. It would have been forgotten very quickly, and we should have avoided all this fuss."

8. *Kommunist*, No. 16, 1957.

9. This attack on the writers, an attempt by Khrushchev and others to break the resistance of the best of them to the reassertion of Party control, was one of the last joint efforts of the old "collective." Molotov, Malenkov, Kaganovich, and Shepilov were all present at the May meeting of the Central Committee. It was later believed in Moscow that it was at the famous garden party that Shepilov, so very much Khrushchev's protégé, fatally blotted his copy-book by going to the help of Margaret Aliger and assuring her when she came round that she should not take too seriously the words of Nikita Sergeievich in a temper. Shepilov was obviously considered a special case by Khrushchev, since the compulsory incantation when referring to the members of the vanquished "anti-Party" group was "Molotov, Malenkov, Kaganovich; and Shepilov, who joined them."

10. Djilas, op. cit., p. 135.

11. Priscilla Johnson, op. cit.

12. Crankshaw, *Moscow v. Peking*, cited above, p. 107.

13. *Pravda*, May 1, 1956.

14. *Pravda*, February 5, 1959. *Unita*, the Italian Communist Party newspaper, carried the full speech on the same day.

15. *Pravda*, March 10, 1963.

16. *Encounter*, London, April 1963. Quoted also in Priscilla Johnson, op. cit. Miss Johnson's work, with the documents selected by her and Leopold Labedz, is indispensable for a proper study of Khrushchev's running fight with the intellectuals during his last two years. Also for an understanding of what the intellectuals were, and are, trying to do. For the earlier phases of the thaw, see Crankshaw, *Russia Without Stalin*, cited above. For a collection of writings of rebellious writers from the early days of the Revolution up to Yevtushenko and his "Babi Yar" see *Dissonant Voices*

in *Soviet Literature,* edited by Max Hayward and Patricia Blake, New York: Harper, 1962. For an example of the limits of Khrushchev's toleration see Alexander Solzhenitsyn's *One Day in the Life of Ivan Denisovich,* the first account in Russian of life in a labour camp, New York: Dutton, 1963. Although Khrushchev let it be known that he had sponsored this book in 1962, it was afterwards sharply attacked. For an example of what he would not tolerate, see *Ward 7* by Valery Tarsis, New York: Dutton, 1965. For a general survey of the whole Soviet era in literature see *Litera ture and Revolution in Soviet Rus-*

sia, 1917-1962, by Max Hayward and Leopold Labedz, New York: Oxford, 1963. I should like to emphasize that it is the cultural battlefront which offers the deepest insights into the minds and the expedients of the Soviet leadership. Deplorable it may be to mix politics with literature, painting, and composing: the fact remains that the only politicians, as we understand the term, in the Soviet Union are the artists of all kinds.

17. Ibid. And here Khrushchev shows how clearly he understood the sense of the final sentence in Note 16 above.

CHAPTER TWENTY

1. Marshal Koniev, whose attack on his late commander was scurrilous in the extreme, was chief among these.
2. The "hundred flowers" had a very short blooming season, a matter of weeks in 1957.
3. Marshal Tito was the first person to relate this story to the world. He had been the chief casualty of the Moscow Conference. It was not publicly confirmed until the Chi nese statement of September 1963. See Crankshaw, *Moscow v. Peking,* cited above, p. 170.
4. *World Culture,* December 20, 1957.
5. *People's Daily,* July 19, 1958, in a leading article with the appealing title: "The Countries and Peoples of the World Who Love Peace and Freedom Cannot Look On with Folded Arms."
6. Khrushchev to Eisenhower, July 18, 1958.
7. Professor Liberman of Kharkov had the honour of being the first man to suggest and outline a detailed plan for building the profit

motive into industry and allowing undreamed-of freedom to individual managements. His first initiative was an article in *Problems of Economics* for August 1962. This was followed up by a major article in *Pravda* of September 9, 1962. Open discussion followed. Khrushchev played with the idea, which was soon elaborated by others, and allowed its experimental application in two garment factories. But he was clearly worried by it, and it was not until he had gone that Kosygin put the whole weight of the Soviet government behind large-scale trials. The best accounts are in *Rise of the Russian Consumer* by Margaret Miller, London, 1965, and *The Soviet Economy Since Stalin* by Harry Schwartz, London, 1965, which also offer very good outlines of the problems of Soviet industry and agriculture generally.
8. This particular imbroglio in fact occurred much earlier. Khrushchev reported it in July 1956. But it was

characteristic of many such disagreements through the years, some of which, as with Belyaev and Kirichenko, led to the downfall of strong Khrushchev men.

9. Even in 1964 about half the milk, half the meat, most of the fruit and vegetables, and over 90 per cent of the eggs consumed by Russians came from the private plots, which Khrushchev never gave up trying to legislate out of existence. For the bad quality of consumer goods, see particularly *Pravda*, April 5, 1963 (speech by Voronov). But Khrushchev's own speeches were full of complaints. Miller, op. cit.; A. Nove, *The Soviet Economy*, New York: Praeger, 1965; and H. Schwartz, op. cit., are all good on this. Crankshaw, *Russia Without Stalin*, cited above, describes the breakdown of the planning system and the operations of the private and semi-official contact men and speculators.

10. The treaties referred to were the Treaty of Aigun, in 1858, and the Treaty of Peking, 1860.

11. August 14, 1963. See Crankshaw, *Moscow v. Peking*, cited above, p. 167.

12. *Red Flag*, April 16, 1960. See *Moscow v. Peking*, pp. 93 *et seq*.

13. *Moscow v. Peking* contains the only

full account of the secret Bucharest and Moscow meetings of 1960 and of secret letters and circulars exchanged between Moscow and Peking; also an explanation of the sources.

14. Ibid., Chapter 12.

15. Theodore Sorenson, *Kennedy*. London, 1965, pp. 544, 548, 549. (New York: Harper, 1965.)

16. Ibid.

17. Ibid.

18. See Note 9 above.

19. Arthur Schlesinger, *A Thousand Days*. London, 1965. (New York: Houghton Mifflin, 1965.)

20. They started, obliquely, at Party congresses of fraternal Parties. Signor Pajetta in Rome in December 1962 had the honour of being the first to state: "When we mean China we have no need to say Albania." He was soon followed up by the East Germans, and then the Russians.

21. *Moscow v. Peking*, op. cit., pp. 117-120.

22. August 14, 1963.

23. For frontier incidents see *Moscow v. Peking*, op. cit., p. 169. "Not all the water in the Volga can wash away the great shame you have brought upon the Communist Party of the Soviet Union."

24. See Note 10 above.

INDEX

Abakumov, 181, 199, 209
Administration, 272, 286
Adzhubei, Alexei, 260–62, 272, 285
Afghanistan, 212
Africa, 269
Agitprop, 262
Agriculture, 44, 57–58, 74, 146, 156–58, 183, 192–93, 198, 200, 223, 286; Khrushchev's policies, 163–65, 169, 173, 174–81, 191, 193–94, 198, 206, 215–17, 247, 271–72, 280, 304; in Poland, 135; pre-Revolution, 176
Agro-towns, 165, 178–80, 270
Albania, 276–77
Alexander II, 4
Alexander III, 10
Aliger, Margaret, 254, 302
All-Union Congress, *see* Congresses, Party
All-Union Party, *see* Communist Party of Soviet Union
Allelulyeva, Nadezhda, 63–68, 81, 296–297
Anarchists, 32
Anders, General, 132
Andreyev, Andrei, 35, 72, 73, 146, 152, 156–57, 161, 163–64, 167, 175, 186
Andrianov, 191
Anti-Semitism, 154
Apparatchik, 36, 38–41, 47, 56, 182, 233
Architecture, 94, 206
Aristov, 211, 232, 251
Armenian Communist Party, 191
Army, 5, 6, 21, 25–28, 30–31, 33, 34, 36, 73, 78, 111, 119, 131–33, 171, 181, 182, 186, 188, 192, 198, 203, 205, 232, 234, 241–42, 271, 280, 286; purge, 83, 97, 109, 121, 129, 149, 198, 228, 250; World War II, 137, 139–45, 151, 154, 158, 160–61, 218
Artists, 63, 78, 115, 119, 125, 128, 134, 155, 190–91, 226; Khrushchev's rela-

tions with, 6, 115, 155–56, 253–56, 259, 261–65, 271, 302–303
Arutinov, 191
Asia, 218, 269, 276
Atom bomb, 184
Atomic energy, *see* Nuclear projects
Atomic Energy Commission, 252
Austria, 242
Austrian peace treaty, 278

Babel, Isaac, 62
Babi Yar, 154–55
Baldwin, Stanley, 95
Balkans, 153
Baltic Sea, 33, 233
Baltic States, 132, 132n., 137, 153–54, 163
Baltic–White Sea Canal, 76, 92
Bandera, Stepan, 151
Bauman District Committee, 67, 72, 79, 85
Bay of Pigs, 281
Beika, 42
Belgrade, 196, 208–209, 211, 220
Belyaev, 211, 251
Beria, Lavrenti P., 15, 21, 73, 74, 95, 103, 107, 121–22, 128–29, 131, 136, 138–40, 142–43, 151, 156, 160–61, 166–167, 169, 170, 172–74, 181, 186–90, 197, 209, 212, 226
Berlin, 41, 276, 278–79; blockade, 162; crisis and wall, 279, 281; East, 149
Bessarabia, 31, 125, 135, 163
Bevin, Ernest, 20
Birmingham, 258
Black Sea, 25, 119, 286
Blitzkrieg, 157
Blobel, Col., 154
Blok, Alexander, 63
Bolsheviks, 4n., 5, 6, 8, 13, 14, 20–30, 33–38, 41, 44, 55, 66, 68, 73, 77, 92, 98,